THE ENGLISH NOVELS DURING THE NINETEEN-THIRTIES

R. B. SINGH

ATLANTIC PUBLISHERS & DISTRIBUTORS

Published by
ATLANTIC PUBLISHERS & DISTRIBUTORS
B-2, Vishal Enclave, New Delhi-27
Phone: 5413460

Sales Office
4346/4C, Ansari Road, Darya Ganj,
New Delhi-110 002
Phone: 3273880

ISBN 81-7156-384-8

Typeset at
APD Computer Graphics
B-2, Vishal Enclave, New Delhi-110 027
Printed in India at
Print India, Maya Puri
New Delhi

Preface

The decade preceding World War II was a period of hope and despair, of darkness as well as new lights. It was a period in which certain factors and tendencies first glimpsed during the Edwardian and Georgian eras came to maturity. It was also a period when certain ideals as well as fears so prominent immediately before and after World War I died. The period was really one of great upheavals and new alignments.

Epic novels like Galsworthy's *Forsyte Saga* or Tolstoy's *War and Peace* might not be written any more; yet collectively novels of a particular period do still have an epical quality. There are many excellent studies of individual novelists of the thirties, but these do not show the totality of the scene. Besides, to be of value, literature requires periodic reassessment; and more than sixty years after *Waste Land* (1922), and about thirty five after World War II seems to have provided a sufficient distance in time for a fruitful re-examination of the thirties novels. The present study is an attempt towards this end.

The first chapter deals with the main predecessors of the thirties novelists, their works and achievements, and their legacies. The second chapter is devoted to the exploration of the main social, political and literary tendencies of the thirties and their impact upon the contemporary English fiction. Chapter three is a detailed study of the works of the novelists of the thirties. Chapter four deals with the technical achievements – plot construction, characterisation, technique and style in these novels. The fifth chapter is about tradition and new trends. It shows the main differences and affinities between the novelists of the thirties and their predecessors. The last chapter is a kind of balance-sheet showing the successes and failures of the novelists of the thirties.

I express my deep sense of gratitude to my guide Dr. Paresh Chandra Bhattacharya, Prof. & Head of the English Department, R.R. Post-Graduate College, Amethi, Sultanpur. His suggestions and guidance have contributed immensely to the successful completion of this research work.

A debt of more personal nature I owe to Prof. Someshwer Singh, Principal, R.R. Post-Graduate College, Amethi, Sultanpur and Prof. Housilla Prasad Singh, M.A., D.Litt., of K.S. Saket Post-Graduate College Faizabad.

I take this opportunity to express my thanks to the Director/Librarian and Staff of the National Library, Calcutta Delhi University Library, B.H.U. Central Library, British Council Library at Delhi and British Museum Library at Boston SPA (U.K.) for the facilities that I was readily provided with.

R.B. SINGH

CONTENTS

FIRST CHAPTER

INTRODUCTION – THE PREDECESSORS

The English novel has a rich and splendid tradition. From the early romances of Lyly, Greene and Lodge, the pastoral novel of Sydney, the picaresque of Nash and the realistic of Dekker, Delony and Nicholas Breton it reached its full stature in the naturalistic novels of H.G. Wells and Arnold Bennet, the psychological novels of James Joyce and Virginia Woolf and in the realistic and parabolic novels of Rex Warner, Graham Greene, Evelyn Waugh and Christopher Isherwood. The novel, which was meagre in form and few in number, to-day looks like a huge banyan tree, overshadowing all the other literary forms which had enjoyed much popularity earlier.

The novel has ever been a perennial source of delight and instruction. A novelist portrays what he sees. In novels we generally find a resemblance to life in the setting, portraiture and in the managing of powerful coincidences. Scott-James aptly comments, "The novel is an art because it exhibits something which the artist believes to be like life, or true to life (not excluding necessarily the marvellous or the fantastic); and because he puts together these elements, in an intelligible external form, for no other purpose than to enable us to see what he has seen and to derive pleasure from it."[1]

Like other literary genres, the English novel, too, has ever been susceptible to foreign influences. And this susceptibility is prominently noticeable in the modern novels. De Vogue's Le *Roman Russe* (1896), a famous Russian fiction, was translated in (1913), : ..... and this work began to exercise an immediate effect on English thinking about fiction."[2] *A Mummer's Wife* (1888), the famous novel of George Moore was modelled on Zola's '*L' Assommoir* (1877). Maugham's first novels namely, '*Lize of Lambeth*' (1897), *Of Human Bondage* (1915), and '*Cakes and Ale*' (1930) also bear Zola's indelible impression. The deep influence of Turgenev is quite apparent in the *Villa Rubein* (1900) of Galsworthy ; and *Under Western Eyes*, Conrad's well known work, also is a proof thereof. Dostoyevsky achieved popularity among English novelists during the First World War and since then the Russian influence has been deep indeed. The English novel, however, is not merely a product of blind imitation of continental novelists. The English novelists, imbibing foreign influences made their novels rich and variegated. The infinite variety, richness and plasticity in style, livliness and dynamism in the delineation of characters, dexterous and multifarious touches to the setting, and commonality in language are the chief distinguishing features of English novels.

Before coming to the novels of the nineteen-thirties, it would be worthwhile to study their predecessors that made them possible. Henry James, the father of modern English novel and the great figure among the generation of novelist,[3] would be a good starting point.

Henry James

The novel before the eighteen-nineties was not a conscious art form. Novelists like Dickens, Thackeray, George Eliot, Meredith, Thomas Hardy and others were not theorists. To them the novel was to please the age. There is an escape from life rather than an escape into life in their novels. But in the eighteen-nineties the novelist became a conscious artist. It could be so, "because the period provided the circumstances which made it possible for him to behave as one."[4]

Henry James started a new era in the English novel by adopting the impressionistic technique that was further developed later by Virginia Woolf. He imitated Zola's realistic approach. A professed chronicler of his time, he dealt with the bare facts of life. Like Ezra Pound and T.S. Eliot, he wedded his art to life; and again like them he maintained attitude of great detachment. His contemporaries, who matured in the eighteen-nineties, could not grasp the reality that found its full expression in his novels.

Henry James was born in New York in 1843, but since 1868 he lived mainly in Europe and later made England his home. Scott-James has pointed out that, "England had long been his spiritual home. There he found the social ease and the manners which pleased him; .... there was the atmosphere whose aroma he savoured, lending itself to delicate and sufficiently complicated human relationships which picqued his curiosity....." [5]

Henry James himself has explained in the second chapter of his *Hawthorne* (1879), why he preferred England over America : "The items of high civilization missing from American life : a court, an aristocracy, an established church, country houses, cathedrals, old universities and schools ; the arts, a political society, a sporting class."[6] However, though living in England, he was not only conscious that he was an American, he actually thought it to be a blessing. In 1867 he wrote : "... we are Americans born.... I look upon it as a great blessing; and I think that to be an American is an excellent preparation for culture. We can deal freely with forms of civilization not our own, can pick and choose and assimilate in short (aesthetically etc.) claim our property wherever we find it .... we must of course have something of our own .... something distinctive and homogeneous .... and I take it that we shall find it in our moral consciousness, our unprecedented spiritual lightness and vigour....."[7]

Henry James was a prolific writer and wrote more than thirty major and minor works of fiction. Besides, he is also known for his critical essays, note-books, autobiography and plays.

Henry James was one of the earliest theorists among the English novelists and his theory of fiction is contained in his well known critical essay, 'The Art of Fiction' (1884). Henry Fielding's declared purpose in writing *Tom Janes* was : " .... to recommend goodness and innocence."[8] For him novel was a history of mankind without any distortion of facts. In `*The Art of Fiction*', Henry James too has remarked that a novelist should be truthful in tracing the history of mankind. The following shows his conviction in this regard:

> "..... the events he (a novelist) narrates have not really happened, and that he can give his narrative any turn the reader may like best. Such a betrayal of a sacred office seems to me, I confess, a terrible crime; it is what I mean by the attitude of apology, and it shocks me every whit as much in Trollope as it would have shocked me in Gibbon or Macaulay. "[9] Thus fidelity to life in the novel is the main point driven home in '*Art of Fiction*', It means, "that his characters must be real and such as might be met within life..... that a young lady brought up in a quiet country village should avoid descriptions of a garrison life...."[10]

The second important point made in the '*Art of Fiction*', is that a novel should be a composite of impressions which the novelist's mind receives in his day-to-day life. The more deep the impression, the more effective and lasting it would be. But the novelist must have full freedom to comit his impressions to writing; only then we shall feel a powerful sway in his impressionistic technique. Whereas Henry James imbibed the influences of such foreign novelists as Balzac, Zola, Sainte-Beauve and Hawthorne, he made himself distinct by his new impressionistic technique.

According to Henry James, ".... English fiction should have a 'conscious moral purpose...." [11] But a novelist should not be didactic in the same sense in which the eighteenth century novelists were. He was of the opinion that the spirit of moral purpose must be wedded to aesthetic sense, ".... it was James's principle that the ethical could be rendered successfully in fiction only when the representation was aesthetically satisfying ....." [12] He imposed a pattern on his novels to create this aesthetic sense so that this moral sense could be conveyed effectively.

Henry James emphasised that the novel should be accepted as a living entity, a growing organism. A novelist should breathe fine spirit in the craftsmanship of his fictive pictures which would always look fresh and entertaining. History can never recreate life, for it deals with dead matters which bear, generally, no resemblance to our immediate life. The novel, on the other hand, is as varied as life itself; and it is its variety that gives special flavour and odour.

There must be selection in the structure of a novel and this selection should be 'inclusive'. It must include all those appropriate words, phrases, coincidences, scenes, settings and other trappings which are required for producing a total effect. There should, however, be no superfluity, for superfluity mars the aesthetic sense. Henry James has pointed out : "Art is essentially selection whose main care is typical, to be inclusive. For many people art means rose-coloured window panes, and selection means picking a bouquet for Mrs. Grundy." [13]

From the earliest till the end we find varient leitmotif running through the novels of Henry James. In *Roderick Hudson*, *The American*, (1877) ; and *Dairy Miller*, (1877) James has portrayed Americans representing diverse sides of life. In *The American* Christopher is a business man. There is also a short glimpse of the rotten aristocracy of France. In *Dairy Miller* there is a fine picture of conflict between Americans and Europeans, showing Americans as 'innocents' and Europeans 'exploiters'. *The Portrait of a Lady* (1861) deals with 'the situation of women' in the society. Simultaneously it also tells about the experiences of the Americans in European countries when they came in touch with the old-world aristocracy. Naturalistic tone is found in his two novels — *The Bostonians* and *The Princess Casamassima*. In the former, strong narrow feelings between the north and the south, reaction trying to thwart reforms, and much dispute over the principles of the feminine and masculine, are the essential ingredients. In *The Princess Casamassima* there is a fine portrait of London life. In fact London plays a major role in this novel and bears testimony to the writer's varied experiences there.

The Ambassadors, *The Wings of the Dove* and *The Golden Bowl* are known for their complexity and allusiveness. In these novels we again find confrontation between the Europeans and Americans. The tragic and comic portions of these novels are finely woven and dressed up. We observe an exact revelation of various facets of the lives of the leading characters.

Henry James selected unlooked aspects of human life as the leitmotif for his novels. His curious searching gaze had not left untouched even the trivial and common events of apparently little value, "He prefers to move lightly, delicately, curiously among the lesser incidents of life, searching as with a microscope for small essences hidden to the naked eye, but so contriving the accumulation of small things as to reveal life in a strange aspect whose strangeness he purposed to evoke."[14]

Every creative genius is an obsessionist. He works by a fixed idea. James was not exception. He was possessed by the notion of 'religosity'. He professed that : "There was no victory for human beings, ... ; you were punished in your own way; whether you were of God's or the Devil's party."[15] He did not, however, have faith in the orthodox Christian religion. Rather, his faith was the product of his own experience. He was in his life the sufferings of both the good and the bad. He felt that 'supernatural' evil is no less strong than 'supernatural' good. Hence the greater part of his works is a dramatization of the conflict between the good and the evil. James believed in the 'idealization of the English society', and, therefore, always took the side of the good in his novels. His characters – Laura Wing in *A London Life*, Rose Tramore in *The Chaperon*, Fleda Vetch in *The Spoils of Poynton*, Nanda Brookenham in *The Awkward Age*, Maisie Farange in *What Maisie Knew* – are all idealists and they struggle against worldly temptations. "Right and wrong are not simple matters for James's great heroes and heroines; they are related to what may be called their life style. At the moment of choice they feel a categorical imperative to behave according to their deepest idea of themselves and of what they owe to self respect regardless of comfort or personal happiness.''[16] The theme of 'human integrity' runs through all the novels of Henry James.

Henry James adopted the dramatic technique and maintained his personal detachment from the fictive pictures of his novels. He wanted to make these pictures concrete, individual and actual. He was a born American and this helped him to feel detached from what he was portraying in his novels. Scott-James has rightly commented, ''He was to wander over the world like an inquisitive God observing with passionless curiosity the strange behaviour of its inhabitants ... his art was to be, in the proper sense of the term, disinterested – that is to say, it was to be concerned exclusively with the matter in hand, to show, to exhibit, a chosen tract of life, to present a theme just for what it was worth an interesting distillation of reality, untouched, unprejudiced by any consideration except that of presenting it perfectly.''[17]

The application of dramatic technique created a rigid pattern in Henry's novels. While it gave maximum aesthetic gratification, it also circumscribed the field of his material a great deal. Novel, if strictly bound by dramatic laws, cannot represent any large segment of life. True novel represents humanity even at the expense of beauty, and Henry James failed in this. He sacrificed humanity for the sake of beauty.

Plot is an 'intellectual aspect' of the nvoel. it is bound by the causal chain. Plot differs in this sense from the story which cannot satisfy the hungry mind, always in search of truth. Henry is well known for his intellect which is the dominant force in his novels, but he did not pay much attention to framing coherent plots. He was an aesthete and brought into play an extravagant care in the cultivation of his art. E.M. Forster has rightly remarked that plot apeeals to our intellect and pattern appeals to our aesthetic sense.[18] The happenings in the novels of Henry James are merely 'episodes'. Mostly we find him revelling in artistic pictorial sceneography that reminds us of his being more a poet than a writer of prose-fictions. In some of his novels he did try to make the plots integrated, but his success was limited. As E.M. Forster has remarked, ''The longer James worked, the more convinced he grew that a novel should be whole ... not necessarily geometric like *The Ambassadors* but it should grow round a single topic, situation, gesture which should occupy the characters and provide a plot, and should also fasten up the novel on the outside.''[19]

We do find a large number of characters swarming in the novels of Henry James, but unfortunately they come from a limited section of the society. Just as he did not pay much attention to the plot construction so also he failed in the delineation of his characters. They are not of flesh and blood. Most of them are types. Forster is right to complain, "They are incapable of fun, of rapid motion, of carnality, and of nine-tenths of heroism. Their clothes will not take off the diseases that ravage them are anonymous, like the sources of their incomes, their servants are noiseless or resemble themselves, not social explanation of the world we know is possible for them, for there are no stupid people in their world, no barriers of language, and no poor. Even their sensations are limited."[20] His heroines are however perfectly fine spirits of freedom. They represent the modern women rather than the victorians.

James adopted a complex style in his novels. Long-winded sentences create difficulties in grasping his meanings. In his early novels we mark some simplicity in style but later, specially in his last three novels *The Ambassadors*, *The Wings of the Dove* and *The Golden Bowl*, he adopted the most virile but obscure style which has made them difficult to understand. Mainly he had chosen the naturalistic style in imitation of Zola ; but being an aesthetic creature, his fidelity to naturalistic style shakes and creeps secretly into the ornate.

To sum up, Henry James was really a great force in the field of English novel. He was the first English novelist who gave a new technique to the English novel that was further developed by his successors. To-day he is remembered as an artist of fine craftmanship. In the words of Scott-James it is true that, "His writing became more and more mannered as he went on, and his habit to verbal refinement led too often to unrewarding obscurity. Preciosity could go no further. But he brought something new into English fiction. After him there is no excuse for judging the novel otherwise than as a fine art. With him English fiction starts again."[21]

H.G. Wells

Herbert George Wells (1866-1946) is reputed for his scientific romances and novels of ideas. He was one of those novelists who live for their consummate ideas to act as intellectual nourishment, and not for their artistic craftmanship. Unlike his predecessors he was a rebel in his artistic performance. Wells followed an untrodden path which, undoubtedly, misled him and for which he had to pay a heavy price. Still he enjoyed a wide popularity in the Edwardian period for his scientific fantasies throbbing with vitality. Like G.B. Shaw he was in his literary persuasion, a mentor who wished to purge the English society of its orthodoxies. Much like Dickens he was a vigorous social reformer who tried to expose the social evils. He breathed a spirit of enquiry among his people who were quite unaware of those vital changes which were then moulding the English life. In the words of Scott-James, ''He had come to some conclusions, provisionally, about many of the problems of that English society which he had been observing and was prepared to analysis and criticse; and he set out to enlighten his countrymen (he was always among the prophets) about the drift of the life they were leading.''[22]

Wells's literary career extends from 1893 to 1945, during which he wrote over one hundred books. These were powerful enough to catch the attention of those intellectual youngmen of his age, who were directly under the impact of Darwinism and who had adopted the agnostic philosophical attitude of Huxley. The very titles of his books such as *The Time Machine* (1895), *Marriage* (1912), *The Soul of a Bishop* (1917), *War and Future* (1917) reveal the fact that he touched almost every important topic current in his time.

A.C. Ward has given a comprehensive list of the principles that formed Wells's theory of novel : ''(a) That the novel is in essence discursive, a tapestry of multifarious interest; (b) that it should be sufficiently elastic in form to take the whole of life within its compass .....(c) that it should be, not a new sore of pulpit, but the home confessional, the initiator of knowledge, the seed of fruitful self-questing, the great central platform for discussion and for the examination of human conduct.''[23]

Wells's theory of novel suited well his literary purpose which was to air his diversified ideas about the contemporary English life that was being swayed by various powerful social, political, scientific and economic forces. But this theory could be seen in practic only after 1911. Before that year his writings were mainly 'fantastic romances'. Only after 1911, the novel became a serious matter to him in which he reflected the dreams, hopes and aspirations of the young generation that believed in the millenium to come in the age of science. In his novels he was the spokesman of his age. Like a saviour he followed the untrodden path and visualised an ideal state. His utilitarianism was like that of Carlyle and Ruskin, who, in their days loudly spoke for spiritual reforms.

Perhaps he was the first prophet who saw man not as a collection of disconnected parts but a single entity. Cazamian is correct to say, "He figured finally as a spiritual guide of suffering humanity, the adviser of nations blinded by their hostilities, of individuals whom their selfishness is making unconscious of.... ."[24]

The novels of H.G. Wells fall into three clear groups–'scientific romances' (before 1900), social comedies (1900-1911) and the novels of ideas (1911 and after). *The Time Machine* (1895); *Wonderful Visit* (1895); *The Invisible Man* (1897); and *The First Men in the Moon* (1901) are his famous scientific romances which are very rich in plastic imagination. He was interested in space, time and evolution, and gave them a new meaning in their social relevancy. Scott-James has rightly remarked, "There was no vision to him more fascinating than that of a struggling changing world, evolving under the ruthless laws of evolution, or becoming modified, for the better, by the will and intelligence of man."[26]

In these novels we observe that Wells maintained a satisfactory detachment, standing at a distance from the existing human life, gazing at its various facets through different corners. These scientific romances are superb in their 'intellectual jeux d'espirt'. They provide the component parts of all the succeeding novels, though many new elements too have been added after the Second World War. As A.C. Ward has remarked, " ... the fantastic romances form an integral part of the whole body of his work, because of their challenging spirit of inquiry and criticism. Though in some sense they laid the foundation of 'science fiction', they cannot be held responsible for the rapid sensationalism in which such fiction became saturated when it attained an uncritical adolescent popularity in the early years of 'The atomic age', i.e. from C. 1945."[27]

Love and Mr. Lewisham (1900); *Kipps* (1905); *Tono-Bungay* (1909); and *The History of Mr. Polly* (1910) are some of the famous social comedies of Wells. In these he followed in the track blazed earlier by Fielding, Smollett and Dickens. He was a second Dickens when he laughed at the gross social ills raging unchecked. Polly and Kipps are the finest creations of his reformatory zeal. He wrote what he felt and experienced outside himself. We mark a fine blending of feeling and thought; idealism and realism budding forth in these comedies. *Tono-Bungay*, like Galsworthy's *The Forsyte Saga*, reveals the disintegration of the old English society. He presents 'a complete cross section of contemporary English life' seen through the keen eyes of George of Ponderevo.

In *The History of Mr. Polly* we find a just criticism of the society, specially in the field of education. *Kipps* is autobiographical in nature and its story is full of many events from the author's own youth.

After 1910 there was a change and H.G. Wells wrote such great novels of ideas as *The New Machiavelli* (1911); *Marriage* (1912); *The Research Magnificent* (1915); *World of William Clissold* (1926); *The Open Conspiracy* (1928); *Homo Sapiens* (1942); and *Mind at the End of Tether* (1945).

In these novels Wells is like an enthusiastic crusader firmly championing the cause of the down-trodden, and pouring out his intense feelings on such topics as social conventions, sex politics, war and the future of the world. A.C. Ward is of the opinion that, "The change was in fact due at least in the first place – to a deliberate departure from methods that had previously satisfied him; .... "[27] These novels, however, reveal a special aspect of the writer's nature. His emotional life was laways at war with his intellectual life. Like Shaw he could not accept that sexual impulse was a 'tyrant'. Therefore, the passions that we do find in such novels are not of the genuine kind. They are the product of his mind and powerful imagination rather than of the heart.

The Research Magnificent (1915) and *Mr. Birtling Sees It Through* (1916) are his two best war novels. *World of William Clissold* (1926) and *The Open Conspiracy* (1928) deal with human progress. *The Work, Wealth and Happiness of Mankind* provides, many rich perspectives, and in *The Outline of History* we find a survey of the past and its rich exploits. He laid down the principle that, "... it is only through a conscious, frank and world-wide co-operation of the man of science, the scientific worker, the man accustomed to the direction of productive industry, the man able to control the arterial supply of credit, the man who can control newspapers and politicians, that the great system of changes that have almost inadvertently got going can be brought to any hopeful order of development."[28]

Wells visualised a better future, grounded in the work and association of men of mature brains. He hoped for an 'open conspiracy' among such talented persons 'to change the laws, customs, rules and institutions of the world'. Wells was an advocate of internationalism for the good of humanity. He dreamed of a world much ravaged by war.

In his seventy-ninth year, Wells was, however, stricken with despair and discarded his rosy optimism. He observed that man was incapable of adapting himself to the fast changing conditions of the world. His last two novels, *The Outlook For Spiens* (1942) and *Mind At the End of Its Tether* are the results of this dejected mood. These novels of ideas had however their contemporary value – for their vital and ennobling ideas rather than for artistic execution.

Wells's aim was to be a journalist in his fictive pictures rather than an artist. Allen is of the opinion, "In the correspondence of James and H.G. Wells we have the classic use of the literary artist *versus* journalist, summed up by Wells when he wrote: "To you literature, like painting, is an end, to me literature like architecture is a means, it has a use ... I had rather be called a journalist than an artist, that is essense of it. "[29] The novel was his favourite channel to communicate his ideas to the common masses who might otherwise have been ignorant of them. He was not bound by those literary devices which were thought necessary in structuring a novel. He expressed himself in any way he thought proper. Except such works as *Kipps* and *Tono-Bungay*, all the other novels are disjointed in shape. They do not also have any character of flesh and blood. We don't remember him as an artist but as a `propagandist' who took to the writing of novels for serving his utilitarian end. The idea is the main thing in his novels and the characters are dominated by these ideas. George Sampson's stricture is worthy of note, "In the novel of ideas, the ideas are apt to come first and human characters are created to give expression to them. No one could call writers like Wells and Huxley unimaginative, but their imagination, their power of invention, is in the realm of ideas rather than of persons...."[30] But the characters of Wells cannot be dismissed summarily in this manner. On the whole they are not unconvincing. They have vigour and are lively. E.M. Forster's comments are more apt, ".... with the possible exceptions of Kipps and the aunt in *Tono-Bungay*, all Wells's characters are flat as a photograph. But the photographs are agitated with such vigour that we forget that their complexities lie on the surface and would disappear if it was scratched curled up."[31] Wells's characters are the direct result of his close observation. He portrayed those characters best who were within his experiences during his early life. Cazamian has clarified this factor very well : "Through the whole of Wells's work the value of the characters varies exceedingly, according to the fund of personal observation and subjective experience which enters into their substance... ."[32]

Wells did not care much to build up his plots which he considered to be a great impediment in laying bare his heart. He wrote arbitrarily without any care for the customary fictive rules; yet he was capable of importing force to his fictive pictures which are powerful enough to catch our attention. Scott-James has commented that, "... the novels of Wells defy all canons of art that are applicable to fiction, and yet ... his strictures still leave that work more convulsed with life and more brimming with blood than any...."[33]

To conclude, Wells was not concerned with 'the art of letters'. He was deeply influenced by the Time Spirit and left indelible impressions on the minds of the present and the coming generation. Wells's thought, keen perception, imagination and homour are the powerful elements of his writing; though mostly they are journalistic rather than literary. According to Scott-James, "He was one of the moulders of opinions in Edwardian and Georgian Britain, and for the historian at least he will be among the greatest of revolutionaries. But his work may date ; for all the vigour, his writing had no polished style to support it.

In the future he may or may not get the credit for what he has done, but the mark he left on the mind of the nation cannot be effaced."[34]

Arnold Bennett

Arnold Bennett (1867-1931) belonged to the pre-war period which produced a good number of other novelists who gave the English novel a new tone and texture. Some of them were pure artists who rested content in the cultivation of their favourite techniques ; and there were others who flung the conventional technique to the winds and devoted themselves solely to the depiction of the age and its problems. These latter could win only temporary success which lasted hardly more than a decade. Arnold Bennett much like George Moore (1852-1933) and Somerset Maugham (1874-1965) has achieved more lasting fame partly because of a naturalistic approach.

Arnold Bennett showed great skill in the development of his art. He was no propagandist. He was no more like a silent painter, holding the brush in his hand and painting while speculating on the many grim and real social problems that loomed large on his mental horizon. He showed no enthusiasm in analysing these problems, no interest in presenting any remedy, no desire to prophesy the future. In this he differed greatly from H.G. Wells. He was an artist observing the dissembling reality and remained content to present it in an artistic manner.

Arnold Bennett was conscious of the new forces coming to operate in the society; so were H.G. Wells and John Galsworthy. Both Bennett and Galsworthy, "Were observed, as Wells was, by the sense of the persistence of change which was altering not only the outward shape of England but having also its potent effect on character and moral values. But whereas Wells was primarily interested in the larger unit of society, with men as its ingredients — as seen through the eyes of one man, himself — Bennett and Galsworthy were interested in the efforts which society had in shaping the character and destiny of individuals."[35]

In spite of much that is similar in the novels of Galsworthy and Bennett, there is a fundamental difference. The grim and realistic pictures of the society as presented by the latter are not as profound in the tragic sense as the moral, dignified and humanitarian social settings by the former. Both have dealt with those new social and economic forces which were disturbing the complacency of the period immediately preceding theirs; both have shown how the old values were still the favourite follies of the nation and how these obstructed the coming of changes. The conflict between the old and new values made situations tense, and this made the novels of these two writers lively and interesting. But in the words of Fraser, "Arnold Bennett had nothing of the high moral dignity, the vague but the real distress about the injustice and unkindness of the world, which make Galsworthy a very attractive figure in spite of his limitations. He was, however, more naturally and completely a creative artist, but an artist crippled, at least in the latter part of his career, by accepting the standards of vulgar success.[36]

Arnold Bennett was born in 1867 at Shelton, and passed his first-twenty one years in cruel privation in one of the six 'sprawling industrial' pottery towns. In 1867 he went to London where he discovered that he could earn money by writing. In 1903 he went to Paris, and for nearly eight years he stayed in France studying French literature seriously. He returned to England and died in London in 1931.

Arnold had started as a hack but soon became a serious writer of novels. His regular literary career began with the publication of his first novel, *A Man From the North* (1898), and continued till 1930 when *Imperial Palace*, his last came out. In his literary devices Bennett was guided by such French writers of his time as Maupassant, Flaubert, and Balzac, who taught him the lesson of total objectivity in art. In the most detached way he succeeded surprisingly in portraying the manifold facets of life brimming over with joy and sorrow and humiliation. There is no personal approval or disapproval in his writings; no preaching of any home-spun truth. If at all there is any self projection, it is unconscious.

In the words of A.C. Ward... his aim was, to record life – its delights, indignities, and distresses – without conscious intrusion of his own personality between the record and the reader. Like his French masters, he was a copyist of life, and only indirectly a commentator, or an apologist.''[37]

Bennett was, however, an artist and not a mere cameraman. The picture of life caught in a camera is flat, mechanical; it can give minute details or broad panaromic views but never the pulsating life underneath. The artist on the other hand blends truth of life with fiction, and presents something which is greater than the transient truth. Bennett's portrayal of society is lively. He was not disinterested, but only dispassionate; not uninvolved or unconcerned, only unconcerned. He followed the injunction of Flaubert and Maupassant given in the preface to *Pierre et Jean* (1881) – ''The realist, if he is an artist, will seek to give us not a banal photographic representation of life, but a vision of it that is fuller, more vivid and more compellingly truthful than even reality itself.''[38]

Bennett's novels are, 'a great bundle of little things' but he did give them excessive touch of humour like Dickens, nor did he give them emotional colouring like Charlotte Bronte. His dispassionate handling gave a special meaning to these little things. According to Compton-Rickett, ''He records the little things in a detached, objective way leaving the reader to trace their relationship to the larger matters – if he will.''[39] Bennett, like his French masters, tried to seek beauty not in the matter but in the manner. He gave a special charm and novelty to the Five Towns novels, the air of which was thick with desperateness and squalor, by a naturalistic presentation. Both Walter Allen[40] and Cazamian[41] have noted that this was due to such foreign influences as of Maupassant and Turgenev. But after the Five Towns novels Bennett almost left this naturalistic tradition because temperamentally he was incapable of sustaining his detachment for long. He could not help but respond to the wonderfully thrilling spectacle presented before him.

Another compelling factor for leaving this track was his own extravagant nature. He knew very well that the naturalistic method could not make him earn sufficient money for his smug life. He was an artist but not a devotee to art; he could not, or would not sacrifice the good things of life for the sake of music. He found that, ''He could produce works of ephemeral entertainment more rapidly and more profitably than works of art. He became famous and wealthy; he began to lead an expensive and gay life....''[42]

The first famous novel of Bennett *A Man From the North* (1898), is perfect in its craftsmanship. It is autobiographical but lacks any distinctive quality. Only when he wrote *Anna of the Five Towns* (1902), he came to be acknowledged as a serious novelist. This novel realistically deals with his early life which he spent in the industrial region of Potteries, though he wrote it sitting far away in London thinking over his past experiences most dispassionately. Bennett has made the novel rich with his own grim experiences. He has described how the towns grew larger and richer day by day. He has given as exact picture of the lives of the people of Five Towns, who were bound by old traditions and were in love with their favourite follies. He has depicted how the scientific inventions were changing the old outer scene. And also in this novel can be seen both his similarity with and differences from H.G. Wells. "Inevitably he felt, as Wells felt, the swift flow in the outer shape of our civilization, so little perceived at any given moment by the average human being; and he felt also, more subtly than Wells, the tragedy of the spectacle of men and women growing old without the power of adaptation."[43]

Arnold Bennett wrote *The Old Wives Tale* (1908) in Flaubertian Style, drawing much upon his previous experiences at Potteries. The scene lies in a small manufacturing town and contains a naturalistic description of domestic life potent enough to convince the reader. Sophia and Constance, the main female characters pass from their blooming youth into horrid wrinkles of old age, but are unaware of the passage of time that has brought about many deaths and decay and many mutations. But this is not all. The novel "combines humour with tragedy, pathos and indignity and ugliness with beauty. The character drawing is excellent and even the trivial incidents are as compulsively interesting as the great events."[44]

Clayhanger (1910) is the first volume of the Clayhanger trilogy and is a remarkable novel. The scene is again laid in the Five Towns. Edwin Clayhanger in whom 'a flame burnt that was like an altar fire', is at war against puritanism and opposes his father who is 'hard, obstinate and unimaginative'. But he himself is not totally free from the old mental sickness of his society. The battle between the resisting old and the irresistible new is fought in the squalid environment of the Five Towns peopled with the homely figures who are absorbed in their traditional rituals and habits.

Hilda Lessways (1911), the second volume of the trilogy is not as remarkable as the first; nevertheless it is good for several reasons. It is absolutely free from those excesses which are generally noticeable in *The Old Wives Tale*. It is potent enough to absorb our attention and sustain our interest. Here Bennett is not as objective as in *Clayhanger*. He takes the side of Hilda and does not care for literary detachment. '*These Twain*'(1916) the last volume of trilogy is peculiarly noted for its artistic devices and verisimilitude. *Riceymän Steps*(1923), a different novel from the novels of the Five Towns, is not of the same stature as *Clayhanger* and *The Old Wives Tale*. Here Bennett does not feel the same degree of intimacy with his characters as he did with the Baineses, the clayhangers and the Orgreaves: Earlforward and the girl Elsie. The novel is undoubtedly drab, but the creative artist in Bennett has lightened its darkness with a sense of beauty. His 'universal sympathy' found beauty even in the most squalid triflings.

Later on when Arnold Bennett became intimate with politicians and journalists he wrote two novels in a satirical vein: *Lord Raingo* (1926) and, *In Later Life* (1930). *Imperial Palace* (1930), was his last important work, noted for its 'romantic human interest' and craftmanship.

Like Hardy, Bennet too was a regional novelist, but with a difference. Hardy's Wessex was a revival of the past and his characters were rooted to that past. This past of Hardy stood for contentment, if not happiness; but Bennett's Potteries resisting changes produced only squalor, ugliness and tragedy. The harmony between the people and their environment so prominent in Hardy is absent in Bennett. Hence Hardy's universality transcends time and space, but Bennett's does not. Walter Allen has underlined this feature of Bennett's novels: "At his best Bennett does achieve universality of a kind, but it is not Hardy's kind. It is, if such a thing is possible, a limited universality, true for a certain kind of a community at a certain point in time, a picture of life not only in the Five Towns but in any industrial community during the last three decades of the nineteenth century."[45]

The plots of Bennett's are devoid of any surprise or mystery and this makes them nude in their beauties. Mystery sustains interest, and producing surprises, makes the reader aware of the several workings of the human heart. A novel without such a mystery is a novel of a few bare arid facts which create boredom.

Bennett's novels lose much of their appeal due to lack of mystery of surprise, yet we can't underrate their value which lies in their graphic portrayal of the regional life. As G.S. Fraser has remarked, "He depicted minutely and exactly the hard surface details of life, ... yet with all its limitations the world of his best books is solid and true and living and, all in all, one of the most accurate descriptions of English provincial life that has even been made.''[46]

Bennett seriously lacked not only in philosophy but also in gracious style. Of course there are many passages picturesque enough in their details and powerful enough to catch our eye, but generally they lack in nobility and dignity which is needed for a great work of art. Bennett's language is suitable and appropriate only for conversation between two characters.

To conclude: Arnold Bennett was a famous exponent of the naturalistic as well as of the impressionistic technique. In his novels we do not find fight of imagination, nor a reflective spirit brooding seriously over the drama of marching humanity, yet they contain an irresistible charm which cannot be removed by the currents of time. Cazamian has opined that the novels of Arnold Bennett might be poor in any respects, but ''they rest upon a solid foundation; their harmony with a certain national and human nature, with some fundamental needs of our instinct of truth, imparts to them the character of what may last.''[47]

John Galsworthy

John Galsworthy (1867-1933), an aristocrat, excelled his two plebeian contemporaries : H.G. Wells and Arnold Bennett in many respects. Well lacked in art and Bennett in sentiment but Galsworthy presented perfect equipoise between the two. His intuitive interpretation of characters, his detachment, his superb piety, and the verve and suavity of his language made his novel, *Forsyte Saga*, a monumental social chronicle. The Chief distinguishing feature of Galsworthy's novels is the juxtaposition of the old and new social values. Cazamian has aptly remarked: ''Thus brought no less clear and no less bold a mind to the analysis of the social order; as representative of his own country as Arnold Bennett, he had more efficiently mingled the national instincts with the lessons of unashamed objectivity which English literature was receiving from the outside world.''[48]

John Galsworthy was born in 1867 and received his education at Harrow, New College and Oxford. He also studied law and was called to the Bar in 1890. He could not however continue practising law for long and soon entered the field of literature. Galsworthy's purpose was solely altruistic. Through Cethru, a character in the novel *The Inn of*

Tranquility (1912), he has defined the purpose of a novelist. It is to expose both social good and evils. Galsworthy, like Cethru, unveiled the rugged and evil, and sometimes dark racesses of human mind without any intrusion of his own personality. Unlike Wells and Bennett he was not obsessed with his own past. He was a realist and, therefore, he dealt with the immediate life with its various facets without any distortion.

In his novels, and also plays, we observe Galsworthy as non-attached chronicler presenting with equal fairness and objectivity all the contending and contradictory elements involved in a situation. *The Man of Property* (1906), the first novel of '*The Porsyte Saga*', presents Soames Forsyte with his sense of possessiveness that includes even the members of his family in conflict with his wife, Irene who was sentimental and vivacious. '*The Country House*' (1907) reveals the tension going on between the two main characters: The squire who was unkind, obstinate and blunt and his wife who was kind, liberal and sharp in mind. In *Fraternity* (1909) and *The Partician* (1911) the novelist has held the balance between several contending forces prudently.

Galsworthy was a follower of the middle way in delineating these contending social forces. He could not condemn such old institutions as the church, state and Government outright. He visualised something of value in them. Nor could be pin his faith in the contemporary age with disintegrated after the First World War. He stood for the blending of the new with the old, retaining whatever is good in the latter and rejecting all that is harmful in the former. R.A. Scott-James has commented, "Thenceforward, Galsworthy was always to be on the middleline, observing what lay to the left and the right of it, in his earlier days laying the emphasis of blame on the right, later shifting it to the left."[49]

In portraying the details of life, Galsworthy followed the naturalistic tradition. His disinterestedness was the direct result of this tradition. He showed an unfaltering fidelity to life, never submitting to his personal whims and eccentricities. Sometimes his powerful emotions lurked just below the velvety surface but without disturbing the balance and always giving a sense of reality. His realism was no doubt scrupulous but always tinged with a humanitarian philosophy. He was not a conscious preacher but a conscious artist who painted his fictive pictures as he saw them in real life and left them to the readers to draw their own conclusions. In the words of Scott-James, "... he was thinking above all of literary technique ... how to present the spectacle of life with gracious impartiality without obtruding the personality of the writer ..."[50]

The first part of *Forsyte Saga* is recognised as Galsworthy's best creation. It consists of *The Man of Property* (1906); *In Chancery* (1920); and *To Let* (1921). The second part titled, '*A Modern Comedy*' also contains three volumes — *The White Monkey* (1924); *The Silver Spoon* (1926) and *Swan Song* (1928). And finally he wrote the third part as a single volume called, *On Forsyte Change* (1930). *The Forsyte Saga* spanned both the Edwardian and Georgian periods. It reflects the changes in the writer's mood caused by the war, and deals with those changes which the war brought in its wake. Unlike Bennett's, the wolrd in Forsyte Saga is that of the upper middle class of businessmen whose main objective in life was to amass riches. Galsworthy has described how this materialistic instinct was directly in conflict with the fine feeeling of human heart and over-rode even personal relations.

Galsworthy produced symbolic characters who stood for certain scrupulous as well as well unscrupulous elements dominant in the English society. Some of his characters are allegorical, yet they are lively and vigorous. In the words of Cazamian, "His studies of characters are very varied ... it would be unfair not to recognise that he has created virile figures, with robust relief ... John Galsworthy has never aimed at the extreme complexity in which some psychologists find their crowning achievement."[51]

Galsworthy, a novelist of feminine temperament, could not handle his plot because of his visionary contemplation; still he showed his skill in imparting great elasticity to the form by his superb technique. His style is suited to his purpose. His poetic temperament has created fine pictures of the earth, sky, air and water of the country-side. His sentences are short but meaningful and are fine example of excellent prose.

To conclude, Galsworthy was a real force in his time, and aroused the whole nation from its drowsy complacency. He was a consummate craftman excelling the other novelists of his time, and long remained a model for the succeeding generations of novelists. He was "devoted to the conception of literature as an art, yet equally convinced that it has a social function to fulfil; ..."[52] His novels would always be considered as the most befitting to the time which produced them, and the best means of making us aware of the social injustices that have smudged the fair face of modern justice.

Joseph Conrad

Teodor Jozef Konrad Korzeniowski, to give Joseph his full name, was born in 1857 of Polish parents in the Ukraine region of South Poland. The family became involved in revolutionary activities and was banished to Vologde in North Russia, where the mother soon died. The child Conrad was shocked, lonely and despondent. It was only 1869 that the young boy and his old and sick father could move to Cracow.

Conrad was a born romantic and cherished the desire of entering the fresh and open life of a sailor. At the age of seventeeen he left Cracow to join a French vessel. He remained there for four years during which, in addition to his duties as a crew, he studied French literature extensively. In 1878 he changed over to the British Merchant Marine and did not leave it till 1894. He settled permanently in Kent and died in year 1924.

Conrad's romantic nature coupled with his earlier Russian and later French studies moulded his literary writings. His studied presentations are realistic but covered with a thin layer of weird kind of charming beauty. George Sampson considers him to be the greatest English novelist of the period between Henry James and D.H. Lawrence, as well as the most remarkable figure in the whole history of English literature.[53] His faith in his fellowmen was so great and his understanding so deep that he could very well imagine the lives of his characters and their locales without feeling any need to call upon his concrete experiences. The resultant picture of life might be slightly blurred but it is certainly clearer than any documentary work. It is not the least fantastic in spite of the romantic elements; on the contrary it is quite convincing, more convincing than an authentic historical record.

Conrad's genius was like that of an untutored but born painter who makes his large canvas a rich tapestry of many colours and shades that never fails to hold the interest of the viewers. To him the story was of secondary importance; he aimed at not to 'say' anything but make his readers feel and see. Consequently his plots are not carefully constructed; they also lack variety and inventiveness. He has, however, maintained proper balance between his matter and manner. He has shown great skill in making his imaginary pictures well proportioned in their contour.

In many of the novels of Conrad the ocean-rippling and smiling in the morning light of the sun, dark and mysterious in the plea moonlight, at times placid and serene like a mountain lake and at others turbulent and deadly like a visitation from the beyond – assume a prominent role deciding the fates of the gallant mariners. The sailor that he was, his imagination was haunted by oceans and women. Both fascinated him; both were puzzle to him. The vastness of one seemed illimitable; the seduction of the other unfathomable. To him the two were the two mistresses of live's values.[54]

Conrad's characters are mostly foreigners to their locales. He has drawn them intensely and dramatically, but has failed to make them really lively and three dimensional. His approach was neither analytical nor psychological. Sometimes they are symbols. By removing them from their normal environment and setting them in a different world of mighty mountains and angry seas he has made them appear dwarfish, unable to cope with the forces buffeting them from unknown quarters. In the words of F.R. Leavis, "... we see the characters from the outside, and only as they belong to the ironic pattern-figures in the futilities of a public drama, against a dwarfing background of mountain and gulf."[55]

Conrad is impressionistic in his technique showing the influences of Flaubert, Turgenev, and Henry James. He was careful in using words and images, and A.C. Ward has remarked in this connection : "The novelist has to strive for the perfect blending of form and substance, aspiring to the plasticity of sculptor, to the colour of painting, and to the magic suggestiveness of music, which Conrad believed, might be brought to play for an evanescent instant over the common place surface of the words; of the old, old words, worn thin, defaced by ages of careless use."[56]

Dante once said that poetry and the language proper for it, are an elaborate and painful toil. Because of his care over the language, Conrad's prose certainly is a poet's prose, rich in sensuous imagery and pregnant with meaning. It is like a verse musical and symmetrical in form. As an artist he tried to combine thought with feeling, humour with pathos. His ironical remarks, though sharp, are artistic enough in their setting. The uncertainty of human fate and suffering human vanities are chiefly the product of his Slav temperament.

Undoubtedly Conrad's art is not perfect. He has failed to explore the relation existing between man and man. He could not give vitality and finer breath to his portraits which do not bear any resemblance to life. Still he was regarded as a major force in the early twentieth century. His beautiful language, masterly presentation of variegated situations and scenes, attractive portraits, and fine blending of romanticism with realism differentiated him from the other great novelists of his time. F.R. Leavis has rightly said, "But he was not only by far the greatest of the Edwardians; there is more to be said than that. Scott, Thackeray, Meredith and Hardy are commonly accounted great novelists. If the criterion is the achievement in work addressed to the adult mind, and capable of as much of engaging again and again its full critical attention then Conrad is certainly a greater novelist than the four enumerated ...."[57]

Rudyard Kipling

Poet, journalist, writer of short stories and novels, and recipient of the Noble Prize for literature (1907), Rudyard Kipling (1885-1936) was more of an Anglo-Indian than an English writer. During his life-time he saw Queen Victoria declared as the Empress of India; he also saw from a distance the South African war and the First World War; and his ideas gradually expanded to make him a prophet of the imperial ideal. In spirit he was one with Curzons and Rhodes, and it is mainly through him that the people of Great Britain became conscious of their extending over many lands and many peoples. They came to believe with Kipling that they were the 'chosen people' divinely ordained to carry the 'white man's burden' of ruling over the 'inferior races' in Asia and Africa. If in the process, they put a few billion pounds belonging to these 'inferior people' in their own pockets, it was their just reward.

Rudyard Kipling was born in Bombay in the year 1865 of Methodist parents. His father was a professional artist and Principal of the school of art at Lahore. His mother too had artistic connections notably with Morris and the Pre-Raphaelists. He went to England in 1877 for education and was for some time the editor of his college magazine. He returned to India in 1882 and became a sub-editor of a local newspaper. When he finally returned to England where he died in 1936, he travelled by the way of Japan and America visiting most of the countries then considered important. His extensive travels gave him experience of many different types and also an international touch to his vision which affected his writings. However, the journalist's touch is found in all his writings except those about India.

Kipling wrote extensively and was enormously popular in his life-time. However, he wrote mainly poems and short stories, and only a few novels. Even of these few novels, *The Light That Failed* (1891), is really a long short story and *Kim* (1901) alone is of any permanent value. In the words of Walter Allen, *Kim*, however, is "without parallel or progeny."[58]

In spite of his long stay in the country, and extensive correspondence with its people both native as well as his own expatriate countrymen, Kipling's understanding of India and Indians was limited. He was handicapped by the prejudices of his fellow Britons in the country; and although he saw much, he divined little. At the same time it must be admitted that while he might not have made India understood by the English speaking people of Great Britain and the U.S.A., he certainly succeeded in making it interesting. And his short stories in such collections as *Plain Tales From The Hills*, *The City of Dreadful Night* and the two *Jungle Books* contributed much more than *Kim*. The image of India in the West – a country of fakirs, snakes, elephants and fabulously rich marriages – comes mostly from this source. He also made the people in his own land appreciate their 'Tommies' better. Previously they took these mercenary soldiers for granted, landed them in theory, but were really ashamed of their profession. Kipling showed that they too were human deserving humane understanding and sympathy.

Kipling was a past master in telling stories, and the straight descriptions in *Kim* and many of his short stories are written with superb clarity and colour. The characters that he has drawn are sharp and clear, but he has not entered very deep into their souls. Only that much is sketched as is necessary for the story. His soldiers – fully individualised but of rudimentary intelligence, school boys and growing men, officers on the Afghan frontier, the civil servants in famine time, the engineer facing a flood and the wonderful sketches of animals – all are distinct but somewhat cold.

Kipling's prose is that of a poet, a poet disengaged from his poetic sensibility. It is sonorous and musical and full of charming images. He selected only the essentials and adopted a conscious style in which every word is expressive. In fact he has shown great ingenuity in the selection and use of words. He has used Germanic words extensively, reinterpreting them and bringing to the surface their original meanings. He has used many army slangs to make his narrations and descriptions lively and authentic.

Kipling's popularity and esteem suffered a sharp decline since approximately 1920 when the great gaps in his understanding of India and Briton's' manifest destiny' in relation to that country (and other colonies) became apparent. A prophet of an ideal can't survive when that ideal is proved to be wrong.

Time has come for a more sober assessment of Kipling's works. In the opinion of G.S. Fraser, "Kipling in fact is a writer who must be rediscovered from time to time and who ... will be remembered for a passionate exactness of language and for disturbing moments of deep vision that every now and again break, with most startling effect, through the compact and jaunty surfaces of his verse and prose."[59]

Virginia Woolf

Virginia Woolf was the main exponent of Bloomsbury tradition that found its full expression in her novels which are filled to satiety with poetry, imagination and sensibility. Her life spanned exactly the same years as of James Joyce and as novelists both worked in the same field, *viz*. 'Stream of Consciousness'. However, whereas James Joyce delved deep into the subconscious, Mrs. Woolf dealt with the psychological reactions to external stimuli. The world of Mrs. Woolf was limited like that of Jane Austen but being concerned chiefly with the mind, she lacked the exquisite detailed craftmanship of the latter in portraying this world.

The more important novels of Virginia Woolf are *Voyage Out*, (1915); *Mrs. Dalloway* (1925); *To the Light House* (1927); *The Waves* (1931) and *The Years* (1937). In addition, she also wrote a few essays in criticism of literature of manner. The subconscious of James Joyce is a witches' cauldron, boiling and bubbling and randomly throwing the ugly, the horrid, and the hateful. The human mind in Virginia Woolf's novels is comparatively more serene and free from turmoil though not exactly orderly and placid.

For Woolf everything was proper stuff of fiction. Every feeling, every thought, every quality of brain and spirit is drawn upon; no perception came amiss. This, however, made here so much engaged with the minor, even insignificant events, nothing memorable happens in her novels. "Her characters do not engage other characters in overt dramatic conflict; rather, they wander through the park, looking at the play of light on leaves and grass, observe the dogs and nurse maids, the banana peel on the gravel path, the crinkled face of a bedraggled old man on a bench, while some tenuous but profound inner conflict plays itself out within their own-selves in terms of this pattern of sensation."[60]

Virginia Woolf was not an objective artist. Her characters lived in her own mind. Therefore, in trying to present the myriad impressions in the minds of these characters, she had to reject the naturalistic technique and adopt the impressionistic one. Her characters are modern Hamlets constantly soliloquising and remaining mere lonesome silent spectators of life's procession.

Coupled with her impressionistic technique, the form of her novels is more of the nature 'hit or miss' similar to that of Thomas Nash's or Lawrence Sterne's. The difference between her and Sterne was that whereas the latter's adventures were in the objective physical world, hers were essentially in the mental. Keeping in mind the formal aspect of her novels, A.C. Ward has remarked, "She was herself one of the important experimenters and though considered purely as fiction, her novels are unsatisfying to those schooled in the traditional mode of the English novelists from Fielding and Smollett to Dickens and on to Wells and Pristley. She undoubtedly extended the boundaries of the novel. For her literary ancestry we should look back to Lawrence, Sterne rather than to the robust stylists."[61]

Virginia Woolf was a sensitive artist as is evident from the delicate shifts and turns in the thought-process of her characters so faithfully and understandingly presented by her. This also has produced many monotonous monologues. These characters belonging to the limited world of the writer and existing mostly in her mind, also lack variety. They belong to the intelligentsia of middle class, feeling and thinking more or less alike. They are articulate and self-conscious but in the absence of physical actions, they do not become lively. They eat their hearts out, unable to communicate even with each other. "They live in a lonely but almost completely self endorsed world."[62] Consequently the world of Mrs. Woolf's novels is a sad one. The language of Virginia Woolf is poetic to a fault and this is her weakest point. There are, however, quite a few sparkling and sensitive passages about which A.C. Ward has rightly remarked, "... she composed numerous enchanting passages which never lack the firmness and clarity of good prose, even when they incite to the mood of exaltation produced by poetry."[63]

To conclude, in the novels of Virginia Woolf we do not find the uncertainty of Lawrence's art, Joyce's exaggeration of savagery and Richardson's dichotomy of unity. Dealing with the minds of middle class sensitivity, she was a very popular novelist in her age. There is no obscurity in her novels and no problems of intelligibility.

E.M. Forster

Edward Morgan Forster (1879-1970), a follower of the Bloomsbury tradition, was acknowledged as an outstanding literary genius of the Edwardian age, although he wrote only a limited number of novels. Rudyard Kipling and Joseph Conrad could not show that balance between aestheticism and moral sense as Forster did. His literary devices originated from no source other than his own mind, and they are thought to be a valid even to-day.

Forster's gross realism is delicately blended with his lyrical language. His intellectual interpretation of human life, his satire and irony and all-embracing sensibility – all worked miraculously solely anchored in the fashion of bygone days. He was a philosopher thinking over those human problems which are ever a cause of vexation to the whole human race. His contemporary Edwardians like Galsworthy, Kipling, Bennett and Conrad lacked this philosophic sense. Like Hardy, human life to him was a serious and mysterious thing though he was neither a pessimist, nor a fatalist, and not even an agnostic. Forster, too, took the human life to be tragic, but not in the sense of Hardy. He did not believe in any superior power like Immanent Will. He thought that man's own frailties were the general cause of his unhappiness. He dealt with those problems of human relationship and morality which directly resulted from man's own narrowness of mind, problems not of an age but for all time. He "is interested in human behaviour in so far as it presents moral problems ...such problems as whether we have been kind and understanding enough to our neighbours, whether we are judging them by the same standards as we judge ourselves by ...."[64]

To Forster philosophy was not mere abstraction, a means to escape from life. He himself has declared, "I cannot shut myself up in a Palace of Art of a Philosophic tower and ignore the madness and misery of the world."[65] He thought it to be the duty of an artist to interpret the disappointing scene before him and give it a coherence and beauty that life itself does not possess.[66]

Forster wrote only five novels in his life-time, each of which is complete in all respects. These are: '*Where Angles Fear to Tread*' (1905); *The Longest Journey* (1907); *A Room With A View* (1908); *Howard's End*; and *A Passage To India* (1924). The complicated but coherent plot, superb characterisation, the subtlety and delicacy of style, transparent and lucid prose – all indicate that these are the product of a mature mind.

Henry James considered the value of a novel to depend directly on, "the amount of felt life concerned in producing it," and ultimately on "the kind and the degree of the artist's prime sensibility, which is the soil out of which his subject springs."[67] Forster like many others, felt that there were things that could not be expressed directly; so he took recourse to symbols. Like Bertrand Russel, he was a liberal humanist and gave full expression to his liberal thoughts in deciding the fates of his characters. He had faith only in things natural and spontaneous, and condemned all the hypocritical social conventions which weighed down the good traits in an individual. In the words of G.S. Fraser, "One might say that Forster is the best modern English novelist of the liberal tradition, the tradition which says it is upto everyman to choose his own friends, his own job, to arrive at his own convictions. Forster realises the almost tragic inner struggle that is involved in living upto this ideal!"[68]

Forster was ever best in the depiction of 'physical vitality', the paganism, the exuberant passion of youth and these excellences made his novels remain fresh and individual even after much rereading, and they will probably remain current for a long time to come.

His villains suffer because of their profane character which issues from their sinister deeds. But he was ever on the same level with his characters, whether he felt compassion or dislike. They belong to English upper middle class of the Edwardian age and represent the values of that class. 'Nullity' is the principal tragic flaw in them. They are nice, dainty, and agreeable. They also possess snobbishness, shams and foibles. Forster has painted them both from the outside and within. Joseph Warren Beach has remarked, "This is a great outstanding feature of technique since the time of Henry James, that the story shall tell itself, being conducted through the impressions of the characters. It is this which finally differentiates fiction from History and Philosophy and science."[69] Forster followed this technique truly. His stories develop through the myriad impressions of the characters. Sometimes the episodes are improbable, but nonetheless convincing.

After *A Passage To India*, Forster stopped writing novels; the society was changing too fast. R.A. Scott-James has recorded, "He himself has explained it by saying that the novel as he conceives it demands a society with some stability resting on something fixed not only in manners but in place ...."[70]

Forster's style is graceful, sonorous and suited to his purpose. It is this individual style that gives unity to his novels. A.C. Ward has commented about it, "E.M. Forster's style is luminous and sensitive, and his books have many beautiful passages; his satire is sharp and penetrating as he deals with conventions and incidents; and there is profound (sometimes bitter) irony in the poising of massive effects upon tiny causes like a monstrous inverted pyramid.''[71]

His notable critical work, ''*Aspects of the Novel*'' (1927) is considered even today to be a standard work on the subject, dealing as it does with such elements as plot, people, rhythm, fancy, and so on. He was a modern Aristotle, laying down sound principles for a perfect novel.

James Joyce (1882-1941)

Impressionism, a product of romantic individualism and modern self-consciousness, is related to the writer's personal reaction to all that constitute life and its environment. It is in a way a projection of his own self, and is therefore unsuitable for any dramatic or scientific presentation. On the other hand, ''Joyce aims at presenting the whole of life, both external and so it gushes up from the depths of the unconscious, in all its wild disorder.''[72] He wanted to rip open the polished painted package of modern civilization and reveal the truth hidden behind the thick wrappers of hypocritical behaviour, external decency and outward fastidiousness. And he wanted to do it not like Jonathan Swift, not with bitterness, not through caricature and exaggeration. His attitude was rather that of a scientist, a psychiatrist-dispassionate and detached, not disinterested and cold but vitally concerned and sympathetic. He wanted to reveal the horrid and the ugly in man's sub-conscious mind, not to condemn but to cure.

The old much used (misused) language – its vocabulary and syntax – James Joyce found inadequate for his purpose. In a work of art the medium of expression should not only objectively manifest or reveal but should also equally objectively represent or signify. Accepting the ideas of Benedetto Croce about expressionism, he felt that there should be as near a correspondence as possible between that which is to be expressed and the medium of expression. As he could not achieve this near correspondence with the language at hand, he sat down, ''... with seventeen foreign language dictionaries, six encyclopaedias, seven pounds of Coffee, an Atlas, and a world Almanac''[73] to forge a new one for his '*Ulysses*'. He also thus founded the cult of unintelligibility in literature.

James Joyce was born in Dublin in the year 1882. After his college education he went to Paris in 1902 from where he went first to Triest (Italy) and then to Zurich (Switzerland) and then again back to Paris.

His important novels are: *A Portrait of the Artist As a Young Man* (1916); *Ulysses* (1922); and *Finnegan's Wake* (1939), although he did write a few poems, short stories, and two other novels *Anna Livia Plurabelle* (1930), and *Haveth Childers Everywhere* (1931).

Joyce was a conscious artist, and in addition to forging a new language, he adhered to the technique of stream-of-consciousness throughout *Ulysses*. This novel deals with the actual sordidness of Dublin life as experienced by the various characters. The personal vision of the writer got mixed up with the interior vision of these characters, who observed minutely the multitudinous activities and the flow of diversified life in such common places as bars, brothels, shops, offices and streets. He looked deep into the minds of men, even into the subconscious, and felt no hesitation in exposing the dirty, squalid and ugly facets of the inner lives of the Dubliners. "It is horrible, but it is masterly."[74] His style was quite appropriate to his subject. When disorder is writ large over the things to be expressed, it is only proper that the language too is freed from the rigid control of grammar and vocabulary. It does not mean that the language of *Ulysses* is irrational or careless. Rather Joyce was extremely careful in this regard. Each word is a complete image in itself, and image follows image in succession producing a paradoxical but symbolical medley full conforming to the seething subconscious.

The figures in the *Ulysses* are mostly archetypes. Bloom and Stephen Dedalus stand for 'humanity in the eternal flux'. They have been shown in a state of 'drunkenness' and reveal their 'fantasia of the unconscious'. They are not well-marked in their outlines; they are seldom seen; mostly their voices are heard while they discourse. Nevertheless they are convincing as characters.

One of the chief characteristic of Joyce as a novelist is his intellectual but exact grasp of the reality," and it is a measure of his superiority as a writer that his concern with the texture of reality should exercise itself in verbal and intellectual rather than visual or descriptive terms."[75]

Joyce had his own idea of the role of novelist–it was that of an omnipresent and omniscient God uninvolved in the lives and activities of His creations. In his own words, "The artist, like the God of creation remains within or behind or above his handiwork, invisible, refined out of existence, indifferent, paring his finger-nails."[76] The texture of reality presented by Joyce is carefully woven. There is nothing superfluous in it. The great care that he devoted to his novels is evident from the fact that he took fourteen years to write *Pinnegans Wake*.

As it has already been said, Joyce also wrote a few poems. He was also a singer with a fine ear for music. Although he did not make any mark either as a poet or as a musician, his prose in spite of its occasional unintelligibility is lyrical. It also possesses structural unity because of the manner in which he has combined or interrelated the parts to the whole.

The judgement about Joyce as a novelist rests mainly on *Ulysses*, but the eminent critics are as unsure of their verdict as the most ordinary reader. He has, however, drawn attention to one very important fact that the modern life as it exists both outside and inside man's mind is so complex that it needs a new technique of expression, if not a completely that it needs a new medium itself.

D.H. Lawrence (1885-1930)

D.H. Lawrence was a great literary force of his time. He invented his own technique, and language which gave a distinct moulding and colouring to his fictive pictures which are still potential enough to arrest our attention. His psychological interpretation of characters, fine dialogues and excellent manipulation of appropriate scenes and situations made him unforgettable to the succeeding generation. For all that he ignored the technique of stream-of-consciousness, he succeeded in the exploration of the dark abyss of human heart through his intuitive powers.

F.R. Lewis eulogises him for his many new experiments covering the different aspects of a novel. ''He is the most daring and radical innovater in form, method, technique. And his innovations and experiments are dictated by the most serious and urgent kind of interest in life.''[77] As a true artist Lawrence explored the inner working of human mind and heart. He was well aware of those psychological truths which Freud had discovered. He wrote in a letter: ''But the conscious life which you adhere to is no more than a masquerade of death: There is a living unconscious life ... we should find reality in the darkness.''[78] Therefore his approach to his characters was from the inside. His characters derive their vitality and liveliness from their inner constituting essence. His `primitive thinking' and `feeling' gave a large dimension to his characters but they are not longer than life. In his essay, `why the Novel Matters', he expresses about the necessity of liveliness in characters: ''In the novel, the characters can do nothing but live. If they keep on being good according to pattern, they cease to live, and the novel falls dead. A character in the novel has got to live or it is nothing.''[79]

Lawrence has depicted the heartfelt feelings and strong emotions of his characters who resemble us and who take us into their confidence. They are mostly proletarians, the class to which he himself belonged. Like Emily Bronte, Lawrence surrendered himself to his sensitivity. Primitive instincts receive full expression in his novels. Certainly he was of romantic temperament, who by accident due to adverse circumstances became a realist. His gross realism ridiculed the contemporary civilization that had kept the body restrained by the mind. He advocated that there was nothing obscene in sex. Instinct must get full scope to work itself out.

We observe a vast pervading mystery in his novels and the significance of his characters depend on how far this mystery resided in them and how far they were aware of this mystery which was surviving at the 'instinctual level'.

At first people scarcely recognised the greatness of Lawrence, but later on he succeeded to gain wide popularity. The succeeding generation of novelists made possible what was latent in his writings.

Aldous Huxley (1894-1963)

Aldous Huxley's was a supple and many-sided talent. His mysticism, cynicism, verve, and sharp penetrating intellect made him a popular novelist during the twenties and early thirties. His prophesies, like H.G. Wells' have not come true, yet his novels strongly reflect the mood of desiccation, disillusionment, frustration, and scepticism so prevalent in the First World War period. He has shown also faith in God in his novels as he had no faith in man. He has shown his firm reliance on renunciation which he assumed to be the best cure for modern maladies. *Crom Yellow* (1921); *Mortal Coils* (1922); and *Antic Hay* (1923) ludicrously give realistic expression to 'The Contemporary Dance of Death' and the 'Gothic grotesqueness' of degrading humanity.

Point Counter Point (1928) shows his stern attitude towards the contemporary political atmosphere which was growing darker and darker due to meanness of the politicians and their dangerous game of real politik. In *Brave New World* (1932) we get a horrible picture of the coming human race which would be a production of the laboratory, 'mechanically conditioned to serve the will of their masters'. Unfortunately the creative talent of Huxley declined towards the second half of the nineteen thirties and his *Eyeless In Gaza* (1936); *Time Must Have A*

Stop (1934); and *Age of Essence* (1948) show this regrettable defect. He lost emotional comprehension and human understanding and felt the contemporary situation to be nauseous. A.C. Ward has commented, "The wise take the world as they find, bettering it as far as they can but yielding to no impulse to vomit upon it. Some part of Huxley's later fiction was more vomitous than satirical."[80]

Huxley was very much concerned with the problem of good and evil. But pity was chief feeling. He has expressed this feeling in a strongly satiric vein. In his novels we observe the artist and mystic constantly at war. Like D.H. Lawrence he clothed his vision in mysticism but the dress had too many gaping holes. Scott-James has remarked about this, "It is disconcerting to observe him, obsessed by the Rabelaisian absurdity of the human race, unable to express himself without ribaldry and constant resort to school boyish naughty talk, and the next moment asking us to survey the scene with the mystical serenity of the saint."[81]

His such early novels as *Crome Yellow*, *Antic Hay*, *The Barren Leaves*, are certainly his most interesting ones. He has displayed his wit and wisdom as well as dismay in a detached but satiric manner. He has described how people's ideas and ideals fail to square with their actual life. He has exposed the various types of intellectual ostentation, mockery and falsehood then prevailing. He has, however, failed to deal with the direct and simple feelings of the people.

The main running theme of Huxley's many novels is to search out a 'workable faith'. He sought salvation in his mystical attitude – the renunciation of ordinary human desires and passions, especially egoism. He was an intellectual who frowned at everything below the level of intellect.

What legacies did these writers leave to their successors – legacies that could be accepted, compromised with, deviated from, or even attacked? Firstly Henry James, and to a degree H.G. Wells, D.H. Lawrence and others, have given a body of sound principles in so far as fiction writing is concerned. The complaint of Henry James (1888) that the English novel, "had no air of having a theory, of conviction, a consciousness of itself behind it – of being the expression of an artistic faith, the result of choice and comparison," [82] no more held true for the novelists of the twenties and the thirties. Henceforth in a novel subject and style can't be separate elements, that it is a work of art depending upon the author's imaginative perception of life and that it is an organic thing, all one and continuous from beginning to the end, like any other organism.

Secondly these writers handed down to their successors a variety of technique for adoption and adaptation. There were naturalistic and journalistic techniques of H.G. Wells and Arnold Bennett, dramatic objectivity of Henry James, impressionistic technique of Joseph Conrad and Virginia Woolf, expressionism of James Joyce and the use of symbols by E.M. Forster.

Thirdly a novelist could no longer avoid social responsibility. He could no longer avoid responding to various currents and cross currents of socio-economic political forces operating in the immediate present. If his genius permitted him, he could look to the past and the present and penetrate through to the future; he could also remain confined to the present itself. He could depict the social conditions in the tradition of John Galsworthy; try to lay bare the mental worlds of his characters like D.H. Lawrence or James Joyce penetrate through the confusing social milieu and expose the basic human problems like E.M. Forster or he could even remain engaged with the flotsam and jetsam on the surface of life's current, somewhat in the tradition of Virginia Woolf. How far the novelists of the thirties were benefited by this rich legacy, can be assessed only after a detailed analysis of their works; before this could be undertaken it is first necessary to see the background in which they wrote the novels.

NOTES AND REFERENCES

1. James, R.A. Scott – *The Making of Literature*, Secker and Warburg (London), 1970 (pp. 365-66).
2. Hollowway, John – The Literary scene – *The Modern Age,* edited by Boris Ford (Penguin Books), London, 1964 (p. 7).
3. Allen, Walter – *The English Novel*, 1963 (p. 262), Hormondsworth.
4. *Ibid.*, p . 261.
5. James, R.A. Scott – *Fifty Years of English Literature* (Longmans), London, 1961 (p. 56).
6. Gifford, Henery – Henry James – *The Modern Age*, edited by Boris Ford (Penguin Books), London 1964 (p. 103).
7. Fisher, William J. – Henry James – *American Literature of The Nineteenth Century* (1970), Eurasia Publishing House Pvt. Ltd., Ram Nagar, Delhi (p. 456).
8. Filding, Henry – *Tom Jones* (1955), Collins (London) (p. 11).
9. Allen, Walter – *The English Novel*, Harmondsworth, London, (1963) (p. 258).
10. James, Henry – *The Art of Fiction* – *American Literature of the Nineteenth Century* – edited by William J. Fisher (1970), Eurasia Publishing House Pvt. Ltd., Ram Nagar, Dellhi (p. 509).

11. *Ibid.*, p. 509.
12. Allen, Walter -- *The English Novel*, Harmondsworth (London), 1963, p. 274.
13. James, Henry -- The Art of Fiction -- *American Literature of the Nineteenth Century*, edited by William J. Fisher, 1970, p. 516. Eurasia Publishing House Pvt. Ltd., Ram Nagar, New Dellhi.
14. James, R.A. Scott -- *Fifty Years of Englsih Literature* (Longmans) (1961) (London) (p. 59).
15. Atkins, John -- *Graham Greene* (London), 1957 (p. 180), Calder and Boyars.
16. Allen, Walter -- *The English Novel*, Harmondsworth (London) (1963), p. 267.
17. James, R.A. Scott -- *Fifty Years of English Literature* (Longmans, London), 1961 (p. 36).
18. Forster, E.M. -- *Aspects of The Novel*, Harmondsworth, London (1970), p. 152.
19. *Ibid.*, p. 162.
20. *Ibid.*
21. James, R.A. Scott -- *Fifty Years of English Literature* (Longmans, London), 1961 (p. 59).
22. *Ibid.*, p. 26.
23. Ward, A.C. -- *Twentieth-Century Literature* (1959) (London) (pp. 24-25), Methuen and Co. Ltd.
24. Legouis, Emile and Cazamian, Louis -- *History of English Literature* (London), 1964 (pp. 1316-17), J.M. Dent and Sons Ltd.
25. James, R.A. Scott -- *Fifty Years of English Literature*, 1961 (Longmans, London) (pp. 25-26).
26. Ward, A.C. -- *Twentieth-century Literature* (London), 1959 (p. 27), Methuen & Co. Ltd.
27. *Ibid.*, p. 24.
28. James, R.A. Scott -- *Fifty Years of English Literature* (1961) (London) Longmans (p. 31).
29. Allen, Walter -- *The English Novel*, 1963 (p. 313), Harmondsworth.
30. Sampson, George -- *The Concise Cambridge History of English Literature*, Cambridge University Press, 1972 (p. 890).
31. Forster, E.M. -- *Aspects of The Novel* (London), 1970 (pp. 79-80), Harmondsworth.
32. Legouis, Emile and Cazamian Louis -- *History of English Literature* (1964), London (p. 1322), J.M. Dent and Sons Ltd.
33. James, R.A. Scott -- *Fifty Years of English Literature*, Longmans (1961), p. 20.
34. *Ibid.*, p. 33.
35. *Ibid.*, p. 34.
36. Fraser, G.S. -- *The Modern Writer And His World*, Rupa and Co. Calcutta, 1966 (p. 51).
37. Ward, A.C. -- *Twentieth-Century Literature* (London) (1959), p. 32, Methuen and Co. Ltd.

38. Quoted by Sampson, George -- *The Concise History of English Literature*, Cambridge University Press, 1972, p. 866.

39. Rickett, Arthur Compton -- *A History of English Literature* (London) (1931) (p. 677), Thomas Nelson and Sons Ltd.

40. Allen, Walter -- *The English Novel* (1963), London, p. 318, Harmondsworth.

41. Legouis, Emile and Cazamian, Louis, – *A History of English Literature* (1964) (London), J.M. Dent and Sons Ltd. (pp. 1335-36).

42. Fraser, G.S. -- *The Modern Writer And His World*, Rupa & Co., Calcutta, 1966 (pp. 51-52).

43. James, R.A. Scott -- *Fifty Years of English Literature* (Longmans), 1961 (London), p. 37.

44. Ward, A.C. – Twentieth-Century Literature (London), 1959 (p. 37), Methuen and Co. Ltd.

45. Allen, Walter – *The English Novel*, London, 1963, (p. 319), Harmondsworth.

46. Fraser, G.S. – *The Modern Writer and His World*, Rupa & Co., Calcutta, 1966 (p. 52).

47. Legouis, Emile and Cazamian, Louis -- *A History of English Literature*, 1964 (p. 1337), London, J.N. Dent and Sons Ltd.

48. *Ibid*., p. 1338.

49. James, R.A. Scott--*Fifty Years of English Literature*, 1961, London (p. 44), Longmans.

50. *Ibid*. p. 43.

51. Legouis, Emile and Cazamian, Louis -- *A History of English Literature* (London), 1964 (pp. 1341-42), J.M. Dent and Sons Ltd.

52. James, R.A. Scott -- *Fifty Years of English Literature*, 1961 (London), p. 46, Longmans.

53. Sampson, George – *The Concise History of English Literature*, Cambridge University Press (London), 1972 (p. 867).

54. Quoted by Leavis, F.R. – *The Great Tradition* (London), p. 182, Chatto, 1962.

55. *Ibid*., p. 201.

56. Ward, A.C. -- *Twentieth Century Literature* (London), 1959 (p. 49), Methuen and Co. Ltd.

57. Leavis, F.R. -- *The Great Tradition* (1962), Chatto, London (p. 226).

58. Allen, Walter -- *The English Novel* (1963) (London), p. 281, Harmondsworth.

59. Fraser, G.S. – *The Modern Writer and His World*, Rupa & Co., Calcutta, 1966 (p. 55).

60. *Ibid*., pp. 73-74.

61. Ward, A.C. – *Twentieth-Century Literature* (London) 1959 (pp. 77-78), Methuen and Co. Ltd.

62. Fraser, G.S. – *The Modern Writer and His World*, Rupa & Co., Calcutta, 1966 (p. 76).

63. Ward, A.C. -- *Twentieth-Century Literature* (London), 1959 (p. 78).

64. Fraser, G.S. – *The Modern Writer And His World*, Rupa & Co., Calcutta, 1966, p. 56.

65. Quoted by Klingopulos, G.D. -- Mr. Forsters Good Influence -- *Modern Age*, edited by Boris Ford, 1970 (pp. 248-49) (London).

66. *Times Literary Supplement* -- Friday, August 20, 1954, -- The Air of Bloomsbury (p. 523).

67. Quoted by Klingopulos, G.D. -- Mr. Forsters Good Influence -- *The Modern Age*, edited by Boris Ford, 1970 (p. 248), Harmondsworth (London).

68. Fraser, G.S. -- *The Modern Writer and His World*, Rupa & Co., Calcutta, 1966, p. 58.

69. Beach, Joseph Warren -- *The Twentieth Century Novel*, India 1965 (p. 16).

70. James, R.A. Scott -- *Fifty Years of English Literature*, 1961, Longmans (London) (p. 71).

71. Ward, A.C. -- *Twentieth- Century Literature* (London) (p. 68), 1959, Methuen and Co. Ltd.

72. James, R.A. Scott -- *Fifty Years of English Literature*, Longmans (London), 1961, p. 134.

73. Eastman, Max -- *The Literary Mind*, 1935 (p. 102), Charles Scribners Sons, New York.

74. James, R.A. Scott -- *Fifty Years of English Literature* (London), 1961, Longmans (p. 134).

75. Kettle, Arnold -- The Consistency of James Joyce -- Pelican Guide -- *Modern Age*, edited by Boris Ford (London), 1970 (p. 302), Harmondsworth.

76. Joyce, James -- *A Portrait of the Artist* (London), 1969 (p. 215), Harmondsworth.

77. Leavis, F.R. -- *The Great Tradition*, 1962, Chatto (London), p. 24.

78. Marshall, Percy -- *Masters of the English Novel* (London), Dennis Dobson, 1962 (p. 201).

79. Lawrence, D.H. -- Why the Novel Matters -- *English Critical Texts*, edited by D.J. Enright and Ernest De Chickera (London), 1970 (p. 291).

80. Ward, A.C. -- *Twentieth- Century Literature* (London), 1959 (p. 65), Methuen & Co.

81. James, R.A. Scott -- *Fifty Years of English Literature*, 1961 (p. 174) (Longmans), London.

82. Wimsatt, J.R., Willian K. and Brooks, Cleanth -- *Literary Criticism : A Short History*, Oxford & IBH Pub. Co., Calcutta, 1964, p. 681.

SECOND CHAPTER

PERSPECTIVE OF THE NINETEEN-THIRTIES

"Eating a Lyon's chop in nineteen-thirty,
And staring through the heavy-lidded pane,
Wondering why they keep their plates so dirty,
And why there's dust in London April rain,
I shall see out of the sick swim of falls,
Huddled beneath umbrellas in the strand,
Dim reminiscence of those betterplaces,
Where my rick Cargo drove upon the sand."[1]

The dark clouds hanging dense and low over Europe and England in the nineteen-thirties were really ominous and by the end of the decade the catastrophe actually came to pass. The economic depression heralded by Wall Street crash of 1929 was no sudden event but had its seed in the Treaty of Versailles (1919) that imposed on unbearable war debt upon Germany which in turn affected the financial structure of France, England and the U.S.A. The war of 1914-18 that was to end all wars "settled nothing, composed nothing, and satisfied nobody", and President Wilson's dream of a world safe for democracy received a severe jolt during his negotiations in Paris with the European Politicians. Whatever little hope he had of a world government finally crashed when he himself was defeated at the nineteen twenty Presidential election and when America opted out the League of Nations.

Political events followed swiftly in Europe. By 1931-32 the military revival of Germany was already much advanced. In 1933 Hitler came to power in that country with his National Socialist followers; the German Reichstag was burnt, and the persecution of Jews and Leftist political leaders began. Three years later an anti-comintern pact was signed between Germany, Italy and Japan and Berlin – Rome – Tokyo axis came into being. The rehearsals of the Second World War soon started. Japan invaded Manchuria and moved south into main China. Italy invaded Abyssinia and Germany annexed Sudetanland of Czechoslovakia.

Austria had already become a part of Germany and Germany soon gave indications of its intention to enter Poland. At the South-West corner of Europe, the democratic forces of Spain fought a terrible Civil War with the fascist forces of General Franco in which many freedom loving Europeans including the British fought directly in the International Brigade in support of the former.

For some time in the midst of the political and economic turmoil of Europe, Russia seemed to remain immune. The Bolshevik party had come to power in 1917, and after a short period of initial uncertainty due to both internal disorder and foreign intervention, it became stablished under the leadership of Lenin. Lenin's death, followed by Stalin-Trotosky rivalry, the latter's escape to Mexico and purgings inside Russia were really interludes in the process of consolidation of power by Stalin. The Five-Year Plans were launched and proved to be on the whole successful. Inflation was kept in check and economic depression that was raging over whole of Europe singularly averted. Many European intellectuals began to think that Communist system would provide a panacea to all their political and economic problems. Then came the severe jolt. A treaty was signed between Nazi Germany and Communist Russia that resulted in Russo-Finnish war of 1939-40 and joint invasion of Poland by Germany and Russia on 1 Sept. 1939. The armageddon that the Second World War was, began on 3rd Sept. 1939 with a formal declaration by Winston Churchill, the British Prime Minister.

The old European days were gone for ever. In the words of Benedetto Croce, "We remember the Old Europe with its riches, its flourishing trade, its abundance of goods, its ease of life, its bold sense of security; we see today the new Europe impoverished, each nation occupied solely with its own affairs, too distraught to pay heed to the things of spirit and tormented by the fear of the worse to come."[2]

Great Britain which had long been an arbiter of world problems, could not play any effective role in the international affairs during the nineteen-thirties. Its economic problems were too acute and majority of its people too worried about their own lives for the nation to have any zest for effective intervation in the affairs of any foreign country. The national atmosphere was charged with squeamishness, sordidness and nostalgia. According to Keith Alldritt, these were, "The years of economic depression and of widespread unemployment, heralded first by the Wall Street crash of 1929 and then again by the financial and political crisis in England in 1931. They are the years that marked the rise of Fascism abroad and the tendency towards appeasement and indecision at home. They are the years of contending ideologies and also of paralysis, not only in political and intellectual life but in the national life as a whole. They are the years that we have learned to patronise if not to scorn."[3]

The first two years of the decade preceding the Second World War were the worst years of economic depression and widespread unemployment. This was, "The time of marches and protests, the misery of slum houses, wretchedness of unemployed men without any hope, and indifference of the government."[4] Though the prices were not high and it was possible even for a common labourer to dress adequately, because of extremely low level of income other necessities could not be adequately, met. One could buy one of the best suburban houses of London by making a down payment between £15 and £30. The irony was that for many these houses were as unattainable as the Buckingham palace. It is interesting to note that in 1931 Sh. 17/- a week was the unemployment pay for a man, 9/- for his wife and 2/- for each child. Of those who were employed, a dock labourer earned between £3 and £4 a week, an agricultural worker £1/10, and a butcher between £3 and £4. A miner's earning was anywhere between £4 and £2/10 a week depending upon the productivity of his pit. The workers engaged in luxury occupation were however better off, a chauffeur could make £4 to £5 and an attendant of the Savoy hotel perhaps the same. Samuel Hynes has given a synoptic description of the situation then prevailing in England: "In the national economy, 1931 was the year in which the Depression seemed to settle permanently over England; more than two and a half million men were out of work by the end of the year, the threat of bankruptcy had caused the fall of one government, its successor had abandoned the gold standard, and the value of the pound had dropped by twenty-five per cent. Outside England, there were violent beginnings of disorders that would continue through the thirties: a revolution in Spain and in Asia, the Japanese invasion of Manchuria, which the European Left saw – perhaps a bit melodramatically – as the beginning of the Second World War. In British politics, it was the year in which the second Labour government collapsed; ...."[5]

The second Labour government formed in June 1929 collapsed two years later and after the general election that followed, a National Government of the Conservatives and Liberals assumed office. The new government, however, was unable to meet the complex national and international situation effectively. More and more people leaned towards Communism as a radical cure to their economic ills. In 1930 the Communist Party of England was a political party only in name. The economic success of Russia and economic ills within their own country increased its membership to a respectable level. Though it still continued to remain a small party, its influence was much wider as socialistic ideas seeped into the Labour, Liberal and even Conservative parties. At first the Communist Party of England and the socialist oriented people opposed whatever party happened to be in power, and this opposition became stronger after Russo-German pact of August 1939; but when Germany involved Russia in June 1941, they changed their attitude and fully supported the then British Government and its war efforts.

While by early 1933 hunger and oppression and chaos and despair were worsening the gathering storms of a catastrophic war really shook the hearts of Englishmen. They felt powerless either to do anything to stop it or to speak out clearly about its nature, extent, and possible consequences. During the First World War the main outcry of the young generation was that the old man, alone were responsible for the war, "but in the nineteen-thirties many who had raised that cry found that they were themselves helpless to avert the danger of war which was going to engulf the whole world."[6]

The expectation of a coming war became an insistent part of the consciousness of the generation of the thirties. "It enters into ... some of the best works of the decade's best writers, as a central image or an offstage threat, as an obsessive metaphor, an image or an illusion; ..."[7] The actual war was not the subject but the language of war came readily to mind, as though war had become a natural metaphor to express relations between man and man. Graham Greene, writing about politics and class in 1934, called his novel, *It's A Battlefield*, and Auden, in *The Orators* (1932) imagined the struggle against bourgeois values as a farcical guerilla war. "Indeed, social, political, and economic conflicts together seemed to amount to another war, a third shadow over the thirties that touched lives and imaginations as deeply as the shadows of those other wars, the one that was past and the one that was coming."[8]

The economic depression, unemployment, revolution and war brought drastic changes in man's outlook. People gave much importance to over those that were really important, for example, personal relationships. When they were in love, they asked whether they were satisfied, and were continually tormented by the thoughts that possibly they were not. Masturbation, homosexuality, following people in the streets, breaking up relationships became common day activities. And "these compensatory activities formed a circle of Hell in which people could never rest from proving that their failures were the same as love."[9] Fortheringham, Powell's main character in *Afternoon Men* (1931), correctly remarks about human life and its relationship with others in the society of the thirties in these words: "... and no one knows better than I that it's (friendship) a quality that in these days is often rated lower than those temporary emotional connections between this or that sex which have their foundations on soil as impermanent as the sand of the sea-shore – when love has come to mean the most boring form of lust, when power means the most useless pots of money, when fame means the vulgarest sort of publicity ..."[10] The social comedies of Powell and Evelyn Waugh reflected truly the disintegration of the inter-war society. People became neurotic and their chief emotions were fear and anxiety. They believed in nothing and their minds had no points of reference except the most obvious. "Food, sex, display, success ... the battle was won; yet how dreary, bleak and forbidding was the conquered field."[11] Their chief desire was "freedom from want and freedom from war."[12] They found themselves in a condition of moral and intellectual anarchy. Therefore, we find intellectuals revolting against religion, the socialist against the hierarchy of state, the agitation of writers and artists against the rotten society. They were seeking a kind of freedom from various forms of constraints that were burden to the human spirit, *e.g.*, "The religious authoritarianism that refused to recognise scientifically ascertained facts, the political backwardness that refused to apply the theory of democracy, the whole outlook of the bourgeoise and `philistine'."[13]

Literature was a socially and politically conscious art in the nineteen-thirties. The writers of twenties were mostly escapists and the main causes of their retreat were, "boredom, disgust, indignation against the herd, the community and the world..."[14] But the writers of the thirties attempted not to save themselves and not to save the community, but to try to save both. Rex Warner has clearly enunciated this affiliation between literature and politics in his, *The Cult of Power* thus: "Moreover, we have learnt that a novel can exercise as much (or even more) political influence as can a procession or an official leaflet. So long as men have the leisure and the desire to read, literature is sure to be a force not only in life but in politics ... this is what may we call the political task – to hold the mirror upto nature ... to instruct, to criticise, to delight, to create and reveal ..."[15] These young writers of the thirties got politics, as their grand parents got religion. The writers of this decade firmly believed that "no art could justify itself except as the handmaid of politics."[16] So the artists thought it their sacred duty to record the suppression, murder, cruelty and the breaking of solemn engagements which were the rituals of the day to day life.

And thus, in the nineteen-thirties, "accounts of the literature revealed the affinity of literature to social questions under various heading like 'Literature and Society', 'Literature and Political Background'. We mark regular references to a possible war and the threat of bombing; and the rituals of cinema-going and the cult of film-star. They form prominent subtexts in novels or poems."[17] Auden, Christopher Isherwood, George Orwell – all had political leanings. Christopher Isherwood took the cause of Otto, the chief character of his novel, *Goodbye To Berlin* (1939) and vividly gave an account how "Otto was a victim of the politico-economic conditions under which he was living and the victims can never be regarded as trivial, especially when they were proletarian; whereas Sally was not a victim, was not a proletarian, was a mere self-indulgent upper middle class foreign tourist who could escape from Berlin whenever she chose..."[18] In the famous drama, *The Dance of Death* (1933), Auden's announcer explained at the beginning what the play was about: "We present to you this evening a picture of the decline of a class, of how its members dream of a new life, but secretly desire the old, for there is death inside them. We show you that death as a dancer."[19]

But Evelyn Waugh who expressed the nostalgic mood of the thirties, professed a contrary view. The Earl of Birkenhead has reminisced about Waugh's stern attitude towards communist ideology, "I remembered then his detestation of communism, which can be seen in his war novels when he describes with revulsion the consecration of the sword of Stalingrad before it was offered to Stalin, whom he believed, with every reason, to be one of the arch-murderers of history .... Our alliance with Russia completely deprived the war of the crusading element which he had first invested it with ...."[20] But his art was not an infidel to the age. Virginia Woolf was right to observe that, "In 1930 youngmen at college were forced to be aware of what was happening in Russia, in Germany, in Italy, in Spain. They could not go on discussing aesthetic emotions and personal relations. They could not confine their reading to the poets; they had to read the politicians. They read Marx. They became communists; they became antifascists."[21] Therefore we are not surprised to see such a propagandist poem in this decade as:

"Unhappy Russia

The URSS
The URSS or as the SSSR
SS how is it SS
SSR SSR oh my dear
Just think SSR

* * *

Each of your breathings begets
Marx and Lenin in the Sky."[22]

But when we read Evelyn Waugh's *A Handful of Dust* (1937), we are reminded of Eliot's famous poem *Waste Land* (1922). We think of them as antipolitical, we find no suggestion in them that politics of the right or the left might avert the end of western civilisation. In Greene's novels of the thirties we mark an overriding sense of disruption, nostalgia, loneliness, fear and anxiety due to the impending war and prevailing unemployment. He was not an antifascist but he always showed his sympathy with the proletarians. His early novel, *Stamboul Train* (1932) is tinged with politics. In, *In The Quiet American* (1955) Greene has presented two opposing forces: communism and colonialism, East and West, materialism and Catholicism for they were, finally, the terms in which Greene saw the conflict. Rex Warner similarly has shown in, *The Aerodrome* (1938) and *The Professor* (1941) how the radicals and reactionaries were at war with each other in this decade.

Thus Graham Greene, Rex Warner, Anthony Powell, Evelyn Waugh, George Orwell, Edward Upward, Christopher Isherwood – all show political consciousness. These artists of this decade were bourgeois artist in revolt; in short, the individualist. Their main concern was to present pictures of a decaying world order.

In the nineteen-thirties reconciliation of art, religion and morality with science was also a great problem, which took diverse forms. There was confrontation between science and religion, between man and the state, between man's mind and the restraints of an inimical environment, between father and son, between the old and the new. This problem has vexed human beings in every society throughout the ages; but in the nineteen-thirties it became quite acute and the failure of the decade to deal with it was "attended with unprecedented catastrophe."[23] The literature of this period is replete with the awareness of this catastrophe, expressing it as the conflict between mind and heart, between reason and faith, between old and new values. The artists of the thirties were conscious of the fact that, "Science is reshaping the world around us, and the poet who deliberately cuts himself off from his life."[24] Science was not successfully attacking even literature. It tried to explain the present tendencies in fiction, to explain, "the modernist poets ... about the nature of poetry, and the future of the literary mind, which demands a thoughtful answer."[25] During this decade science moved at a tremendous speed. "Great discoveries were being made every year, facts being patiently accumulated, the laboratories had never been so active."[26] The practical application of scientific knowledge had resulted in great improvements in railways and motorcars, wonderful means of communication by telephone and wireless, undreamed sources of recreation through the cinema, and also helpless insecurity to life in the midst of immense material wealth.

The writers of the thirties were excited by aeroplanes and other technological innovations and tried to identify these with a 'change of heart'. Like the Futurists they were excited by the unfamiliar beauty of machinery. In 1912 Marineth, the father of Futurist movement, opened his Technical Manifesto of Futurist Literature with this arresting sentence –

> "Sitting on the gas tank of an aeroplane, my stomach warmed by the pilot's head, I sensed the ridiculous inanity of the old syntax inherited from Homer."[27]

Futurism came to maturity in the late thirties. So came the streamlined ships, the Tear-drop cars, "those classic trains like the Burlington Zephyr – and finally a whole streamlined future expounded in a series of exhibitions culminating in a locus-classicus of Futurism."[28] The new inventions of science such as train, cinema, aeroplanes and radio stirred the imagination of the artists of this decade. They searched beauty in man-made machines and new architecture instead of in nature. The sound of a running train appealed to them more than the song of a cuckoo. It was a part of the Futurist creed to insist on superiority of mechanical beauty.

Aeroplanes could write advertisements attractively in the sky; they could also drop bombs, and it was this latter use that dominated the literary imagination as the thirties passed and the international situation worsened. Aeroplanes, together with the car, the sofa, and the new highway came into focus in literature, 'as things, not symbols of the things'. The new styles of architecture also received much attention from the writers. In *Good Bye To Berlin,* Christopher Isherwood describes the house of the wealthy Bernsteins family which was 'built entirely of glass'.

Cinema was 'the greatest social force in existence', in the thirties. Films had entertaining, educative and often refining influences. It was an instrument well-suited to the age. But it ceased "to propagate human values and began merely to mirror human shortcomings, since the sins of our neighbours are supposed to be of most vital interest and therefore good box-office."[29] Many of the films pictured "the standards of adult life, action and emotions, cheapening, debasing and distorting adults until they appear in the eyes of young people perpetually bathed in a moral atmosphere of intrigue, jealousy, wild emotionalism and cheap sentimentality."[30]

Hollywood, the movie capital of the U.S.A., came to symbolise the shallowness and extravaganza of the cinema. The writers of the thirties were very much influenced by Hollywood. Some of them became professional filmscript writers and film-critics. They adopted film technique in the structure of their novels. They noted how cinema going was the main ritual of the decade. Evelyn Waugh was a regular film-goer throughout his life and in *Vile Bodies* (1930) he provided an early reference to the then famous film actress, Greta Garbo. Greta Garbo was the rage of the period, and there are many mentions of her not only in *Vile Bodies*, but also in George Orwell's *Keep The Aspidistra Flying* (1936), Graham Greene's *England Made Me* (1936) and many other novels. Her coiffeur, way of walking, voice, dress, mannerisms and so on set the standards of contemporary feminine style.

The poets and the novelists of the thirties made use of the ultra-modern imagery instead of conventional ones. They brought in machines, pylons, dynamos as well as Freudian symbols: "Wireless and aeroplane in the physical world, Jung and Freud in Psychology, Fascism and Communism in politics, the slump in economics. All of these, though they might not have altered human nature, have profoundly modified the stuff of consciousness..."[31] In Graham Greene's novel *A Gun For Sale Anne*, the chief female character thinks, "This was war too; this chaos through which the train moved slowly, grinding over point after point like a dying creature dragging itself painfully away through no man's land from the scene of battle."[32] In those days aeroplane was a symbol of modernity for the Futurist imagination, and also intimately associated with the new architecture. It tended to be a right-wing rather than left-wing symbol. It was also an impersonal symbol of power, speed and beauty.[33] Images of bombing became increasingly common in the writings of the late thirties when aerial bombing was widespread in the Spanish civil war.

As the thirties progressed the frontier became a strong preoccupation with the English writers. In Christopher Isherwood's *Mr. Norris Changes Trains* (1935) the hero complains in the opening chapter, "All these frontiers... such a horrible nuisance."[34] We mark the various forces that work on the minds of persons living at an international border in Greene's *The Lawless Roads* (1939).

In Anthony Powell's novel, *Afternoon Men* (1931), Pringle, a painter by profession, "Stood in the corner of the room and bit his nails."[35] Pringle's nail biting stands for his gloominess and nervousness. Neurosis was the most common disease of the thirties. The anti-heroes of Evelyn Waugh and Anthony Powell stand for the modern man without any dynamism or purpose. Consequently the novels of these writers, which are really anti-novels, are uneventful and passive, and in them things appear to be accidental and grotesque. Skill for manipulation and architectonic count for little in these novels. These novels and their heroes sum up, "modern man's literary and social sense of powerlessness."[36]

During the thirties foreign influences came not so much from France as from Germany. Both the mode of thought and the forms of writing Rainer Maria Rilke and Franz Kafka affected the more sensitive of the English writers of the decade. "The intricate and in fact insoluable moral problems that were the basis of Kafka's stories found a strong response in a generation haunted so powerfully by the image of general guilt that they were unable to work for any particular good. Rilke's lyrical genius and elegiac tone had a limited but powerful influence upon spender."[37] The works of Franz Kafka were being translated into English during the thirties by Edwin and Willa Mir. *The Castle* appeared in 1930, *The Great Wall of China* in 1933, *The Trail* and *Metamorphosis* in 1937 and lastly *Amerika* in 1938. All these works of Kafka were accepted at once as significant for the time. English prose writers in the thirties were influenced by Kafka mainly because "life-like Kafka's heroes they were aware of guilt without being able clearly to discover its nature; like them, were in rebellion against the authority which they respected, and to which they desired to submit: 'If an authority is good why should it not be feared?' K. asks in *The Castle* and this was a question that fellow-travelling artists asked themselves. Yet the opposite view which may also be found in Kafka, `All virtues are individual, all vices social', was again in a way exactly felt."[38] The artists of this period, after reading Kafka, told the truth of the time symbolically. They applied, "Kafka's apparatus of ambiguity that could be used for all sorts of purposes, comic, tragic or merely mysterious, and that such a technique might produce anti-fascist, fairy tales of great power and beauty."[39]

In the thirties Edward Upward was thought of as the potential English Kafka, the young writer who would make English Marxism imaginative. According to him, "Literary allegories and fantasies have survived the test of practical experience in former centuries when a more realistic view of the world could only have led to despair or to futile rebellion; ... But a modern fantasy cannot tell the truth, cannot give a picture of life which will survive the test of experience; since fantasy implies in practice a retreat from the real world into the world of imagination..."[40]

Surrealism came into vogue in late 1935 and 1936. The movement started from France and existed there for more than a decade. But surrealism was not successful in England chiefly because it requires "a degree of self-dramatisation and egotistic gaiety in its practitioners of which these young writers were simply not capable."[41] Hence in 1936 the poet David Gascoyne could be described as "England's only wholehearted surrealist."[42] Skyes Davies, most intellectual of surrealist writers, is chiefly known for his surrealistic prose work *Petron*. Petron takes a journey, surveying various scenes like a murdered woman, an old man who divides his fingers into tiny fingers, a field of growing hands that open by day and close by night. The writer said, "Until we can conquer those realms, we are always in danger. We wish to make this private world public – to put an end to loneliness."[43]

Thus surrealism provided a means of expressing not political ideas, but the emotions behind politics of the thirties – "The fears and anxieties, the sense of unknown and terrible dangers, and of possible violence and courage beyond the projections of reason: in short it provided a parabolic method for the social nightmares of the time which reflected in the main works of Greene, Isherwood, Waugh and Warner."[44]

In the thirties the literary tendency was toward something which "for want of a better name, literarymen called it classicism, a higher and clearer conception of Reason and a more severe control of the emotions of Reason."[45] The word classical, when applied in relation to a writer, means: "a writer of worth and distinction ... a writer who is of account, has real property and is not lost in the proletariat crowd."[46] It means classy, and naturally became identified with law and order and restraint. The thirties were the hightime of economic and spiritual depression and deepening dejection in a world impermeable to optimistic idealism; so at length it devalued the Romantic fervour and hailed a generation of writers of whom some desired a revival of classicism, others a new era in which the scientific spirit of the modern world should be exalted over all else, while some others attended at the rebirth of the metaphysical temper which had been dominant in English poetry since the 17th century.[47] Although Wyndham Lewis was of the opinion that, "the conditions have so radically changed that it is otiose almost to make use of these terms classical and romantic any further ... the notion of the "classical revival" is an essentially romantic notion,"[48] the few that there was still "a continuation of the world of Greece and Rome ... in most of our English and European intellectual and applied science..."[49] cannot be overlooked. James Joyce's *Ulysses* (1922) was a classical novel of the twenties but the thirties could not produce any such monumental work. The works of the novelists like Waugh, Warner and Anthony Powell who wrote social and political allegories and satire, were more like those of Defoe, Swift and Fielding of the eighteenth century.

The times called out for such comments on the contemporary society by imaginative prose writers as Ben Jonson was able to make on the Elizabethan, a cartoon as vivid and same as Jonson's of the world in which he lived. But there was none such. Anthony Powell could look back to the age of Robert Burton (1576-1640) and imitate the classical tradition established by him and Browne (1605-82). Like Burton and Browne, Powell too expressed the melancholy mood of the thirties in the reflective vein.

Because of the classical tendency, the novels of the thirties were solid and not gaseous, "Aristotelian rather than Platonic; public rather than private, objective rather than subjective; inclination to action rather than to dream; sensuous rather than ascetic; smack of common sense in place of metaphysic, to be universal rather than individual; to lean upon intellect rather than upon nerves."[50]

The greatest social allegorist of the thirties was Rex Warner, "a classical Scholar".[51] In his famous book, *The Cult of Power*, he laid emphasis on the classical spirit "that was needed to the thirties whose progress seemed to have more danger than delight, when, as humanitarianism made its gradual conquests, whole cities were destroyed in a moment and when, in bewilderment at the appalling contradictions between the teaching of religion and the actual facts, people increasingly take refuse in various kinds of dogmatism or in a suspension of all belief whatsoever."[52] Like John Bunyan he too showed in his novels spiritual and social forces belittling man in his ordinary relationships. Evelyn Waugh another classicist was satirist. He was a subtle moralist and too sophisticated a chronicler to ignore the comic and ridiculous in human misfortune.

The Writers of the twenties and the thirties assimilated the findings of psychoanalysis and were experts in linking the unconscious with the conscious. We mark, "the influence of dream upon reality and reality upon dream. Art revealed a variety of levels on which people lived."[53] James Joyce and Virginia Woolf in the twenties and Graham Greene, Isherwood and Rex Warner in the thirties sought to reproduce the flow of man's thoughts, feelings and reveries. "They were forced to track down the sinuosities of these underground rivers: free association, dream imagery and, study of symbolic acts."[54]

But before the thirties, "no other generation had shown so close an interest in mental and spiritual disturbance as to create a growing assumption that most men and women are cases to be diagnosed, that the world is a vast clinic and that nothing but abnormality is normal."[55] The ideas of death-wish, the supremacy of the unconscious, repression and guilt, the conflict between ego and super-ego, anxiety and instinctual life, neuroses, and oedipus complex abound in the novels of the thirties and testify to the influences of Freud, Groddeck, C.G. Jung and D.H. Lawrence. Freud had shown the effect of interaction of the various elements in man's mind upon his activities. He had also asserted that the unconscious is the major and more dominant level of the mind, being the reservoir of our dreams and desires and the source of our instincts. But to Groddeck, "The unconscious is a part of the psyche, a part of the It."[56] The It being the "deepest nature and force of the man," accomplishes "everything that happens with and through and in man; it is responsible for his existence."[57] The "It", therefore, is something similar to Shaw's 'Life-Force', and Auden used this idea of the creative life-force in his early poems. The diseases in us, according to Groddeck are indeed the means of self-punishment and self-cure and not caused by external factors.''[58] Groddeck's theory of illness and Freud's theory of the neuroses or Love's psychosomatic theory of diseases as well as of the harmful effects of repression were well noted and they got their proper reflections in the literature of the thirties. C.G. Jung opened new roads along which the writers could travel hopefully. The Jungian unconscious is not negative, a mere lumber room attached to the mansion of the conscious mind. It is positive and creative and it is the ''objective psychic'' providing us with our inner experience; and it signifies a dynamic, demurgic force in life, without which human relationships are robbed of depth and magic, art is a mere pretty toy, and religion is so much empty ceremonial and arid moralizing.[59]

D.H. Lawrence's unconscious is the creative energy in every individual. Life according to D.H. Lawrence's 'unconscious' is the creative energy in every individual. Life according to D.H. Lawrence can be lived vitally and spontaneously only when we know how the unconscious ''habitually unfolds itself'' because we ''determine its laws and process in our lives: than at last we can begin to live from the spontaneous initial prompting instead of from the dead machine principles of ideas and ideals.''[60] According to him repression or a compulsory ordering of the free flow of the unconscious results not only in ''dislocation or collapse of the great voluntary centres, a derangement of the will''[61] in us but also in a vital damage to ''the life-flow of those connected with us.''[62] In these ideas of Lawrence authors could find a convincing scientific explanation of the moral and spiritual degeneration of the individuals as well as of the collapse of a social order.

The common point, that emerges from the ideas of these psychologists is mainly their defiance of the restrictions and repressions which lead to inhibitions that hamper the natural free growth of man. In fact these ideas, collectively and separately strengthened the writers' clinical view of the sick and disintegrated life of the thirties and became guiding principles in their literary works. In the preface of his novel, *Down There On A Visit* (1962), Christopher Isherwood remarked, ''down there refers to that nether world within the individual which is the place of loneliness, alienation and hatred. The novel in four episodes describes characters shut up inside private hells of their own making, self dedicated to a life-long feud with the authors. The author laughs with them – for even hell can be funny – but he is forced to realize that his visits to them are, at the same time, visits to the down there inside himself.''[63] Graham Greene entered the field of psychoanalysis and pathology in the powerful accounts of those tortured souls which seem to be composed of equal parts of Freud, Dostoyevsky, the thriller, and the movies; *The Power and the Glory* (1940), and *Brighton Rock* (1938), are studies of morbid psychology. Rex Warner, Powell, Orwell and other novelists of the thirties also studied neurotic men and women of their times under the guidelines of Freud and Jung. They were concerned with the drama of the soul in their works and took delight in its presentation.

Some philosophers like T.E. Hulme, John Kierkeggard and Reinhold Niebuhr impressed the writers of the thirties by their thoughtful speculations. Hulme popularised the idea that man is limited, sinful creature, bitterly aware of perfection, but aware, also, of how much he falls short of perfection. By strict discipline he can achieve a limited decency, but it is folly for him to dream of a world in any however distant future of 'men like gods'.[64] This attitude was taken over, refined and elaborated by T.S. Eliot and then handed down to the writers of the coming generations. Graham Greene, Evelyn Waugh, Auden and Powell were aware of this imperfection of man. The thirties was the decade of anxiety – a mood that was then called angst, a word borrowed from Soren Kierkegaard, a Danish religious thinker of the early nineteenth century. Kierkegaard was the father of existentialist philosophy. His belief that one is not a Christian till one allows oneself to remain a victim of despair[65], appealed to some writers of the thirties and paved the way for their full acceptance of Christian faith. In Kierkegaard's idea of 'Dread' as well as of "leap into faith" they found a convincing solution to the problem of guilt and anxiety that possessed man's mind. They held that Kierkegaard's teachings were all the more valid for the thirties when "the smug bourgeois Christinandom, he announced, has crumbled and what is left is an amorphous, despairing mass of displaced persons and paralysed Hamlets."[66]

According to Reinhold Niebuhr faith does not "endow the believer with a superior wisdom which will enable him to escape errors, miscalculations, and faulty analyses of the common life of man."[67] He opposed the idea that "man should be examined as if he were no more than of the many objects in nature which the scientific method will be able to comprehend fully, if only its tools are sufficiently precise and the scientist is sufficiently objective."[68] It was in Niebuhr that the writers of the thirties found the most convincing interpretation of Christian faith which viewed man both as a spirit and a finite creature involved in the flux of nature. From Niebuhr they learnt that, "The issue of Biblical religion is not primarily the problem of how finite man can know God but how the sinful is to be reconciled to God and how history is to overcome the tragic consequence of its false eternals ..."[69]

Thus, these philosophers provided a new religious attitude to the writers of the thirties. The most successful and purely artistic development of Kierkegaard's ideas was to be found in the strange novels and tales of Kafka who was in turn imitated by the English novelists of the thrities.

NOTES AND REFERENCES

1. Greene, Graham -- *Early Poem* 1930 -- Quoted by John Atkins in his critical work -- *Graham Greene*, Calder and Boyars (1970), London (p. 14).
2. Croce, Benedetto -- Of Liberty -- *Foreign Affairs*, New York, Oct. 1932 (p. 17).
3. Alldritt, Keith -- *The Making of George Orwell*, Edward Arnold (London), 1976 (p. 1).
4. Symons, Julian -- *The Angry 30s* -- Picture File, Eyre Methuen (London), 1976 (p. 1).
5. Hynes, Samuel -- *The Auden Generation,* The Bodley Head Sydney, Toronto, 1976 (p. 65).
6. Ward, A.C. -- *Twentieth Century Literature* (1901-1950), Methuen and Co. Ltd. (London), 1959 (p. 18).
7. Hynes, Samuel -- *The Auden Generation*, The Bodley Head, Sydney Toronto, 1976 (p. 20).
8. *Ibid.*, p. 41.
9. Spender, Stephen -- *The Thirties And After,* 1978, Willian Collins Sons & Co. Ltd. Glasgow, London (p. 116).
10. Powell, Anthony -- *Afternoon Man*, Heinemann (London), 1931 (pp. 61-62).
11. Warner, Rex -- *The Cult of Power* (1946) (Borisnwood) (p. 15) (London).
12. *Ibid.*, p. 124.
13. *Ibid.*, p. 14.
14. *London Mercury* -- The Ivory Tower, December, 1938 (p. 119).
15. Warner, Rex -- *The Cult of Power* (1946) (London), p. 129.
16. Ward, A.C. -- *Twentieth-Century Literature,* Methuen and Co. Limited, 1950 (London) (p. 16).
17. Bergonzi, Bernard -- *Reading The Thirties*, (1971), The Macmillan Press Ltd. (London) (p. 6).
18. Isherwood, Christopher — *Christopher And His Kind* (1976), London (p. 9).
19. Auden, W.H. -- *The Dance of Death* (1933), The Hogarth Press (London) (p. 9).
20. The Earl of Birkenhead -- Fiery Particles -- *Evelyn Waugh And His World*, Weidenfeld and Nicolson (London), 1973 (p. 149).
21. Woolf, Virginia -- *The Moment And Other Essays*, The Hogarth Press, 1947 (London) (pp. 115-16).

22. Aragon, Louis, *The Red Front*, New Verse, May, 1933.

23. Warner, Rex --*The Cult of Power* (1946), Borisnwood (London), p. 39.

24. *The Times Literary Supplement*-- Science and Literature Editorial Note July 1954, p. 457 (London).

25. Eastman, Max -- *The Literary Mind* (1935), Charles Scribners Sons, Newyork (p. 11).

26. *The Bookman* Vol. XXXIV, 1933, p. 160.

27. Marineth -- *Selected Writing* (London), 1972, p. 84.

28. Bergonzi, Bernard -- *Reading The Thirties* 1971 (London), The Macmillan Press Ltd., p. 96.

29. Cousins, E.G. -- 'Cinema And Propaganda' -- *The Bookman,* Vol. LXXXIV, Oct. 1933 (p. 481).

30. Leavis, F.R. and Thompson, D. -- Men and Machines -- *Culture And Environment*, 1948 (London) (Chatto and Windus), p. 144.

31. James, R.A. Scott -- Editorial Note, *London Mercury*, April, 1935 (pp. 522-23).

32. Greene, Graham -- *A Gun For Sale* (1977) (London), Penguin Books (p. 182).

33. Bergonzi, Bernard -- *Reading The Thirties* (1971), London (p. 104), The Macmillan Press Ltd.

34. *Ibid*., p. 66.

35. Powell, Anthony -- *Afternoon Men* (1974), Heinemann (London) (p.104).

36. West, Paul -- *The Modern Novel*, Vol. 2, 1967, Hutchinson & Co. Limited London (p. 431).

37. Symons, Julian -- Of Crisis And Dismay -- *A Study of Writing In Thirties* (1945) (London), p. 96, Rajan, B. & Pearse, A.D. Dobson -- Focus one -- Photocopy Service, British Library, Lending Division.

38. Symons, Julian -- *The Thirties : A Dream Revolved*, Faber and Faber (London), 1975, p. 132.

39. *Ibid*., p. 133.

40. Upward, Edward -- *Sketch For A Marxist*, Interpretation of Literature, in C. Day Lewis, ed., *The Mind in Chains* (London : Frederick Muller Ltd.), 1937 (p. 48).

41. Daiches, David -- *The Present Age After 1920* (London), 1964 (p. 106).

42. Notes on Contributors -- Contemporary Poetry and Prose No. 1, May 1936, p. 15.

43. Davies, Hugh Sykes -- Extracts from the lecture : *Biology and Surrealism,* International Surrealist Bulletin No. 4, Sept. 1936 (p. 13).

44. Hynes, Samuel -- *The Auden Generation* -- The Bodley Head, 1976 (London), p. 226.

45. Eastman, Max -- *The Literary Mind* (1935), Charles Scirbners Sons, Newyork (p. 15).

46. *Ibid*., p. 125.

47. Ward, A.C. -- *Twentieth-Century Literature,* Methuen and Co. Limited (London) (p. 196), 1950.

48. Lewis, Wyndham -- Classical Revival In Endgland -- *The Bookman* Review, No. 517 Vol. LXXXVII, Oct. 1934 (p. 10).
49. Hight, Gilbert -- *The Classical Tradition* (London), 1949 (p. 344), Clarendon Press, Oxford.
50. Lewis, Wyndham -- *Classical Revival in England,* The Bookman N. 517, Vol. LXXXVII, Oct. 1934 (p. 10).
51. Fraser, G.S. -- *The Modern Writer And His World,* Rupa and Co., Calcutta 1976 (p. 92) (India).
52. Warner, Rex -- *The Cult of Power,* 1946 (London), p. 154.
53. Nin, Anais - *The Novel of the Future,* 1969, Peter Owen, London (p. 8).
54. *Ibid*., p. 83.
55. Ward, A.C. -- Twentieth-Century Literature, (1959) (Methuen and Co. Limited), London (p. 37).
56. Groddeck -- *The Unknown Self,* Second Edition (C.W. Daniel Company), 1932 (p. 43).
57. *Ibid*., p. 40.
58. *Ibid*., p. 97.
59. J.B. Priestley -- Jung And the Writer, *The Times Literary Supplement,* 6 August, 1954 (p. iii) (London).
60. Lawrence, D.H. -- *Fantasia of the Conscious and Psychoanalysis and the Unconscious Life* (London), 1961 (p. 212), Phoenix Edition, Heinemann Ltd. (p. 212).
61. *Ibid*., p. 48.
62. *Ibid*., pp. 221-22.
63. Isherwood, Christopher -- *Down There On A Visit* (London), 1962, Methuen and Co. Ltd. (p. 2).
64. Tindall, W.Y. -- *Forces In Modern British Literature,* Vintage Books Inc. (1947) (p. 217).
65. *Presenting Kierkegaard* in the Living Thoughts of Kierkegaard, New York, David Mckay, 1952 (p. 3).
66. *Ibid*., p. 14.
67. Prof. Neibuhr -- The Two Cities -- *Times Literary Supplement* (The) London, Sept. 17, 1954 (p. xxxii).
68. *Ibid*., (p. xxxii).
69. Auden, W.H. -- The Means of Grace -- *The New Republic,* IV, June 2, 1941, p. 766.

THE MAIN NOVELISTS OF THE THIRTIES AND THEIR WORKS

GRAHAM GREENE

During the thirties Graham Greene established his literary eminence as a novelist, by creating a world of "myths of social decay out of the individual crisis."[1] He took for granted what Henry James once professed, that "... the object of the novel is to represent life", and "to make all descriptions ... so clear that each situation could be visualised readily by any reader precisely as he saw it ..."[2] Greene showed his excellence in bridging the gap between head and heart, always exalting the latter at the expense of the former. His novels are eminently readable although, "... their subject matter is unpleasant, depressing, and tinged with occasional intrusions of his Catholicism..."[3]

Like other novelists of the thirties, he too dealt with all the problems that come as the aftermath of the First World War – the problems of economic depression, fascism, unemployment, resettlement of ex-servicemen, post-war morality, class-consciousness and socialism. The public was eager to read any novel which disclosed some key to the riddle of the human mind, and undoubtedly Greene's novels gratified this desire of theirs. They (Greene's novels) proved to be a mirror of the age, "but a special kind of mirror that reflected not merely the external features of the age but also its inner face, its nervous system and conflicts which swayed it."[4] He took such elements as hallucinations, nightmares and legends, and fused them together to contribute to the feeling that his characters and events stand for something more than what they appear to be.

Greene was not only a realist but also an artist who sought to give us not merely "a banal photographic representation of life, but a vision of it that is fuller, more vivid and more compellingly truthful than even reality itself."[5] We measure his greatness as a novelist by the essential characteristic of "a Christ like all embracing compassion."[6] Even today his novels enjoy wide popularity. "His prestige is due not merely to the vividness with which he conveys distinctly twentieth-century scenes, but to the difference of tone with which he pervades them by what has become for many people an unusual hypothesis – that God is not dead."[7]

Graham Greene was born on 1 October, 1904, son of the Headmaster of Berkhamsted School. He received his education first at his father's school, then at Balliol, and lastly in Oxford University. He longed to go to the East which, then, lured many young men looking for "adventure, money and sex." He took a job with a tobacco company since it offered the prospect of three years in China. His longing was not, however, fulfilled, and next he got a job with the Nottingham Journals without salary, `just for the experience'. At that he became familiar with a Catholic priest, Father Trollope, and other three months he accepted Catholicism in 1926. He joined the *London Times* in 1935, serving first as a film critic and then as a literary editor. In 1941 he joined the British Foreign Office and remained there till the end of the Second World War.

Graham Greene started his literary career as a poet but after the first volume, he changed over to novels. *Babbling April* (1925) , a collection of poems, dedicated to his parents, disclosed mostly life's dinginess and impressed those young men and women of the twenties and the thirties, who were enmashed in a death-wish.

Four years later, in 1929 came his first novel, *The Man Within*, and he is still at work. Till 1939 he wrote novels, three of which are counted as 'juvenile' as mere entertainments or thrillers. Greene himself has differentiated the 'serious' from the 'thrillers' in these words : "The (serious) novels were written slowly and the entertainments quickly ; that the novels were the products of depressive periods and the entertainments manic, that the entertainments were crime stories, the novels something more.[8]

The title of the novel, *The Man Within* was adopted from Thomas Browne's, "Theres's another man within me that's angry with me."[9] It is extremely romantic, and was written before the writer realised that romance without faith could give satisfaction to no one, before he turned to realism. It was really an "apprentice work" and it was fortunate for Greene that it was at all published. It is, however, by "no means a bad novel."[10] We mark a psychological subtlety in the character of Andrews. He, an antihero, is lost in self analysis. And this heart searching of his lifts the novel, "out of the rut prepared for it by easy virtue and hotel beds."[11] Andrews strongly feels that mystery of self leads us away from day-to-day excitement and action. He hates himself because he is not only timid but also insincere. The other characters, however, do not appear as authentic. Elizabeth and Lucy are mere, "sexual extensions of Andrews inner dualism, are crude stereotypes of pure and carnal love."[12] There are also some marvellous thrilling scenes in this novel – especially the one where Andrews stands still in the midway in the encircling fog when his would-be murderers are searching for him within a few feet. The novel bears all the signs of immaturity. It is "incomplete, naive and crude",[13] being the first work of its kind.

Greene's next novel, *Stamboul Train* (1932) is certainly better though the author himself has labelled it as 'entertainment'. We do not find it to be merely sensational; it is more acute in its overbearing sense of guilt, failure and death-wish than *It's A Battlefield* (1934), its successor. Greene's unpleasent attitude to sex is dominant here, squalor rather than ecstasy is the overriding sense of the novel. It describes a sensational episode involving the fortunes and misfortunes of the travellers on the Orient Express, running from Ostend to Istambul. Dr. Czinner despaired Communist revolutionary, Myatt the Jewish merchant, and Coral Musker young dancer are the main characters who make the novel lively and interesting. The minor characters: a murderer on the run, a lesbian journalist, a clergyman and some English tourists are the interesting personages who make the story saucy. Journey is main structural device that knits the various strands together and obliges some of the characters to get involved in the fates of the others. Some scenes like the one in which Dr. Czinner is lying in the store, mortally wounded and in great consternation, counting the last moments of his life, and Coral Musker giving him all protection and care, risking her own future, are very impressive. Although the writer professedly, "set out to write a book to please, one which with luck might be made into film..."[14], yet the title does bear a deeper meaning – it stands for the "thin protection of civilization."[15] When Coral left her safety and entagled in various tests and trails, she became disengaged from Myatt, her would-be husband. She was rescued and fell into the grip of the lesbian Marbel Warren. This journey tells us that "One had to be very alive, very flexible, very opportunist" [16] in the train. We mark oppressive sordidness not only in the author's mind but also in the world about him and this is because the novelist tended to be a realist and contemporary.[17]

Certainly the *Stamboul Train* opened a door for Greene, the novelist and let the future in.[18]

It's A Battlefield (1934) another 'hot pot' followed *Stamboul Train* and brought in its sweep clashes of benighted armies, betrayal, guilt and loneliness. The novelist took the idea of this novel from Kinglake's description of the Battle of Inkerman, in '*The Invasion of the Crimea*'.[19]

The metaphor of a battlefield is picked up again and again throughout the novel: "Politics is a battlefield, London is a battlefield. The world is a battlefield."[20] The Assistant Commissioner thinks of his duties as in war.

> "He was like a General left alone at headquarters to study the reports from every company; they littered his clerk ...; the front line was only a hundred yards away where the trams screamed down the Embankment and the buses circled Trafalgar Square. It was hard, he thought to get any clear idea of a war, carried on in this piecemeal way throughout a city."[21] Conrad Drover, the deranged clerk who attempts to kill the Assistant Commissioner, fancies about his situation likewise: "... he might have been at the edge of a great army hidden by mist; and for a moment it was not a shoe, a fire, a lantern slide which held his thoughts, but a faint memory of his secondary school, of a Latin lesson, of any army which waited on a hillside alone a lake while an invisible enemy marched in the mist below."[22]

Greene's first notion for this novel contained in a note book entry of Sept. 1932, was that it should be, "... a large inclusive picture of a city, the connecting link the conviction of a man for the murder of a policeman. Is it poetic to hang him? And the detectives go out through the city listening..."[23] And so the novel gives a picture of an historical city, situated in real time and space–real London in the early thirties. Greene produced this sense of historical reality by harnessing together manifold imaginative incidents but very near to reality, and mixing with these names and places that were historical. In the novel the characters lead their personal lives, going through their own private joys and sorrows. They struggle hard to fulfil their strong urges of love and hatred and revenge – but they fail and become frustrated. The stories of their personal lives show that man's desires cannot be the governing factor of man's destiny but the enormous pressures of historical reality. The novel shows clearly how law, justice, police, jury, civil service had all collapsed. At the end of the novel the captain says, "I cannot stand human justice any longer. Its arbitrariness. Its incomprehensibility."[24] The attack on human justice is all pervasive in the novel. Injustice, "was as much a part of the body as age and inevitable disease. There was no such thing as justice in the air we breathed, for it was those who hated and envied and married for money or convenience, who were happy."[25]

Greene wrote this novel under the influence of Conard's *The Secret Agent*, we find, "The same sordidness, the same bitterness and dark intensity, the same sense of defeat, of hopelessness.."[26] pervading the novel. Greene's own sense of insecurity, insufficiency and failure and sexual maladjustment is dominant for the first time in this novel.

In *England Made Me* (1935), the first 'serious' work of Greene, he showed himself to be a really great novelist. The novel is well wrought and well porportioned in its many aspects. The characters are finely sketched with splendid observation, with the limitation that they are not free to develop themselves. Like Hardy's characters they are dwarfed by the narrowness of the sphere within which Greene puts them. Kate, Anthony, Minty and Krough work and behave like marionettes due to the deterministic principles held by the writer. Greene gives, here, fine pictures of boredom, fear, disgust and bodily discomfort. Krogh, whose finances run into millions, symbolises the ruthless impersonality of a financier. He is a slave of his own success and is hardly able to enjoy pleasure, being constantly involved in the mad pursuit of wealth and making his industrial empire more and more extensive. The novel ends with the death of Anthony. He is pushed into the river on a fogy night by Hall, a henchman of Krough who could not bear the presence of Anthony as his bodyguard because Anthony was the brother of his mistress Kate. Kate loved his brothers and this Krough could not tolerate. Thus, evil succeeds, but this success is only on the surface. The real victory, victory in defeat, is achieved by goodness in the heart of Anthony who took his stand for righteousness before his death. And this satisfied Greene's religious faith. The novel appropriately ends in a hopeful note:

> "... the missal in the cupboard, the Madonna, the spider withering under the glass, a home from home."[27]

Journey Without Maps (1936) is an accurate description of Greene's own travel in the savage, unsavoury hinterland of the Republic of Liberia. The journey was not an ordinary one. It was a "parabolic journey ... into the self and into the past, in search of meaning."[28] The journey began at Freetown, in Sierra Leone. From there Greene and his companion and their African porters went inland, crossed into Liberia in the remote interior forests, and returned to the Liberian Coast and civilization at Manrovia. The journey was, "the worst boredom I had ever experienced, the worst fear and the worst exhaustion."[29] The life Greene found in African forest was unfamiliar, non-dramatic and without any excitement, a replica of what lay under the surface of life in England and Europe – the dark interior and "the waste land", of "the seediness of civilization."[30]

In this novel Greene's approach to life is evident from the following:

> "To-day our world seems peculiarly susceptible to brutality. There is a touch of nostalgia in the pleasure we take in gangster novels, in characters who have so ageeably simplified their emotions that they have begun living again at a level below the cerebral. There seemed to be a seediness about the place you couldn't get to the same intent elsewhere, and seediness has a very deep appeal even the seediness of civilization, of the sky-signs in Leicester Square, the 'tarts' in Bond Street, the smell of cooking greens off Tettenham Court Road, the water salesman in Great Portland Street."[31]

Greene was aware of the many absurdities which made Gerhardi view life with disgust and boredom. This was also the dominant mood of the people in mid-thirties. Greene wrote the novel just after his journey and incorporated therein this mood of the time. Bernard Bergonzi is correct in saying: "... the book seems to me stamped unmistakably with the atmosphere of the middle thirties – Hitler is quite new, dictatorship is only a tang on the breeze blowing from Europe; in England ... depression and a kind of metroland culture."[32]

The novel is also a metaphor. It is not simply a journey of exploration like Livingstone's in the dark and mysterious interior of a *terra incognita*; it is "a kind of jungian night-journey into the darkness of self and of the racial memory."[33] The novelist, here, like a psychiatrist, is aiming "to bring the patient back to the idea he is repressing, a long journey backwards without maps, catching a clue here and a clue there ... until one has to face the general idea, the pain or the memory."[34] In the same context Greene wrote further: "... here in Liberia again and again one caught hints of what it was we had developed from."[35]

A Gun For Sale (1936) was also one of the best and most important novels of the ninteen-thirties. Greene wrote this novel in order to provoke by producing disgust and other disagreeable emotions. Nothing here is noble, splendid or charming except some moments of love seeking expression. Greene was a topical writer of the thirties, and this novel was the result of this topicality, encompassing as it does the economic depression of the time, capitalist monoplies, war-scare, sky-scare, ghastly murder and chasings by the police. As in *Journey Without Maps* in this novel too Graham Greene adopted the device of a parable to put forward his personal views of the contemporary life. The story is set in the seedy atmosphere of the contemporary England. Raven, a professional murderer, kills the minister of a foreign state, at the behest of his employer, Sir Marcus, an English aramament manufacturer. This murder is done to force a war in Europe. The murder is purely for promoting commercial interests. The hovering threat of war is the main cause of fear and tribulation of every character. The characters discuss it, newspaper headlines give report about it, it is spoken of in radio broadcasts and written on moving neon signs. There is also a parallel war, the war of the powerful against the weak, the rich against the poor, notice in the two chief characters of the novel. Raven, the son of a hanged criminal who had seen his mother cut her throat, is defaced by a hare-lip and is 'unloved and incapable of love'. Anne, a girl of the working-class, is faithful to her class. She too is at war with her deplorable economic condition. The world in which these figures move, is described in battle-field images – the 'dark wounded ground' of the factory section, Anne's train moving through the industrial wasteland is, "like a dying creature dragging itself painfully away through no man's land from the scene of a battle."[36] The novel ends with the death of both Sir Marcus and Raven. Anne is reunited with her lover, Mather, and the war comes to an end. The reader is left with a sense of the evils of war, and of the futility of man's effort to avert it. Rosamund Lehmann's comments in *The New Statesman* about this novel deserves extensive quoting:

> "Beneath its title. ... To my mind, it (the novel) more closely resembles a long elaborate dream-experience. One of these dark disorganising circumstantial dreams which unwind in more or less logical sequence: dreams of immense conspiracies, with oneself moving against an enemy unseen all powerful; oneself in the predicament of being obliged to save the world. They are all there – the wicked faces, the shots, the solitary figures in the streets

suddenly there and then not there, ... Mr. Greene has a remarkable capacity for building up and sustaining a Dark Tower atmosphere. Every detail is significant. Icy wind from the north, rain freezing in the gutters, fog, winter streets, train lines, shops decorated for Christmas ... all seems saturated with the menance of flight and pursuit.''[37]

Brighton Rock (1938) brought Graham Greene into the front rank of living novelists. It has many faults, yet Greene succeeded to invoke an intensity of mood, which made it very popular. Rose, Hale, Pinkie and Kite are all neurotic beings. They are mostly engaged in paring their nails, and this paring of nails is a symptom of oppressive tension pervading their small world. Anne betrays Raven in *A Gun For Sale*, for she realises that he is more evil than she had fancied, and Rose betrays Pinkie here, because she is afraid and stunned, and believes that she is acting rightly. Greene's natural sexual urge was possibly acute at this time of his life, and also possibly he was beginning to feel a repulsion from it. This repulsion is clearly marked in Pinkie's attitude towards sex which to him is like sickness and dirty act. Pinkie is a puritanic bachelor abstaining from drinking, smoking and betting.

Greene had already become a catholic and modelled Pinkie's belief on his own. ''Why'', he told Rose, ''it's the only thing that fits. These atheists, they don't know nothing. Of course there's Hell, Flames, and damnation...''[38] The main stressing point in the novel is the world of man, pulled in two opposite directions – good and evil. Each man's world is limited by his mental horizon, and he knows right from wrong in this limited world. But there are wider issues like war, general good and wider evil. Sex is one of the evils because of which priests abjure it, and the institution of church alone can lead to redemption. The church of Pinkie and Rose is the inner world and everything else stands apart in the outer darkness. But as the story proceeds we find that Greene is bewitched and horrified by his own religion. He is found indulging not in the description of life but in the display of ''intimate paraphernalia, such as chamber pots, belches, dirty laundry and smeared soapdishes.''[39]

The Confidential Agent (1939) is also one of those 'Entertainments' of thirties which would ever haunt the readers' imagination. Greene clearly declared when he started to write this novel that ''... he had in mind only a certain vague ambition to create something legendary out of a contemporary thriller.''[40] The world of *The Confidential Agent* is that of madness; whereas the world of *Brighton Rock* is of evil. D., the hero, is entangled in a mesh of intrigue and violence, plausibly unravelled against the background of an outwardly calm and reassuring England. He is a confidential agent in whom no one has confidence, and who can have confidence in no one. He announces that the modern world presents us with a hopeless choice. We must choose between one side or the other, there is no mid-way and there is no escape. D. knows that he too has to make a choice and at last he does so hoping to find decency in England. But he is disillusioned and finds beneath the smooth surface indecency and malice.

The Confidential Agent is not generally accepted as one of Greene's Catholic novels, although the same motif that lay behind *Brighton Rock* and *The Lawless Roads,* is also dominant here. There is pity for the downtrodden. Because of his profession, D. is well aware of the unhealthy mores and malaise rampant in society. He sees that in this society rich and comfortable people like his enemy L. desire to make their lives safe and secure; that their hearts are made of stone. He does not have confidence even in the trade-union leaders whom he sees as not genuinely interested in the welfare of mankind. His reaction is disbelief and savagery; his preference betrayal and anarchy.

The Lawless Roads (1939) is a splendid travel book which is enriched with Greene's "personal impression of a small part of Mexico at a particular time, the Spring of 1938.[41] At the beginning of the novel, the novelist quotes the following lines from *Wit's Recreation* (1640), which suggested to him the title of the novel:

> "What made the change? The hills and towers
> stand otherwise than they should stand,
> And without fear the lawless roads
> Ran wrong through all the land.
> Man's like the earth, his hair like grass is grown,
> His veins the rivers are, his heart the stone."[42]

Just as *Journey Without Maps* was an actual journey treated as a parable, similarly the author's real journey is Mexico, full of many hardships and dangers, has been given a metaphoric meaning in this novel. The author muses silently on seeing too much of squalor, poverty and misanthropy in Mexico.

The novel is explicitly Greene's catholic propaganda: "I have no sympathy with those who complain of the wealth and beauty of a church in a poor land ... in church the democracy is absolute. The rich man and the poor man kneel side by side for communion; the rich man must wait his turn at the confessional.''[43] It is however not all propaganda; it is an artistic creation wrapped in poetic vestures and rich romantic colourings, above all, his speculations on seeing the `Godless state':

> ''Far below Tabasco spread out, the Godless state, the landscape of a hunted man's terror and captivity – wood and water, without roads, and on the horizon the mountains of chiapas like a prison wall.''[44]

The Lawless Roads is a story of a ''land of skyscrapers, of stone stairs and cracked bells ringing early; one was aware of fear and hate, a kind of lawlessness – appalling cruelties could be practised without a second thought; one met for the first time characters, adult and adolescent, who bore about them the genuine quality of evil.''[45] Actually *The Lawless Roads* is an interesting transcript of contemporary history of man, which is full of bloodshed and gigantic ruins. The author starts his journey from San Antonio and visiting several cities in a Mexico, gives an accurate and exhilarating account of his travels in an unknown land devoid of religion and human ethos. The novel ends at the polemic note ''Is it easier to say your sins be forgiven you...?''[46]

It is quite evident that these novels of Greene written in the thirties were concerned with political crisis and depicted Europe as a place of cruelty, violence, and restlessness. They present vivid and horrid pictures of prevalent economic depression and menance of war:

''... a picture made up of people anxiously watching news flashes, people demonstrating, people looking for jobs, people turning over second hand clothes, jerry built housing estates, `To Let' and `For Sale signs', desolate slag heaps, the pervasive evidence of decline and despair.''[47] After an unsuccessful experiment with the stream-of-unconscious technique, he evolved his own fictional mode that was serious, using devices of journalism and the cinema. His novels are shot through with the sense of ''social and political crisis, were in accord with the literary programme of Auden, Isherwood, and their associates.''[48] He was one of the first novelists who realised how serious was the loss of religious sense in modern fictions; hence, he restored this sense and justified the novel in moral as well as aesthetic terms. Even the thrillers of the thirties were not merely episodes of crime and violence but they were set in ''patterns and conventions of classical tragedies.''[49] In the words of Greene himself, these novels are concerned with: ''The hunted man who becomes in turn the hunter, the peaceful man who turns at bay, the man who has learned to love "justice by suffering injustice."[50] Greene was a sincere artist. He never showed infidelity to his imagination and involved himself in a certain disloyalty to the church. He never cared for religious prudence and the interests of ecclesiastical propaganda in his pursuit of artistic ends; and so some of his novels displeased the catholics as much as the non-catholics. In *The Power and the Glory* (1940), for example, there is serious condemnation of the Holy office itself. David Lodge is correct to comment, "... in Greene's fiction Catholicism is not a body of belief requiring exposition and demanding categorical assent or dissent, but a system of concepts, a source of situations, and reservoir of symbols with which he can order and dramatize certain intuitions about the nature of human experiences... Greene's Catholicism may be seen not as a crippling burden on his artistic freedom, but as a positive artistic asset."[51]

It can now be summed up that Graham Greene in the thirties was a reputed novelist whose novels at that time were quite satisfying in their aesthetic and moral approaches. He was of the Auden Generation, and so could not escape the gigantic influence of Audensque style which is quite perceptible in his practice of cataloguing important facts from immediate life and arranging proper words and images to substantiate them. The compelling story, the relaxed style almost colloquial and unemotional though capable of conveying thrilling emotions, the convincing figures and well knit plot, and, above all, plausibility, are the main causes of his popularity.

CHRISTOPHER ISHERWOOD

Christopher William Isherwood Bradshaw (1904–) received high praise even from his contemporaries who called him as "the most promising novelist of his generation",[52] "who held the future of English novels in his hands"[53], and whose departure for America with Auden in 1939 provoked the remark, "With Isherwood left the hope of English fiction."[54] His Berlin stories have been interpreted, "as the epic Isherwood intended, and stressed Isherwood's flair for fantasy and grotesque."[55] These are notable for rich and varied feelings, distinctions of characters, and subtlety of observations.[56] His mythopoetic powers have been underlined by David Garnett who has compared the impact of his Berlin novels with that of Blake's *The Marriage of Heaven ad Hell*. Like Blake he had, "the distinguishing mark of original writers and painters, the mark of imaginative greatness, and that he is able to impose a personal vision.''[57] Isherwood's world, whether its action took place in London, Berlin or in Hollywood, was the same everywhere.`David Pryce-Jones has aptly stated, ''His writing is concerned with himself and his own development, and not with abstratctions or ideologies.''[58] What Isherwood wrote of his friend upward was true of himself also: ''wherever he is all the places are the same, because all places became part of himself.''[59]

Throughout his career Isherwood remained a revolutionary. He revolted against the romantic conception of war; against the romantic idea of the hero, and against heterosexual dictatorship of the establishment. By that revolt he built his antimyth in his fictions and non-fictions.[60] Before the war Christopher Isherwood was best known by his novels – *Goodbye to Berlin* (1939); and *Mr. Norris Changes Trains* (1935). His serious intention, ''the use of the novel form to clarify tragic situations'', was made earlier manifest in such works as *All the Conspirators* (1928); and *The Memorial* (1932).[61] Until the mid-sixties his novels continued to appear at irregular intervals. He had chosen to devote much of his time also to such other interests as Indian mysticism, screenplay writing and his personal life. His wide travels in and intimate knowledge of London, Berlin, the Far East, South America and United States enriched his novels with vivid, varied and striking events. His friendship with such prominent literary figures as W.H. Auden, Stephen Spender, Aldous Huxly, E.M. Forster, Virginia Woolf, Thomas Mann and the actress Greta Garbo distinguished him also in the literary circle.

Isherwood was born on 26 August 1904, in his parents' home about twelve miles south-east of Manchester. The infant Christopher's world was one of provincial upper-middle class respectability, in which affluence was enjoyed but which lacked the extravagance and ostentation of great wealth.[62] His father Frank was interested in novels, Oriental society, Buddhism and theosophy and this Isherwood received in heritage. Both he and his younger brother Richard were to follow in their father's footsteps as far as religion was concerned, and this led him through ''agnosticism and the Quakers to the Indian Philosophy of Vedanta.''[63] His mother Kathleen advanced his liking for literature, and produced with him a small book called *The History of My Friends* (1910-11). During this period he also started learning French, but soon grew to hate it, and ended up with a mental block against it.

Isherwood received his early education at St. Edmund's school, and there he met Wystan Auden, aged eight. But the two did not really get to know each other until Isherwood's last year there. Christopher left St. Edmund in late 1918 and in 1919 he went to Repton, a fairly middle-of-the-road public school where he met with Edward Upward, a year older than he. Upward's romantic attractiveness and idealism attracted him. Like Christopher, Upward who later became a famous novelist was writing poetry at Repton. In the same year Isherwood and Upward went to Cambridge together for the scholarship examination in which both did well. While at Cambridge in January 1925 Isherwood completed the first draft of the novel, *Lions and Shadows* based mainly on his own life, but it was published only in 1938.

Christopher Isherwood visited Germany for the first time in 1928. It was a short visit of about seven to ten days to Bremen. His second visit to that country was in 1929 urged by his friend in Berlin, W.H. Auden, whom he called 'Hugh Wyston' in *Lions and Shadows*. Although Christopher mentioned that his chief motive for going to Berlin was to meet Layard, an anthropologist, really, "It was Berlin itself he was hungry to meet; the Berlin Wyston had promised him. To Christopher Berlin meant boys."[64] He himself has admitted in his autobiography his tendency towards paederasty since school days thus: "... he had fallen in love with many boys and been yearningly romantic about them. At college he had at least managed to get into bed with one."[65] He went to Berlin because he could not relax sexually with a member of his own class or nation; he needed a working class foreigner. He had become clearly aware of this when he had gone to Bremen. This Bremen trip provided him with materials for a novel, written many years later – *Down There on a Visit* (1962). Isherwood's infatuation for Bubi, Otto, Heinz and other German boys, was the main force working behind his German novels. His later novel *A Single Man* (1964) is an open picture of this subculture of paederasty. Very explicitly Isherwood has given reasons for his liking of the boys: "Why do I prefer boys? Because of their shape and their voices and their smell and the way they move. And boys can be romantic. I can put them into myth and fall in love with them."[66]

Isherwood's first novel, *All the Conspirators* (1928) is an intensely private novel, showing a hapless mother's boy unable to break his ties with his home and his mother. Only Christopher and his friends could understand "all its allusions with its clipped language, filled with phrases from their own jargon, and incidents taken from their lives."[67] Isherwood has shown both the Edwardian manners of the bygone generation and the sensibility of the younger generation 'as bogus and smug'. This novel is, "an autopsy of a malignant family with Isherwood a Coroner, dissecting the great malody, horror of one's home."[68]

Times Literary Supplement adversely criticised the book: "It is a first sketch of a novel rather than the complete and rounded novel itself. Mr. Isherwood has collected various parts of a machine but he has not succeeded in putting them together."[69] At that time Isherwood himself had imagined, "... a novel as a contraption like motor bicycle, whose action depends upon the exactly co-ordinated working of all its interrelated parts ...."[70] This coordinated working is absent in *All the Conspirators*. The novelist adopts jerky, cinematic technique and Hemingwayesque dialogue to unfold the episodes.

Isherwood was at the time interested in the exciting new technique of Woolf, Forster and Joyce, and his chief preoccupation was the fate of the artist in the bourgeois society. When the novel opens, Philip Lindsay, a mock Stephen Dedalus, has made the first of two grand operative gestures : he has quit his office job and with his cynical friend Allen Chalmers, has fled to a remote island. There he imagines himself as an artist in exile. His conversation and mannerisms however expose him as an imposter and a fool. Isherwood mercilessly discloses Philip's disguised sensibility, showing him as a pseudomartyr of the arts. The relationship between him and his mother, Mrs. Lindsay is very complex. Without him Mrs. Lindsay is grim and morose. Philip cannot even begin a painting or a work without her. She shows her disinclination to take tea with Philip when he returns from his holiday.[71] For a while Philip fecklessly pursues the romantic life of a misunderstood artist; but unable to endure his mother's abrasive seclusion and silence, he surrenders and childishly asks, "what do you want me to do?"[72] His mother wants him to, and because he must comply he returns to his loathed office job.

In this first novel Isherwood's method is to start in the middle of a scene and then, as the chapter advances, provides the missing information. However, the novel totters because it lacks in integrating unity. The incest between Joan and Philip and the affair between Joan and Allen carry nothing through. Similarly Philip, sick with brain fever, runs through thick fog, down dirty streets, among crowds of ill-disposed people; but it does not advance the plot. The following passage in which Philip rents a room, burlesques the conventions of outrageous melodrama:

> "A fat woman, with a prospect of gaslit hall and staircase behind her, eyed his bedraggled figures coldly, but admitted

> that she had a bed to spare. She called shrilly for a consumptive-looking man-servant, whom Philip followed thankfully up flights of rickety stairs to a bed room, a tiny garret under the roof.''[73]

Cyril Connolly however valued the book because it, ''reveals the nature and peculiarities of the author, and the nature and peculiarities of his time. Like Prufrock, which was a key to T.S. Elio.... This first novel is a key to Isherwood, and the twenties .... (It) introduces a dominant theme of his work, the Evil mother, fierce, obstinate, tearful, and conventional, who destroys her son....''[74]

Christopher's second novel *The Memorial* (1932) was a novel of a lost generation. Once he had thought 'The Lost' as the title of the novel, and wrote in his diary: ''The link which binds all the chief characters together is that in some way or other each one of them is conscious of the mental, economic, and ideological bankruptcy of the world in which they live. And all this must echo and re-echo the refrain: It can't go on like this. I'm the lost, we are the lost.''[75] It is divided into four parts, in a non-sequential time pattern 1928, 1925 and 1929. It deals with a group of middle-class people trying to come to terms with the aftermath of the First World War. Members of the family of a squirearchy find themselves in straitened circumstances and are unable to adopt to the new situation. There is a tendency for the younger elements to turn to a Bohemian life: The atmosphere is one of *apres moi le deludge*. Several of the characters are clearly recognisable borrowings from Isherwood's own family and friends. Mary Seriven leads an active musical and artistic life with her daughter. In London there is also a morose, artistic widow, Lily Vernon (Kathleen), obsessed with memories of her heroic husband Richard (Frank), who was killed in the war. Richard had also been an amateur water-colourist, and had lived in a large house up in Cheshire near the village of Chapel Bridge. Courageous in her `reactionary romanticism', Lily has a son Eric, who is like Christopher himself. He is handicapped by strong glasses and a stammer and his ''sexuality is ambiguous, despite his barely suppressed and aggressive desire for his female listener. Angrily he warns Edward to moderate his interest in his male cousin, yet he realizes his only motive can be jealousy.''[76] Eric gives help to Mary Seriven to carry on with her little concerts, after leaving Cambridge at the time of the General Strike. Eric is always oppressed by his mother Lily with whom he no longer lives, yet he is aware of the absurdity of her effect upon him. Lily keeps a diary and her attitude towards her environment as well as the villagers is exactly that of Kathleen's youth might condemn Lily's cult of her dead husband, but he was the truly strong man. His opposite the Truly Weak Man, is represented by Edward, his great friend, a homosexual who did heroically in war and got injured in an aeroplane accident, although his bravadoes were a sham.

In Lily Vernon, Isherwood presents a masterful portrait of the "Evil mother, fierce, obstinate, tearful and conventional."[77] Isherwood's method here is a sophisticated refinement of the jerky, stop-go cuts in *All the Conspirators*. He composes like a film editor, but in *The Memorial* he lengthens his vignettes, clarifies his dialogues, varies and develops his characters.[78] To avoid the dull chronological approach of most epic novels, Isherwood start in the middle, goes backward and then forward. In the first shot, Isherwood presents his characters in 1928, a year earlier than the book's present; then he turns back the picture album eight years, three years, then to 1929. We see the character at four critical periods through the subjective eyes of other characters and through the writer's own descriptions, what emerges is a series of chilling family portraits. Lily emerges as a contradictory figure. Although she appears to be no more than thirty, she is surrounded by a "curiously mature air sadness and quietness."[79] Dressed in black for mourning, she has, "absolutely the look of a child, smiling sadly and yet gaily."[80] For Major Charleswoth, Lily is a martyr, widow and siren, for her son, she is all of these as well as the perfect mother. Her son accepts all her monthly treatments and answers her questions but wonders all the time: "Why need we go through this? Which of us wishes it?"[81]

In his Berlin stories Isherwood brilliantly recorded what he saw and felt. His method is to catch the unrest and shabby chaos of the larger life around him in the microcosm of the individual. John Lehmann was the first to spot this capability "Isherwood was one of the first prose artists of his generation to receive the full impact of Europe as the Fascist tidal wave began to roll over it, and one of the very few who neither turned their backs on the catastrophe to write of other subjects nor were deflected by it... he absorbed the whole scene into his imagination, 'without a single hiccup of indignation that one can detect'."[82] As the political situation deteriorates, Isherwood's portraits darken. There is an increasing sense of suffocation, a sinking of human consciousness, as people discover themselves in helpless situations, trapped by the approaching horror of Nazism.

The two Berlin stories taken together can be considered as an epic as was intended by Isherwood. The first, narrated by Isherwood's name sake, William Bradshaw, was published in London in March 1935 under the title – *The Last of Mr. Norris*. But not long after its publication, he decided to change its title to *Mr. Norris Changes Trains*. It was intended by the author to mean, "that Mr. Norris keeps changing trains – that is to say, keeps having to change countries in a hurry, to escape his creditors and the police – but also that he keeps changing allies and political affiliations, jumping from one band-wagon on to another."[83] *Mr. Norris* has for its background the rise of Nazism and the collapse of the German Communist Party, and gives us information about the psychological condition and growth of Isherwood. "Norris is an essentially comic character, a colourful flaneur delighting in mysteries, dabbling in Communism and Fascism, revelling in the decadence of wings and scents and vintage wines."[84] Frank Kermode labels him as "Dickensian".[85] Isherwood wanted to make the reader experience Arthur Norris just as he himself had experienced Gerald Hamilton.[86] In order to make his reactions to and feelings towards Hamilton convincing he assumed the role of Bradshaw, the narrator.

The novel opens with the meeting between Mr. Norris and Bradshaw in a third class compartment of the train that is taking Bradshaw to Berlin for the first time. Very early in the narration Norris is identified with Hamilton:

> "My first impression was that the stranger's eyes were of an unusually light blue ... this smile had a great charm. His hands were white, small and beautifully manicured. He had a large blunt fleshy nose and a chin which seemed to have slipped sideways.... his forehead was sculpturally white, like marble. A queerly cut flinge of dark grey hair lay across it, compact, thick and heavy."[87]

Arthur Norris is a political operator in Berlin, where he plays the dangerous game of profiteering from the stormy unrest of the early nineteen-thirties. He is not very successful because of his harsh, unpleasant male secretary, Herr Schmidt. He foolishly fondles with the masochistic pleasures offered by stern young ladies in leather boots, and gladly takes for granted other peopl's perversions, predilection and dishonesty, unless it offends his sense of decency. Everything in the book paints that Norris is an heterosexual. If he had been sketched as a homosexual like Hamilton, it would have given a different turn to the

Bradshaw's feelings for Norris are characterised by unwilling respect and affection. Though he knows that Norris has caused great economic losses to his own friends, he cannot condemn him. He forgives and protects Norris, and sometimes feels sorry for him. He says to Norris, "I don't condemn you. As for my standards, if I ever had any, you've muddled them up completely. I expect you're right. In your place I'd probably have done just the same."[88] The reader's attention is focused on Norris's comic inferns and Bradshaw's amused toleration thereof. In the early chapters there are occasional hints of the public realities of the time. The public political world enters Bradshaw's life – at first at the personal level. He meets the Nazi Baron Von Prenitz, Otto, the Communist and his girl, Anni - a homosexual, a pimp and a whore. Hitler is mentioned, the winter 1931-32 comes and Bradshaw's narrative turns into a kind of history of a city in a state of civil war: "Hate reploded maddenly, without warning, out of nowhere, at street corners, in restaurants, cinemas, dance halls, swimming baths, at mid-night, after breakfast, in the middle of the afternoon."[89] Election results are quoted, and scenes occur at public meetings and in the public streets. It is 1933: Hitler is in power, the Communists are hiding or in prison, Bayer has been murdered in the Spandan barracks, Von Pregnita has committed suicide. Mr. Norris has fled to South America after being disclosed as a double agent, and Bradshaw has returned to England. Most of these events are observed and recorded by Brandshaw coldly, as a news-reel firm might report them.

It can be seen that *Mr. Norris Changes Trains* is a novel of a traditional private theme that expanded beyond the private lives of its characters. William Plamer remarked, "It has value as a view of Berlin during the years preceding Hitler's triumph, and accordingly as a study of social disintegration and upheaval, and it has a deeper meaning than that, for it may be taken as a comment on the state of civilisation in general during these last few years, and it may be that in the figure of Ludwig Bayer, a Communist leader, we are tentatively to anticipate the possibility of a cleaner and better behaved world."[90]

Isherwood's own idea about the novel was, however, different. He wrote to his mother Kathleen on March 12, 1935 from Copenhagen:

"... I am much shocked at the callousness with which they (the reviewers) all completely ignore the tragedy at the end. They seem to find German politics just as one long laugh .... Indeed I felt that Mr. Norris, far from being modern in conception, is almost too faithful to the English Comic Tradition...''[91] Forster's Comments (11May, 1935) after reading the novel are also revealing:

''.... it is not altogether my sort of work -- (it) dwells on the contradictions rather than the complexities of character, and seems to reveal people facet by facet ... It's marvellous too the way you've maintained standards of right and wrong and left Norris an endearing person. And you've made him both silly and witty, like a character in Congreve. He's awfully good. The necessity of combining knowingness and honesty in William renders him more of a problem, for in art there are uneasy bad fellows.''[92]

Goodbye to Berlin, the second of the Berlin novels was published in 1939. It began and ended with Isherwood's two Berlin diaries. Isherwood has remarked about this novel in the introductory note:

''It is a work about the first years of the thirties that was written in bits through the decade and published in the last year; so in a way it ... expresses the whole period. Even in its form it seems expressive of the time...''[93] One finds *Goodby To Berlin* as a fine depiction of the failure of feeling in ''an impoverished, demoralised, bankrupt city.''[94] No great event happens nor any public figure appears in the novel. The last, the poor, the weak, the neurotic, the lonely and the unloved, living their sad private lives, are the personages. Like T.S. Eliot in *The Waste Land*, Isherwood presents the grim picture of Berlin, out of fragments of the lives of its inhabitants – a cabaret singer, a whore, a working class hunter, a bar tender, a Jewish merchant. ''It is a city in which no one acts, and no one feels, a frozen and lifeless place, like the bottom of Dante's hell.''[95] But it is also a city; it belongs to the thirties, as Eliot's belongs to the twenties; and it provided a fertile ground for fascism.

Goodbye To Berlin is a fine meeting place of the opposites. Rich/poor, Jew/gentile, fascist/communist, German/alien, homosexual/heterosexual meet but they still remain isolated. Sally Bowles, the Nowaks and the Landauers remain in separate groups. ''Human relationships falter and fail, love is sold, friendship is lost or betrayed.''[96] The city of Berlin does not foster human relationship. The structuring principle is the first person narrator, but there is total objectivity. Isherwood asserts: ''Because I have given my own name to the ''I'' of this narrative, readers are certainly not entitled to assume that its pages are purely autobiographical, or that its characters are libellously exact portraits of living persons.''[97] He assumes the role of ''a camera with its shutter open, quite passive, recording, not thinking. Recording the man shaving at the window opposite and the woman in the Kimono washing her hair.''[98] On the surface, then, *Goodbye To Berlin* is a documentary, but it is also a personal testament, a record of the author's own life. The first section, for example, `A Berlin Diary' Autumn 1930 begins:

> ''From my window, the deep solemn massive street cellar-shops where the lamps burn all day, under the shadow of top-heavy balconied facades, dirty plaster frontages embossed with scroll work and heraldic devices. The whole district is like this. Street leading into street of houses like shabby monumental safes crammed with the tarnished valuable and second-hand furniture of a bankrupt middle class.''[99]

The story in the section, 'The Nowaks' moves round the conflict between love and hate. In this case the lovers are homosexuals – Otto and Peter Wilkinson – observed by the narrator. Peter is a ''wrapped, hypersensitive Englishman, about Christopher's age, unable to cope with the shallow, but violently sensuous Otto: they snap and claw at each other until Otto leaves.''[100] Otto's mother, Frau Nowak is sick with tuberculosis and goes to a senatorium. Herr Nowak returns home drunk every night, victimized by Berlin's infection and social dissatisfaction. Lothar, the elder son who has joined the Nazis, comes home only to eat and sleep. Otto manages his living in the streets. The daughter, Greta vacantly passes her days. The condition of the family becomes worse after the departure of Frau Nowak to the sanatorium. The family falls apart: Otto reverts to the cabarets; Lothar disappears; and Herr Nowak and Greta lapse into a primitivistic life. Christopher finds Herr Nowak drunk and Greta, ''shaking like a jelly with tears of laughter pouring down her cheeks.''[101]

The best story is in the section, 'The Landauers'. The Landauers are a wealthy Jewish family, owners of a huge department store. Chris tutors their eighteen-year-old daughter, Natalia. The story shifts to Bernhard Landauer, the cousin of Natalia. He tells Christopher that:

> ''I am getting out of touch with existence. That is bad, of course ... one must preserve a sense of proportion.... Do you know, there are times when I sit here alone in the evenings, amongst these books and stone figures, and there comes to me such a strange sensation of unreality, as if this were my whole life? ...''[102]

Bernhard never speaks candidly and without circumlocution.

In *Goodbye To Berlin* there is enough of symbols. In the opening diary, the objects in Frau Schroeder's living room augur the ferocity of Nazi Germany, "the hat stand is made of three halberds heavy and sharp enough to kill."[103] The candlesticks are "shaped like entwined serpents,"[104] from an ashtray emerges the "head of a crocodile,"[105] a paper knife is copied from a Florentine dagger. Isherwood's cool curiosity changes into horrified incredulity: "The sun shines, and Hitler is the master of the city ... and dozens of my friends ... are in prison, possibly dead."[106] The author ceases to be an impersonal recorder; he gets identified with the city:

> "Berlin is a skeleton which aches in the cold: it is my own skeleton aching. I feel in my bones the sharp ache of the frost in the girders of the overhead railway, in the iron work of balconies, in bridges, in tram lines, lamp standards, latrines."[107]

Thus in *Goodbye To Berlin* Sally Bowles, Peter and Otto, the Nowaks, the Landauers, and others shuffle through their shabby cabaret choreography.[108]

The Herr Issyvoo of *Goodbye To Berlin* as the reviewer for the Times Literary Supplement notes, acts like highly successful lenses "through which to focus a real or imaginary world, an expert use of the first person narrator, bettering the achievements of rival practitioners in this mode like Maugham.[109] Isherwood's own remark about this novel in 1939 was:

> "*Goodbye To Berlin* ... does contain a lesson in history. It tells us that poverty kills feelings, and isolates one man from another like freezing weather; that love and hate are political terms, and that hate feeds on human separateness; that violence is the energy of frozen hearts; that passivity and detachment are cold virtues...."[110]

To conclude, *All the Conspirators*, *The Memorial*, *Mr. Norris Changes Trains* and *Goodbye To Berlin* as well as the later novels of Isherwood are fine "autobiographical glimpses – blurred, darkened, partial into mirror. Taken together, these glimpses coalesce to form a reflected image of what might be called the essential Isherwood always investing his life with epic proportions, always the antison of Kathleen and Frank."[111] Besides, he distinguished himself in the thirties by writing novels of epical stature, mini in size but larger in spirit. To call his novels simply as documentaries, is to underrate him who worked in an alien country in pure artistic Mephistophelian spirit.

REX WARNER

Rex Warner was one of the important novelists of thirties. His novels are read even to-day for their high spirited entertainment and cursive and fluent style. Unfortunately some readers enjoy the *The Aerodrome*, *The Wild Goose Chase* and *The Professor* mainly as thrillers, completely failing to grasp their deeper significance. They miss his strong feelings for social justice, his awareness of the deeper moral currents, his sense of the spirit of ivory at work in history, and the myth making power of his imagination. His Kafkian technique to deal with his tales, gave a universal appeal to his works. His passion for dreams, visions, the grotesque and madness reminds us of Dickens and Dostoievsky. He was true to what he professed to be the real task of literature : "... to hold the mirror up to nature, to show men how they live and what is meant by their own words and manners, to investigate everything under the sun, to retain the tradition of the past and to explore the future, to instruct, to criticise, to delight, to create and reveal."[112] When his *Poems* and *The Wild Goose Chase* were published in 1937, he immediately established himself as one of "the more accomplished, versatile, imaginative and erudite of the pre-war generation of writers."[113]

Since then he has produced over thirty published works, covering every genre, including short stories, plays, allegorical novels and fictionalized biographies. He has, however, shown his special talent in the treatment of "politics, war, literature, love, the intrigues of bureaucratic man and the pains of economic man..."[114] The stories of Rex Warner compare favourably with those of Wells, but Rex Warner,[66] ... is less journalistic in invention; and is, indeed, far more inventive in portraying human behaviour. Wells is warmer, but Warner is less of an egoist. Wells' invention has not suppressed things like Warner's fantastic hermaphrodite intellectuals who start their love affaris at the end;..."[115]

Rex Warner was acutely aware of the tragic reality. His intellectual activity had centred largely on the periods of classical antiquity, and he had notably absorbed much of the Greek mentality. The form of two of his best novels – *The Professor* and *The Aerodrome* bears the marks of tragedy as Aristotle viewed it.

Reginald Ernest Warner was born in Birmingham on 9 March, 1905, son of a clergyman belonging to a typical middle class family. His uncles tended to be, "philosophers, birdwatchers, gentle eccentrics,"[116] and it was possibly from them that he himself developed an interest in ornithology that can be seen in his poems on birds and his novel, *The Wild Goose Chase*. After attending St. George's school, and winning a classical scholarship at eighteen, he went up to Wadham College, Oxford, where he read both classics and English. Cecil Day Lewis has written nostalgically of Warner in those days in his autobiography, *The Buried Day*:

> "Rex ... in photographs of this period looks like a sort of a Pre-Raphaelite curate–kept his more earnest side well concealed. A son of the rectory, he was now beginning to revolt against many of the things he had been brought up with, to swing more and more widely between ideal and real, his brilliant brain often at the mercy of the emotional pressures which it imperfectly understood and reacted to feverishly. ... At this time Rex liked to see people in the broad outlines of caricature – a single feature, ludicrously standing for the whole man."[117]

Warner graduated in 1926 and took to teaching as this profession which he kept, with occasional breaks, till 1949. It was during his stay in Cairo as a teacher (1929-32) that he completed the manuscript of *The Wild Goose Chase*. For a decade or more after 1949 he devoted full time to writing and doing radio and television work; and in 1962 became a visiting Professor of classics at Bodwin College.

The first novel of Rex Warner, *The Wild Goose Chase* was published in 1937, and the reactions of the critics were typical. One condemned the author as a mere left-wing propagandist and communist apologist; another viewed the book as dealing with outdated liberal sentiments; and a third suggested that a new writer of ineffable merits had appeared to brighten English Literary scene.[118]

Lehmann, a famous literary man of the thirties remarked, "... a new dimension had been added to the English novel in our time."[119] It opens with the following explanatory lines:

"For our contention is not with the blood and the flesh, but with dominion, with authority, with the blind world rulers of this life, with the spirit of evil in things heavenly .... *The Wild Goose Chase*, I made you a symbol of our saviour, with your fierce indifference to bye-laws and quiet flying ....''[120] The novel bears clear mark of Kafkian influence. In an article of his own in *Penguin New Writing* Warner draws attention to what he calls, ''two of the most common uses of allegory: first ... to give vigour and vividness to a definite belief; second to attempt fantastically to throw some light on what is beyond the ordinary reach of words.''[121] Bunyan and Swift practised the first kind whereas Dostoevsky and Kafka followed the second. *The Wild Goose Chase* is of the second kind in allegorical pattern. Warner's allegory or symbolism is to act upon the reality imaginatively until its solidity departs to reveal the truths that reality hides. It takes the familiar tangible symbol, as Melvile took the whole, Dostoevsky the family, and Kafka the processes of law, and ''projects the imagination from the springboard of that familiarity into regions of fantasy, until by methods which may seem wayward and irrational it arrives at a truer estimate of the significance of those symbols in the life of mankind than could have been attained by pedestrian rational methods.''[122] Melvile and Dostoevsky were the first great novelists to apply to the structure of the novel this essentially poetic creative method. Kafka elaborated the form as an imaginative tract for his own times. In *The Wild Goose Chase* Warner took over from Kafka two of the chief attributes of this form of fiction – first, the detailed and commonplace realism; and second, the imaginative distortion of it. The beginning of *The Wild Goose Chase* might be effectively summed up in a sentence – once upon a time there were three brothers who set out to find the wild Geese – and the tradition of a fable is adhered to in making the youngest brother, George the successful one. The initial realism is sustained, except for the undefined nature of the quest and the hint of exaggerated caricature in some of the characters. This is deliberately done. It is not Warner's purpose to pass off *The Wild Goose Chase* as realism; he knows that the more circumstantial is his fantasy, the more cogently will his imaginative treatment of it operate on the willing reader.

Warner's longing for social order is a paramount influence on his art. He is prepared to let form of that art to be determined by what may be broadly called political preconceptions. The symbol of the wild goose is an echo of the Holy Grail and the hero, George, is something like a socialist Galahad. George, Joe, Pushkov, Andria, Freda Harison and Goholov are the revolutionaries who are in pursuit of love, beauty, strength and freedom. They wage a war against the fascist town-government which stands for tyranny, subjection and death to the weaker. George enumerates the abuses of this government to Marquata, "... your senseless morality, your lunatic police, your oppression, your deliberate cruelty, your stupidity, your jigging, it is sufficient reason for me utterly to condemn your Government...."[123] Like George, Joe's wife Freda Harrison too had pursued the wild geese that stand for freedom, but had died facing the enemy. Goholov encourages the other revolutionaries, "So I say, love life. Hate your enemies .... Keep yourself whole. Help your comrades. Lead them if you can.... Do not rest till you have destroyed those kings. Help the revolution."[124] Pushkov, another revolutionary, points out what has been done by the town-government and its corrupt officials to the subjugated peasantry:

> "A great portion of our people was taken away into slavery. Inside the town they now work in factories, making beads and cigarettes for us, and for the townsmen instruments of science, utility and torture. Consequently, since our district was annexed, the wealth and power of the town have grown enormously ... who feeds the town? We do ... you ask me about the policeman. Simple fellows they look, laughing at everyone, but their cunning is diabolical, and they have no notion of morality."[125]

Three brothers one after another set out in search of the wild geese that "Would bring to their discoverer riches beyond dreams, and a despotic control over the armies and women of other states."[126] Rudolph the eldest and David, the second fail because both deviate from their primary objective. George, the youngest brother succeeds. The regime of the three kings is overthrown with the help of the revolutionary peasants party, and George assumes a position of authority in the new government. He speaks to the assembled men and women, "Well then, this government, this intellect has been overthrown. The masses, the despised body, have taken its place. Do you not see what this means ? It means a new life, something which has not been heard of before ... we shall choose our own way of living and it will not be the way of kings or scientists ... we shall make use once more of time and space and shall be particularly attached to the earth and to the sun. The government which we destroyed was of air and water. Ours will be earth and fire...."[127] Rex Warner himself realized that, "The fight against fascism was a fight against a dark, medieval obscurantist tyranny which was infinitely more dreadful, hideous and paralysing than any tyranny man had experienced before."[128]

In spite of its strong communistic overtones, making it a veritable "Marxist Pilgrim's Progress"[129] the novel, unlike the Russian novels of the Stalinist era, contains many non-communistic passages; to wit:

"On creaking boards George went on tiptoe, knowing not why, opened the door and saw Joan standing upright before a long mirror, naked, fingers plaited behind head, not admiring herself, but sleepy-eyed surveying; and motionless she stood as he entered, raising only heavy eyes in ordinary welcome. Closing door swiftly instepping George confronted and circling arm .... He pressed close and his arm gliding upward sank into the moist dip. Kisses are like iron in flowers, and soon they lay lovingly at ease...."[130] The bloody scene in which Bill, the husband of Joan, is killed by Andria[131], is a thrilling. One and the combat between the peasants army and the mechanical toy-soldiers of the town[132] is pure fable and very entertaining. And lastly, George's encounter with the king[133] at the close of the story, is nothing short of a melodrama.

These scenes along with the personal stories of Don Antonio, Bob, Goholov, Joe and Andria finely weave the texture of the novel. Though the story is allegorical, the characters are real human beings and not shadowy intellectual abstractions. Of course some of them do appear larger than life because of their symbolic significance. The kings stand for evils, George for truth, beauty and strength, Joan for simplicity and virtue, Bob for flattery and empty geniality, David for the modern youngman who wishes to get the experience of both sexes like Tiresias, and Marqueta, the King's mistresses, stands for counterfeit love. The intelligibility and plausibility of their discourses make the story easily comprehensible. The plot is coherent, well knitted though large in its dimension. Each and every episode is fully integrated. George is the narrator of the story, and the novelist records what he hears from the mouth of George. He remains behind curtain so long as the story goes on. His subjectivity never distorts the personalities of his imaginative creations. His detachment is true test of his living a classical genius. In this way the novel is not an "uncrafted window on life – the reader is supposed to look straight through the words at the pictured characters and settings just as one peers out through a spotless pane on one's next door neighbour."[134]

In 1938 three political parables were published: Spender's *Trial of a Judge*, Auden and Isherwood's *On the Frontier*, and Warner's *The Professor*, "... each book is, in its way, an elegy for a lost liberal idea of European civilization. This is essentially a tragic theme, and the characters who express it best are Spender's Judge and Warner's Professor. Both are publicmen with public titles and reputations, who are defeated because they are liberals in a port-liberal time ....''[135] They are heroes but not of chivalrous feats; they are men of values, and of worth. Samuel Hynes has pointed out that, ''It is a curious phenomenon of the late thirties that liberalism, which has been buried so deep by the left in earlier years, should seem to rise from its grave like Banquo....''[136]

The Professor is about the failure and death of liberalism and triumph of fascism. Like Spender, Warner was a communist for a time, a Party member; and again like Spender he took the view in his book that liberalism was out of date, and that revolution was the only line of action left for the opponents of fascism. But his Professor is heroic and a compelling one in his defeated liberalism. ''Above all, Warner's undying faith in the humanist ideals and his essential optimism (in spite of the tragic end of the Professor) reveal his progressive and revolutionary weltanschanung.''[137]

The story of the novel takes place in a European country at a time of political crisis when the fascists and the communists are very near to a civil war, with the armies of a neighbouring fascist state waiting on the borders for an invitation. At this juncture, the Professor, a classical scholar, ''a man whose integrity no one had ever questioned ... a man who had shown himself in his speeches and writings to be able to understand the best aims of all parties, and yet who was attached to none; ... one whom neither brow-beating, cajolery or false alarms would be likely to turn from a course of the strickest honesty and widest sympathy,''[138] is offered the chancellorship of the country. He accepts the position, and is swiftly and easily overthrown by the fascists; the foreign army enters the country and as he attempts to escape he is betrayed, imprisoned, tortured and shot in the back.

''Much of this is highly dramatic, and Warner handles it with the rapid, terse intensity of a thriller. But the most dramatic passages in the book are not moments of physical action, but the passionate monologues and debates, in which men holding different political positions argue them, and in so doing pass judgments on the Professor's liberalism.''[139]

The debate begins in the first scene itself in which the Professor, lecturing to his students on sophocles, digresses on the word 'Polis' – ''an enclosure,'' he explains, ''a safety zone or outpost against the Greeks (and in a very real sense their view was correct) was actually the barbarism of others who were outside this on the whole liberal organisation.''[140]

Two more dialogues are of particualr importance. In one the Professor meets an old school mate who is now a fascist officer named Julius Vander, and who argues strongly with the Professor about the relevancy of fascist creed:

> "... all I require is food, drink, women and a certain sense that I am controlling my own destiny ... you say you want to make men brothers. What you really want is to make them ants .... Your Christianity, your Platonism, your intellectualist culture... are, as I have said, unnatual and unfitted to real men ... the only freedom that you offer is economic freedom, a barren slogan which no one who is not an intellectual even understands."[141]

In the second the speaker is an elderly cobbler whom the Professor meets during his flight from the invading fascist army. He argues in Biblical terms, and reproaches the Professor for his liberalism.

"... neither war nor poverty is so dangerous to mankind as is your liberalism. For you, in your detachment, endeavour to legislate for the abstract man. What a terrible insult to real living and tortured men and women: What a denial of God! ... Believe me when I say that the world is alive. It lives in suffering, and that suffering calls not for regulations, not even for understanding, and for love."[142] The cobbler reproaches the well-meaning scholar for his detachment, and tells him that damnation is the fruit of his moral blindness, for the denial of the Christian faith that God is love, that "all misery is created as a field in which love may move."[143] Here we catch a glimpse of Warner the modernist. Conformity to liberal and secular ideals has been juxtaposed to catholic Christian tradition creating a situation in the Aristotelian sense of tragedy.

The Professor shows the context of the problem of the age that there is no security; that the ideals of liberalism as well as orthodox Christianity are ineffective in face of blatant force of aggressive fascism. As has been hinted above, besides being a political parable, *The Professor* is also a classical tragedy. The Professor's dream is rooted in the classics, that of the democratic Greek Polis, but his hamartia, or tragic flow is his devotion to abstract justice. He refuses to arm the workers against the Legionaries. He refuses or is unable to understand that the sword is mightier than the pen. He, then, is a tragic hero and his action brings the final catastrophe.

Warner, the classicist is also seen in the plot of this novel. The beginning of the narrative contains the seeds that produce the conclusion:

> "The last week enjoyed, or rather experienced by Professor A may be reconstructed with tolerable accuracy from two sources."[144]

The reader learns immediately that : "We shall see a man quite unfitted for power .... He believed against all the evidence, scholar though he was, not only in the existence but in the efficiency of a power more human, liberal, and kindly than organisation of metal. He believed not simply in the utility but in overriding or pervasive power of the disinterested reason."[145]

Warner adheres closely to the Aristotelian notion of high tragedy, and also to Elizabethan tragic drama. The story of *The Professor* produces pity and terror resulting in catharsis. The tragic hero realises his own folly. In the prison he looks as miserable and pathetic as King Lear.[146] His stubborn resistance in face of torture and suffering produces admiration. He says to Colonel Grimm, "I must give you credit for some sincerity, but I can only hate everything for which you stand. You cannot change my mind, I reject your proposal."[147]

But the novel shows imperfection in the delineation of characters who are nameless and faceless. They are sketchy and pantomimic, and are mere spokesmen of their respective idealogies. They debate too much on topics which are boring and disgusting to the readers. There is no interplay of powerful feelings, and even love is very cold and lifeless. There is no humour to lighten the seriousness of the tragedy. Nevertheless the novel can be read for leisure. It can also appeal to those who are interested in the struggle among the power hunger for world domination. Ronald Mason aptly remarks, "... Warner has not yet written a more compact and, within its limits, compelling novel. In its own right it should be read as a fascinating demonstration of the power of ideas to give form and life to a novel on their own;..."[148]

Rex Warner's another notable novel, *The Aerodrome* was published in 1941. *The Wild Goose Chase* was the story of humanity's assault upon tyranny, but *The Aerodrome* profiting by the disillusion of the late thirties and employing a shrewder realism, is the story of tyranny's assault upon humanity. The encroachment of tyranny in the Aerodrome is not so much upon communal life as upon personal freedom and friendships and desires. As in *The Wild Goose Chase*, in *The Aerodrome* also there is antagonism between the village and the town. The village cannot understand the aerodrome, and the aerodrome despises the village. To each the other is unreal. Thus, as far as the flight Lieutenant is concerned, shooting the Rector is no more deplorable than overturning the teapot. But this dichotomy grows out of a fundamental unity. "It is from the incalculable power of love that have developed both the Aerodrome with its ruthless in human efficiency and the village with its sensuality, its muddle and stupidity."[149] This underlying unity is suggested by the movement of characters between the aerodrome and the village, and also by the ambiguous and complex family relation. The hero, as the Vice-Marshal's son, connects the village with the aerodrome. Bess's love for the Flight Lieutenant points to a totality in which both factors included. The incest which turns out to be no incest suggests that crime is merely the perversion of creative forces by a self-imposed dichotomy.

There is a similarity between Warner and Kafka in that both use the village or the country as the base from which the central character sets out to struggle against the opposite: The authoritarian influence represented by the castle, the city, or the aerodrome. Kafka's K. wishes to enter the castle; similarly, in Warner's the brothers see the city as a way to the wild goose, and Roy sees the aerodrome as the means to gain freedom. This freedom sought by Roy is not merely freedom from the old family ties and Bess but also the wider freedom which Antony, the Air Vice Marshal, promises his followers, the freedom they will attain through the conquest of power. Disillusionment, however, awaits him. The aerodrome proves to be the death rather than the attainment of his desires. The Air Vice-Marshal talks of freedom, but the power by which he proposes to attain it turns mercilessly upon the people with whom he has had the most human relationships. Roy realises that, with all its disorder, the life of the village is more desirable than that of the aerodrome.

In both *The Wild Goose Chase* and *The Aerodrome* the heroes realize that, not only will the city, or the aerodrome fail to bring them freedom they desire, but these will actually destroy the very roots of humanity from which freedom grows. In *The Aerodrome* the Flight Lieutenant preaches a sermon in which he tells the villagers that the Aerodrome has only done them harm, while Roy accepts a technical breach of the rules of the aerodrome, for which he is not directly responsible, as a possible means of escape and recommencement of his life with Bess. In the struggle with Authority, Warner repeatedly uses symbols recognised by modern psychology as pertaining to a conflict. In the final denouement in *The Aerodrome*, Roy discovers that the Air Vice-Marshal is both his and the Flight Lieutenant's father, so the two men struggling against authority are also sons struggling against a father. In the struggle against authority the sons win. The Air Vice Marshal is killed on the eve of attaining his great ambition when his plane crashes, being sabotaged by the Flight Lieutenant. But the winners realized that mere overthrow of tyranny is not the attainment of their real aims. Roy realizes that the death of the Air Vice-Marshal and his own subsequent liberation mean only the beginning of the development of his life and relationship with Bess.

The Air Vice-Marshal is the most memorable character in the aerodrome. He is larger than life, trying to transcend the inconsistencies in his nature. He is also a human father wishing to spare his son. He fights the corrupt villagers, his motive being revenge on the Rector, who as a youngman had tried to kill him and steal his betrothed. He is a revenge tragedy, but it is not in the tradition of Seneca.,By obliterating the present as produced by the past and replacing it with a new present structured according to his fascist ideas – perfect but arid. He would take revenge by clearing away what he thinks to be falsehood. His aerodrome society is to be an elite one, consisting of men who deny the creative role of fatherhood, and who live for their man-made system. He is a tragic figure conforming in every respect to the Greed models. He falls because he cannot be true to his own fatherly nature (home love) and also to the objective reality of his self-created way of existence. He simultaneously tries to do his son Roy a favour by taking him out of the village life and advancing him at the aerodrome; but the son returns to the village. And his illegitimate son, Flight Lieutenant, also rejects the aerodrome because his woman has been destroyed because of it. He tampers with the plane and sends his father, Anthony to his flaming death. Lear disowns Cordelia; Macbeth kills Duncan; Oedipus strives to know the one truth about his father's murderer. They all bring tragedy on their heads. Similarly, the Air Vice-Marshal attempts to eliminate the festering multitude of evils in the village and fares no better.

As in *The Professor*, in *The Aerodrome* too Warner has worked according to the classical concept of tragedy, making it relevant to the twentieth century through contemporary reference to the phenomenon of Fascism. We sympathise with the Air Vice-Marshal's yearnings to be free of the filthy encumbrances of human existence. Here for the first time does Warner demonstrate notably the ambivalence which is found in his characters. The Air Vice-Marshal does not seek evil; he seeks to rise above it. The villagers are corrupt, and he would forge from incorruptible material a new way of being, clean and hard as his aeroplanes. The embroilments in the story, the sordid sexual involvement, and the Rector's agonizing confession at the beginning of the novel in the form of a soliloquy are a few of the Jacobean elements in the novel.

In summing up we can say that Rex Warner's novels of the thirties are "a series of long, sustained, passionate arguments worked out in prose which is at once noble, majestic, evocative and electrifying. There is not only limpidity and clarity, as in George or Wells, or power and passion, as in Arthur Koestler, but also a strong poetic verve and a turn for a highly original, metaphysical language,"[150] His plot construction, characterisation and technique are splendid. His allegorical fantasy is highly inventive. It is at once poetical and logical. He succeeds fully in conveying the political phantasmagoria through symbols. He owes nothing to Wells, but a great deal to Shaw and Kafka.

EVELYN WAUGH

Evelyn Waugh wrote in 1962 that, "Novels are mere shadows compared with the real world,"[151] and shadows sufficed for him. He saw the pre-war world as absurd, little, humble, of antagonising forces; and he set out to record it with no more than the "scrappy, half-educated `sense of period' which he shared with his contemporaries."[152] He believed that "superficial acquaintance" was "one of the materials of the writer's trade"; that the artist responds to "the amorphous, haphazard condition in which life presents experience" like a carpenter whittling "a rough piece of timber into shape."[153] Waugh always liked representational work which exhibited technical virtuosity, rather than vision,[154] and like Charles Ryder, a character in his novel, *Brideshead Revisited* he thought of modern art as `bosh'.[155]

In 1946, he made the famous and surprising declaration that he was not a satirist. Satire he maintained needed a society with homogeneous moral standards.[156] This statement helps to know his literary lineage. It places him, "among writers like Swift, Thackeray and Shaw, who all achieved considerable rapport as entertainers with a very large public, but who felt, like Waugh, morally estranged from the world that applauded them."[157] "The novelist", Waugh wrote in the Preface to *Helena*, "deals with experiences which excite his imagination", and much of what he found exciting he knew to be ugly and unlawful. He had been an active homosexual, an appalling bully, a drunkard and a snob. Equally integral to his personality, of course, were his love for order, friendship, reason, good workmanship, honour and purity of life. He was in fact at odds with himself temperamentally to an extreme degree, just as he was at odds with the values and beliefs of most of his contemporaries; and certain issues seem to have made him actually aware of the tensions and contradictions inside himself. Of these one of the most potent was racialism."[158]

He holds his religion in reserve relentlessly, and in this he is unlike Graham Greene. Waugh's novels refuse to be didactic; but if there is a lack of an ideological framework, there is nonetheless a powerful unifying principle. His novels focused "on his fascination with nudity, barbarity, urbanity, cynicism and graceful selfishness; his preoccupation with anarchy and death; his love of order, verbal elegance, structural deftness, his capacity for complex and humiliating feelings of envy and lust; his moral sensitivity and respect for innocence; his cold heartedness; his exact sense of moral principle; and his utterly unprincipled capacity for cruel glee."[159]

Evelyn Waugh was born in Hampstead in 1903, second son of Arthur Waugh, publisher and literary critic. His elder brother, Alec Waugh, was a popular novelist. As childhood ended, Evelyn marked that men of letters were all round him. His father's publishing firm was small but distinguished. Alec, his elder brother found fame with his sensational novel, *The Loom of Youth* which had an immediate impact on Evelyn Waugh before he had reached his teens. He received his education at Lancing and Hertford College, Oxford. In 1927, he wrote his first work, a life of *Dante Gabriel Rossetti*, and in 1928 his first novel *Decline and Fall*. Then followed at regular intervals *Vile Bodies* (1930); *Black Mischief* (1932); *A Handful of Dust* (1934); and *Scoop* (1938). During these years he travelled widely in Europe, the near East, Africa, and tropical America. Probably this was the 'wide travel' that made him love, "... distant lands and barbarous places, and in particular the borderlands of conflicting cultures and states of development".[160] In 1939 he was commissioned in the Royal Marines and later transferred to the Royal Horse Guards, serving in the Middle East and in Yugoslavia. In 1942 his novel, *Put Out More Flags* was published, in 1945 *Brideshead Revisited*, *When the Going was Good* and *The Loved One*, and in 1950 *Helena*, his historical novel. Evelyn Waugh turned to the Roman Catholic church in 1930, for he thought that "...life in England or anywhere else was unintelligible and unendurable without God."[161] He was married and had six children and lived in the West Country, where he died in 1966.

Waugh's first novel, *Decline and Fall* (1928) is a brilliant account of the rise and fall in the fortune of its hero, Paul Pennyfeather. The story is funny from first to last. "Its bland, destructive brilliance lights up a world of comic happenings through which people move with the lunatic logic and inconsequence imparted to them by their creator's ironic vision of mankind."[162] The novel presents Paul as a passive, inert and uncritical being, registering no kind of attitude to his own experience. His most typical feature is a sort of blankness. Margot Beste-Chetwynde announces her intention of ditching him for a more successful man, and he is pained not at her loss but how little he was pained. The author himself remarks, "This book is really an account of mysterious disappearance of Paul Pennyfeather so that readers must not complain if the shadow which took his name does not amply fill the important part of hero for which he was originally cast."[163] This shadowy quality of Pennyfeather, partly because of this shadowy half-presence, emerges as less eccentric, more directly normal, than the high society caricatures among whom he moves. He is more moral than other characters, even though that morality is satirised as a form of callowness: when he is asked to say why he has been sent down from Oxford he resorts, 'true to his training', to honesty. The significance of Paul's blankness is two-fold. It allows the novel's real concerns – the life of upper-class society– to emerge 'objectively', as a neutrally descriptive record than as part of a more personal, inward, evaluative history; and it deftly prevents this experience from being unduly criticised by the man who is its sacrificial victim.[164]

Paul has been sent down unjustly from Oxford and is sentenced to seven years' penal servitude as a scapegoat for Margot Beste Chetwynde's crimes of prostitution. His inability to belong to his own experience prevents him from articulating anything remotely approaching a protest. In the meditative quiet of his prison-cell, he is torn between two principles: "On one side was the dead weight of precept, inherited from generations of school masters and divines. According to these, the problem was difficult but not insoluble. He had 'done the right thing' in shielding the woman : so much was clear, but Margot had not quite filled the place assigned to her, and he was shielding her, not from misfortune or injustice, but from the consequence of her crimes...."[165] This conflict is essentially between a sense of morality and a sense of style. Paul's moral conflict over Margot and the self sacrifice to which it leads, signify a seriousness and gentlemanly honour which no other character in the book would be capable of showing. And in this sense

Paul is still a butt of the novel's satire. We are asked to approve not only his attitude towards Margot, but also the solemn absurdity of the love-struck heroism which motivates it. The novel satirises Paul's position on the one hand while on the other it seriously condemns high society. Paul's moral gesture saves Margot, but reveals him as an `outsider', too passive and gentlemanly and serious to survive in the jungle of Mayfair.

The upper-class values are satirised but not dismissed; they are fraudulent and hollow, but there is really nowhere else to turn. The incidents are reported rather than presented, and this is itself significant. The surface-texture of flippant observation is intact, but the deeper forces also are exposed. However exposure implies a sort of controlled objectivity which is hardly there at all; the Prendergast incident is really a mixture of distrubance and indulgence. It is distrubance in so far as it indicates, not any significantly, 'objective' reality in the novel but an uncontrolled reflex of fantasy on the part of the novelist; it is indulgence in so far as it signifies a quite gratuitous sensationalism, done entirely for its own sake. But the book is, apart from the sparkle of its wit and its baroque details, an excellent and coherent story. It moves from start to finish with experienced ease.

Vile Bodies (1930) is, ''more crowded, less classic and clearcut in plot, more dispersed in interest, more of a revue show ... it proved a dazzling Kaleidscope of brightest Mayfair, brilliantly fantasticated.''[166] This novel is similar in tone and technique to *Decline and Fall*, but the mood is more intense.

Events in *Vile Bodies* occur in rapid fragmentation in which everything is at once ordinary and alarming. Deaths, suicides and the fall of a government are caught up randomly in the general whirl. The society gossip-columnist Simon Balcairn is driven to suicide by the pressure of his career, but the event is too trivial to imply any indictment of the society as a gesture, it has the histrionic unreality of the world it is rejecting. In the midst of disintegration is the elusive figure of Father Rothschild, the mysteriously omniscient, inscrutably knowledgeable Jesuit. Father Rothschild is offered as a centre of spiritual value, but a centre which is necessarily suggestive rather than realised.

Like *Decline and Fall*, *Vile Bodies* contemplates a world which it can in no sense adequately interpret. Upper-class values are false, but the offered alternative is a vision of ordinary life which is equally despicable. The novel is set in actual London. The topography is well drawn. The street names in the novel are real and in the right places. But it is a London novel only in the sense that the waste land is a London poem, "The city itself is an unreal city, a fantasy of modern life lived in the absence of values."[167] This is an allegorical world where we meet Mrs. Ape who appears with angles: Faith, Fortitude, chastity, and so on through the sacred virtues to Divine Discontent. Other characters' names also confirm this point : Lord Chasm, Lady Throbbing, Mary Mouse, Walter Outrage, and Miles Malpractice. The world of *Vile Bodies* is a waste land; only it is a waste land inhabited mainly by 'bright young people',[168] who are of post-war First-World War generation, inheritors of the post-war mood that Richards had described as "A sense of desolation, of uncertainty, of futility, of the groundlessness of aspirations, of the vanity of endeavour ...."[169] Lacking causes or vocations, they spend their time going to parties: "... masked parties, savage parties, Victorian parties, Greek parties, wild West parties, Russian parties, Circus parties ... dull dances in London and comic dances in Scottland and disgusting dances in Paris – all that succession and repetition of massed Humanity ... those Vile Bodies."[170] This passage gives an image of depression analogical to the processions in Dante's Hell, although here it is simply a catalogue of nonsensical events. The word that the 'bright young people' use again and again is 'bogus'. "People are bogus, love is bogus, sex is bogus, politics is bogus, even the bright young people are bogus...."[171] Mr. Outrage complains about the wantonness of the young, and Father Rothschild replies:

> "... they don't make the best of a bad job nowadays. My private school master used to say, 'If a thing's worth doing at all, it's worth doing well'. My church has taught that in different words for several centuries. But these young peple have got hold of another end of the stick, and for all we know it may be the right one...."[172]

Vile Bodies is "a parable of bogusness that ends in the greatest bogusness of all, the war that is inexorably approaching. It is also a definition and a defence of the generation ... though it is full of satiric sketches, we cannot call it a satire; it is rather ... a surreal or expressionist attempt to record reality when it seemed more and more to be any rational observation, unreal."[173] The novel reflects in true sense the mood of helplessness and aimlessness which dominated the period *entre deux querres*. Waugh was not satisfied with the structure of the novel. He himself remarked in an interview: "Of *Vile Bodies* .... It was a bad book, I think, not so carefully constructed as the first separate scenes tended to go on far too long .... It was second-hand too.''[174] Nevertheless the novel is perfect from the viewpoint of verisimilitude. The rackets, the vices, the chatter and the jokes make the novel saucy. Situations and persons are flung on the scene with lavish extravaganace, and this extravagance gives double appeal to the novel.

Vile Bodies was followed by *Black Mischief* (1932). Its locale is Africa, and it is as easily read as the former two. A spirit of heartless, morally feather-weight farce ensures that Mr. Youkoumian's indifference to his wife's atrocious suffering is simply funny. Equally disarming is the imposition of European social and political institutions on a primitive society. The novelist takes great delight in distributing titles among his Africans, and the humour results out of this also. When the Earl of Ngumo threatens, 'to dismember any man on his estate' from his peers, it is reminiscent of the noises made by middle-aged dominant males in English country families. Again, like its French counterpart, the Nestorian church has its little nest of fascists, eager for 'a whack at the modernists and Jews', who are supposed to be responsible for the birth-control programme. All this blends finely with the farcical triviality of life at the British Legation, the machinations of Mr. Ballon, and the adventures of Dame Mildred and Miss Trim. The novelist does not show the complexities of Connolly's inner life, nor of Black Bitch's and nor of the youkoumians. He has plainly arranged their marraiges as a joke. Seth has the hopeless task of representing personal decency in Africa, of fusing with his primitive consciousness, the notion of the human individual of intelligence and goodwill. But in the task he fails. He says, ''I have seen the great Aldershot, the Paris Exhibition, the Oxford union. I have read modern books ... at my stirrups run woman's suffrage vaccination. I am the new age. I am the future.''[175]

This absurd speech implies that Africans cannot really understand the complexities of Western thought. But Seth is not simply a joke. His loveliness is serious and symptomatic:

> ''Seth lay awake and alone, his eyes wild with the inherited terror of the jungle, desperate with the acquired loneliness of civilization. Night was alone with beasts and devils and the spirits of dead enemies; ... Seth could not expand to meet the onset of fear. He was alone, dwarfed by the magnitude of the darkness, insulted from his fellows, strapped down to mean dimensions.''[176]

The last phrase reverses our view of Seth. It is sharp, precise and powerful in its indignation at the way he and Africa have been diminished by civilizaion:

> "It is as if Waugh were scathingly opting for barbaric terrors and barbaric communion."[177]

The other source of moral unease in *Black Mischief* is of course Basil seal. Seth and Basil are well matched, both showing their charming immaturity. Basil is a debauched worldling with the heart of a ruthlessly invulnerable adolescent. He steals his mother's emerald bracelet and escapes but our pleasure in his wickedness becomes rather less comfortable when he becomes the secretary of innocent Seth. Connolly, the British General who knows Seth and Basil well seems to offer some assurance that Seth will survive Basil's depredations, and our fears are further allayed when Seth comes to know of the affair between Basil and Prudence. The celebrated love-scene in Basil's room reminds us of the seediness of Graham Greene's Africa:

> "The atmosphere of the room was rank with tobacco smoke. Basil, in short-sleeves, rose from the deck-chair to greet her. He threw the butt of Burma cheroot into the tin hip-bath which stood unemptied beside the bed; it sizzled and went out and floated throughout the afternoon, slowly unfurling in the soapy water.[178]

Thus the novel deals with the incompatibility of western civilization, and all its attendant and deplorable ills, with African barbarism. As the novelist professed in an open letter to the Archbishop of Westminster in 1933: "The plan of my book (Black Mischief) throughout was to keep the darker aspects of barbarism continually and unobtrusively present, a black and mischievous background against which the civilized and semi-civilized characters performed their parts ... hoping to prepare the reader for the sudden tragedy when barbarism at last emerges from the shadows and usurps the stage. It is not unlikely that I failed in this; the transition was too rapid, the catastrophe too large."[179] The book is full of flippantly brief allusions to cannibalism, public executions, nudity and slavery. The notorious master stroke by which Waugh removes the blinkers after Seth's death and Prudence's disappearance is all the more appalling for the vivid economy of his prose:

"Basil shook him violently "Speak, you old fool, where is the woman?' The headman grunted and stirred, then a flicker of consciousness revived in him. He raised his head, "The white woman? Why, here", he patted his distended paunch, "You and I and the big chiefs – we have just eaten her." Then he slumped forward into a sound sleep. Round and round circled the dancers, oclare and blood and sweat glistening in the firelight; the wisemen's headgear swayed above them, leopards feet and snake skins, amulets and lions' teeth and the shrivelled bodies of hats and toads, jigging and spinning. Tireless hands drumming out the rhythm; glistening backs heaving and shivering in the shadows. Later, a little after midnight, it began to rain."[180] Malcolm Bradbury praises the assured handling of "desparate materials, tones and events in the novel, but finds Waugh's approach so tangential that it is difficult to find the centre of the action and be sure of the effect he is trying to produce."[181] The actions centre on civilization and barbarism, and one of the favourite images in the novel is of the civilised society under siege; but they are so dispersed that it is difficult to see the novel as a coherent aesthetic whole, and to that extent the above criticism of Malcolm Bradbury is correct.

A Handful of Dust was published in 1934. The novel seems upto a point quite unexciting, for it deals with real life: "It is a social novel about adultery, treachery, betrayal, tragic and sordid desolation."[182] Characters seem to lack motive and awareness. The central theme is the destruction of a simple, dull and honest lover by his wife – a cad without heart or affections. The social scene is one of dreary squalor and unkindness.

The sparkle of *Vile Bodies* "is replaced by a neat, crisp, jabling bitterness and the tragedy of meaningless silly lust."[183] Grim events follow one another; wit is not lacking, but it has become furious and much mature. The novel is thought as a serious one because it sets out to explore a contemporary mood of breakdown and futility in terms of collapsing relationship of Tony and Brenda Last. The novel offers an account of trivialised and insubstantial relationships; yet both qualities belong as much to the technique of the novel as to its content. In this respect, the novel has more in common with *The Waste Land*. There is a sense in which the novel exploits the fact that it deals `objectively' vacuous relationships and responses to explain away its own superficiality of treatment. We are asked to believe that Brenda Last is in love with John Beaver. The novel hinges on a deep emotional crisis – the sudden death of the Last's son, John Andrew – yet it takes refuge in the upper-class convention of concealed emotion to ratify its own evident incapacity to handle genuine feeling. The tragedy of the death has to be left implied, reflected in objective consequences such as Brenda's desertion of Tony. We are meant to sense, throughout the event, a sort of significant emotional blankness. At the point of explicit feeling, Waugh withdraws quickly to the style of the early satires.

John Andrew's sudden death has some plot relevance also, in that it helped in the final sundering of the relations between Brenda and Tony. Yet the incident seems too dramatic for its functional role within the narrative. Its literal and metaphorical meanings seem curiously disjunctive. The last section of the book, however, gives the tragedy a new and wholly original baroque twist; the dull and ill-used hero, born to be betrayed, is left the victim of a fate contrived with devilish ingenuity, and will pass the rest of his life a slave, reading Dickens a loud to his master in an Amazonian jungle. It is no doubt a brilliant terrifying *tour-de-force*. Later the author wrote an alternative ending, of a more ordinary cynical type. It is more probable and less remarkable; it has closer coherence with the rest of the book.

Thus Waugh shows in this novel that within a situation where people act ruthlessly and selfishly, tragedy, as it were, may be distributed over their lives, though each may be incapable of feeling its intensity. John is the most sensitive and live person among these rather dead people. When Brenda, first hears of his death, involuntarily she exclaims, "Thank God", and one feels that it is this attitude of her which killed him. Waugh's powerful imagination invents situations poetically and this is true of the ending of this novel. As a satirist he caricatures, but he never distorts the fact and, therefore, he never loses, the sympathy of his audience.

Scoop (1938) is journalistic in its spirit. The novel is mainly a jigging of episodes in John Courtney Boot's life that seeks its fulfilment and perfection in a literary career. Boot's entanglement with Katchen and Julia, is very funny and ridiculous. In this novel as elsewhere Waugh as a narrator is usually neutral, concealing his attitude behind a front of impersonal reporting. Sometimes, however, he is more open, and the result is interesting:

"Various courageous Europeans, in the seventies of the last century, came to Ishmaelia, or near it, furnished with suitable equipment of cuckoo, phonographs, opera hats, draft treaties and flags of the nations which they had been obliged to leave. They came as missionaries, ambassadors, tradesmen, prospectors, natural scientists. None returned.

They were eaten, everyone of them; ... and in the nineties humane counsels prevailed. The European powers independently decided that they did not want that profitless price of territory; ... accordingly, by general consent, it was ruled off the maps and its immunity guaranteed."[184] This caricature of the benefits of civilization typifies the spirit of much of *Scoop*. Lady Metroland, Lord Copper, Mr. Salter, Lady Cockpurse, Mrs. Algernon Stich, Sir Jocelyn – all represent the folies and foibles of the upper middle class Britons. The novelist's acute observation makes the landscape a rich tapestry which redeems the novel from banality. At intervals, we also notice emotionalism brimming over the theme.

Thus the novel is carefully composed, but lacks the earlier sparkle. In spite of a fine and delicate vein of comedy there is a sobriety, almost a solemnity of mood. The style is quiet and full. The novel stands on the border between fantasy and actuality.

Through these peculiar novels, we recognise Evelyn Waugh as a novelist of the disillusioned twenties, in that he shares the prevailing obsession of the decade with barbarism and vitalism as the alternative to rational civilization; it is an essential part of his comic thrust and subject matter. "He is throughout his work, a devastating explorer and recorder of the frontiers of civilisation and barbarism, of the places that generate disintegration and the people who live by it; his great heroes and heroines from Margot Metroland to Basil Seal and Trimmer, are people of change and high points of comic invention."[185] Waugh's world is contingent and arbitrary yet cogent. His position as a narrator strikingly well 'concealed, cool, hard and detached.' Like other writers who began in the twenties – Evelyn Waugh too is obsessed with the world of an irrevocable modernity, a world of psychological stress, dissolving relationships, new life-styles, novel technologies and environments. We find unity and diversity in these novels of Waugh because they are all concerned with the same situation: "The contrast between an England still creaming of its past greatness, whose memory is evoked by country houses and the country side, and an England of the twenties and early thirties in which people lived their lives as though they were part of another, and absurd dream. Beyond these two dreams of the old England and the Bright young things, there is the awakening of the will into a nightmare reality beyond which there lies yet another dream of the renewed greatness of England."[186] Thus Evelyn Waugh in the thirties emerged as a great comic genius. He saw a great dearth of comic writers in this decade and mentioned in the preface to *Vile Bodies*:

> "There were not many Comic writers at that time and I filled the gap."[187] Indeed his comedy is `the voice appropriate to a world without any notable salvation to offer, and many indeed have its own salvations – so Paul Pennyfeather, in *Decline and Fall* is protected by a comic good fortune that takes away his identity but allows him survival."[188]

ANTHONY POWELL

Powell, "one of the most important living English novelists',[189] differed from the writers of his generation like Auden, Orwell and Isherwood, by keeping pace with the liberals. He wrote in the manner of Evelyn Waugh. He declared: "But you cannot write about something that is not, so to speak, in you already .... If you are straining too hard, you cannot write. I used to play a game as a child in which you jumped little horses along a ribbon in a race. If you jerked the ribbon, the horses fell down. If you did not jerk it hard somebody else won ... you got to give out just the right amount."[190] The interview reveals how Powell was careful in the construction of his novels. We mark in Powell's novels that they engagingly look at surfaces, at the same time suggesting that it is by means enough. The surface is continually disturbed to show much more. On their quiet way they direct us towards a good, practical unextreme general philosophy of life. They give us the sense of life through character, caricature, fine humour and invention and a largely humane point of view.[191] We notice further a fine blending of naturalism, fantasy, comedy, farce and occasional tragedy in a single volume. Powell employed, "an elaborate linguistic craft to fix and indentify the uniqueness of every individual experience[192] and this gave authenticity and plausibility to his novels. Powell believed in history, but in his early works, he permitted his historical vision to be occluded. Powell introduced history by various means – first person recall, time-skids and allusions, and patient delineations of background. In this way Powell shows that his structural powers are enormous.

Bernard Bergonzi has said recently that, "Because of his lack of mythic or obsessive preoccupations Powell's fiction is less clearly patterned or structured than Waugh's."[193] The feel for myth and the talent for merging it with historic realism and moral insight is not strong in Powell. Powell's real mark of achievement as a young writer, was his, "astonishing maturity of approach both to the problems of love and sex which preoccupy most young novelists, and to the feminine protagonists who exemplify such problems....''[194] One feels, then, a plea throughout Powell's books for the natural warmth and vitality of life to be allowed their expression. It is this belief which gives the platform on which Powell's humour, elegance and disclosures rest, and which provides the books with the solid ground to support their charm.

Anthony Powell was born in 1905, the son of a regular army officer. He was educated at Eton and Oxford, and now lives in Somerset. After Oxford he worked for Duckworth, the publishers, who brought out his first four novels. He gave up publishing to become a film script writer for a short time, and from 1925 to 1958 was the literary editor of Punch. At present he reviews regularly for the *Daily Telegraph*. During the war he served in the British army and became a Major. He is a D.Litt. of the University of Sussex (1971), was married in 1936, and has two sons.

Afternoon Men (1931) is first novel of Anthony Powell. The title comes from Burton's *The Anatomy of Melancholy*: "They are a Company of giddy-heads, afternoon men.''[195] The novel shows a group of mainly young people between the wars at a fairly common level just above the middle-class London society. Although we do see and hear something of their work, the book is mainly concerned with their social and sexual lives. The novel is asking: what place genuine feelings can have in the empty world under examination, and regrettably there is no answer. William Atwater, the hero of the novel, reveals the sombre truth. Although he is not at all striking in appearance – a weedy-looking man with straw coloured hair and rather long legs....''[196] he gets involved with a number of women. Of these, Susan Nunnery, a beauty, affects him most. She is very much a part of the rootless and wilfully superficial life. Atwater and Susan came together briefly, and almost at once she begins to move away. From the start we know she is inconstant apparently she has just given up living with a man called Gilbert.

Eventually, she and Atwater go out to dinner together, but the restaurant is crowded. Others join them from time to time, talking banalities, that prevent any real intimacy, although Atwater does attempt to woo Susan during the dinner. It is one of the funniest scenes in the novel. What Powell wants to say in this scene is what he tells us throughout the novel: "The relentless trivia of social life may kill any deeper relationship, probably before it starts.''[197] Susan continues to drift from him. She is an empty creature incapable of feeling. She intends to run from seriousness such as Atwater wants to run from superficiality.

Finally Susan leaves London for America with Verelest, a Jew, apparently of independent means. Deserted and dismal Atwater is seen at the end about to take up where chapter one began – preparing for another party. His search for something deeper has failed and, we gather, will go on failing. Atwater's love with another woman, Lola, is also a failure. Here, the sex is flat, meaningless and absurd. Atwater's affair with Lola ends untouched by feeling. Atwater has also a fleeting, though consummated, affair with Harriet Twinning, the mistress of his artist friend Raymond Pringle. Farce or heavy irony predominates. They make love in a wood, having just watched unwittingly what the reader takes to be Pringle's suicide. Again there are the deadening, impersonal and mechanical preliminaries.

Harriet says:

'This is silly'.
'Not at all'.
'Wait a moment'.
'That's better'.[198]

At once Atwater is disappointed, 'Curse you for giggling', he tells her. The lives of other characters are also sexually empty. In fact Powell is concerned not only with the sexual emptiness, but also with the dire frailty of social assumption after the First World War. It is very nearly true to say that no settled sexual relationship is shown anywhere in the novel. Barrow, the painter debates amusingly about which of the several girls he should marry, never citing love as a factor. There are characters who are, or have been married, but their spouses are missing. Susan lives with her father, and we meet no Mrs. Nunnery. There is only one permanent relationship, and that is between Mr. and Mrs. Chalk. But they are of different class from the chief characters.

The dialogue in this novel is almost always laconic and, by intent, generally trite and laborious. Through it Powell conveys much of his amused criticism of this aimless society. Lola explains to Atwater how she spilled her drink over Pringle:

'Is your husband angry?'
'Yes'.
'I was looking for my bag'.
'Were you?'
'It was suddenly knocked out of my hand
all over him.'[199]

On many other occasions throughout the book Powell's object is to hold back the narrative, stretch the emptiness, often by repetition:

> 'What would you like to eat?'
> 'Anything'.
> 'Anything?'
> 'Oh, yes, anything'.[200]

These sluggish formula conversations excellently catch the pattern of such lives.

Sometimes Powell uses monosyllabic, repetitious conversation to convey for more than what is actually said, a skill crucial in realistic fiction. Susan telephones to say she is not coming to meet Atwater:

> 'So sorry, I shall n't be able to see you to
> night I'm in the country.'
> 'I see.'
> 'I cannot get away.'
> 'Cannot you?'
> 'You don't mind, do you?'
> 'Yes'.
> She laughed.
> 'No, you don't really'.
> 'Allright, I don't.'[201]

Thus *Afternoon-Men* is a store of remarkable qualities despite some signs of immaturity. Characterisation is not highly developed; but Atwater and Susan have their intricacies of personality, and even the comic figures like Pringle and Fatheringham are liable to individuality and dignity. James Tucker remarks, "... the novel is very funny, combining understated wit, farce and what might be called comedy of mannerisms."[202]

Powell's second novel, *Venusberg* (1932) like the previous one, also moves in something of an ironic and deflationary circle. It is almost funny, but the flavour has become more subtle, and the novel's world is wider. In a superficial sense the book may be seen as a love story. Lushington, the hero, loves Lucy. But Lucy loves Lushington's friend, Da Costa who does not love her. Lushington's pain is further sharpened when he goes as a foreign correspondent to a Baltic city where Da Costa is a diplomat, and is thus constantly reminded of his failure with Lucy. On the boat Lushington starts an affair with Ortcud Marvin, and this continues when they arrive at their destination. Ortrud's husband, a professor of psychology, comes to suspect that she is unfaithful to him and asks for a talk with Lushington on the subject. Lushington is afraid of being exposed, but it turns out that Da Costa is the suspect. Prof. Marvin believes that Ortrud actively dislikes Lushington, regarding him as a rival of Da Costa for her affection. After a ball, Da Costa and Ortrud share a cab to go home, but on the way they are shot dead by assassins aiming at the local police chief. Da Costa is thus removed, and we are to infer that Professor Marvin will assume that, since the two were together, his suspicions were correct. Lushington returns to Britain, and takes over Lucy who also believes that there was an affair between Da Costa and Ortrud. Lushington's involvement with Ortrud remains secret.

Thus, the novel seems to say that life may at any time become violently disjointed, and that those who come out on top may find that the way they do so is not the way they intended; that the result is less spectacularly desirable than they had hoped. Here, we do find some touches of fatalism, even of cynicism.

Some of the characters have also been affected adversely by the Russian Revolution: Count Scherhatcheff, for instance, talks of the last luxuries once enjoyed by his family. We are among wrecks of a massive social collapse. One of the results of this is that "Much of the irony and humour came from contrasting the chaos of reality with the fixed protocol and arrogance of those who believe themselves still socially eminent."[203]

Count Bobel illustrates Powell's technique. Above all Michael Bobel is a magnificently comic creation. Of much disputed Russian lineage he now operates as a commercial traveller, selling face-cream. He is present at the killings, and is actually arrested as a suspect. It turns out that he was drunk and waving a cardboard pistol given by a night club. It is Bobel who speaks what may be the novel's anarchic theme: "In Russia we have an expression – nitchevo ... It means nothing or, more freely, what does it matter? ... I tell you (Lushington) this because I think this is a moment when such a philosophy of life might be of value to you."[204] Pope, another wonderfully comic figure, seems to stand for some elements of British social stability among the emigres and conspirators. His very job suggests hierarchy. As an aside, almost, during Bobel's last appearance in the book, he mentions that Flosshilde is pregnant by him. Love seems here savage and irresponsible, feelings almost absent, and in any case, not likely to find a response. Lushington like Atwater is looking for a real emotional experience, and we approve and sympathise with him.

This novel provides a remarkable advance in Powell's creation of people. Even caricatures like Pope and Bobel have some stature, and poignancy. Other minor figures like Wallermar and Scherbatcheff are given convincing depth in fairly brief and very assuming treatments. It is in Ortrud, though, that we find sexuality, arrogance, coquethishness, vulnerability and a touch of dorm – all combined marvellously, creating a credible, beguiling and complex woman.

The following passage describing Scherbatcheffs illustrates a notable feature of Powell's early style: "Now that his eyes have become accustomed to the half-light Lushington saw that a youngman was lying at full length on the ground immediately under the window and in front of the man with the shaved head. This young man was writing in an exercise book by the light thrown by the oil-stove. He was writing lethargically with a stampy pencil. The girl at the piano still played her finger exercises ..."[205] The style is rigorously simple, sometimes to the point of flatness. The prose is controlled, a sensitive instrument capable of holding tragedy and farce in a single grip.

From A View To a Death (1933) is another social comedy of Powell. The novel deals with the country-house society. The early sections are more like clever, sharp, witty sketches than the organised stages of a novel. The central figures are poorly sketched, but they have their own power and dynamism. They possess ironic minds. The absurdities of those they describe are taken by the reader not as impartial observations, not the whole story, but only as aspects of some one which amuse and fascinate the speakers.

In this work we find the style less mannered than the first two, a more straightforward instrument for telling a story. It is, "brisk, occasionally witty, still offhand and antidramatic."[206]

Lastly *From A View To a Death* does reveal some of the accomplishments of Powell, but lacks the charm and carefully maintained single flavour of *Afternoon Men* and *Venusberg*. "The qualities which Powell prizes – tolerance, humanity, decency – have gone on leave for this novel, and he is showing us the dispiriting result."[207]

Powell's next two novels, *Agents and Patients* (1936) and *What's Becoming of Warning* (1939), deal with segments of English upper-middle-class and middle-class life in a very witty and precise manner. *Agents and Patients* is quite funny; but *What's Becoming of Warning* has for at least three quarters of the book a suspenseful and intricately shaped plot, something very unique in Powell's novels. Maltravers and Chipchase in this book recall Bobal. They are occupied with the problem of not only surviving in a rough and anarchic society, but also like Zonch, reaching rather a higher level. They already have style if not status. Cash is the problem. Their method is to involve a rich innocent in the mysteries of professions (psychiatry and film making) somewhat in the manner of Jonson's predatory alchemists. Although lacking in character development, Zonch, Maltravers and Chipchase are interesting outlines of recognisable types. They have pretensions and elan but not much else; men with professional ambitions but rather no liking for hard graft.

Money and need for they press more in *Agents and Patients* than in any of Powell's previous books as the title of novel suggests, it is concerned with humour, extravagance and freedom. Blore Smith has a private income, but feels incapable of realising his ambition. During an early sequence he matches a street display in which a man tries to escape from fetters, and sees this as a symbol of his own life. 'He that is not free is not an Agent, but a Patient'; says the Wesley Sermon. He tries to step out of the bonds of ignorance and inexperience and does shed his innocence at a French brothel. Later he is more or less abducted by a malapert woman though she eventually leaves him. Blore Smith at the end neither learns style, nor acquires confidence, but only becomes cagy. He has been systematically fleeced. He has not greatly liked his sexual awakening either. At any rate, Blore Smith's stature has not dramatically changed.

In these novels of the thirties, Powell planned to express in contemporary terms his feelings about life and love. "These terms, as first conceived, were to have a background of dances and country houses, as well as the parties, night-clubs, pubs, which with a modicum of office-life, eventually provided most of the scenario."[208] Powell worked under the influence of Balzac who opined that a novelist can use anything for material, say anything in his own way. He could adopt the naturalistic method of Balzac but possibly he could not recognise Balzac's grasp of human motive, sense of conflict and knowledge of life. The study of these novels shows that Powell was also influenced by Dostoevski. In his own words, "Dostoevski's characters and situations have one of the qualities I prize highest in a novelist, the ability to be at once grotesque yet classical, funny and at the same time terrifying. It seems incredible, having once discovered the Russians, that I should take so long to appreciate Dostoevski.''[209] Powell seems to have been most interested in capturing the almost unrecordable deed spots in life. In the early novels (discussed here) he does it through ''an unweighted, unpunctuated prose'', but in the later ones the style becomes radically different. However, ''In the last resort, his true originality as a stylist depends on realism, not exaggeration.''[210]

Thus, like his other contemporaries, Powell did his best to record faithfully the depression and decadence of the middle class people in the thirties in the fashion of a realistic novelist. His concentration on abstract emotions seem to develop out of ''a totally different realm of experience (from the visual) – the realm in which the mind dramatises, at a given moment, its feelings towards a whole aspect of life.''[211] In fact Powell's fidelity to life and art gives a plausible reading to his novels which do not hinge on parables which are much in common with the symbolic novels of George Orwell.

A short survey of the other novelists of this decade

George Orwell (1903-1950) like other writers of his time expressed the shabby England of depression, war and austerity; the social and political issues of his time formed the themes of his writings. His novels during the thirties were *Burmese Days* (1934), *The Road to Wigen Pier* (1937) and *Inside The Whale* (1940). The social and political themes of his time formed the themes of his writings.

Some critics have adversely remarked about *Orwell*. According to Keith Alldritt, ''... except *Ninteen Eighty-Four* (1949) Orwell created no valuable work of literary art, rather his contribution was to literary culture.''[212] O.D. Leavis has also remarked : ''Mr. Orwell must have wasted a lot of energy trying to be a novelist .... I think I must have read three or four novels by him and the only impression those dreary books left on me was that nature didn't intend him to be a novelist.''[213]

Orwell's novels, however, do have literary value. In spite of their vague symbolism, these enormous naturalistic novels with unhappy endings full of detailed descriptions and arresting similes show considerable forte in characterisation. These characters are not just 'derived formulas'.[214] They are life-like and convincing, although, as has been said by Harry Levin, Orwell ''is interested more in characteristics than in characters, less in temperament than in milieu."[215] To quote George Wickes, "... what makes Orwell so convincing in his sense, ordinary common sense, matter-of-fact, tone of voice. He has a remarkable gift for making revelation soul like common place. There is no nonsense about him, nothing pretentious; ... everything he says rings true."[216]

In the thirties when almost all the intelligentia of England was engaged in liberal politics, Orwell was typical rather than unique. What distinguished him from all his contemporaries was his extraordinary 'candour, integrity, and staying power'.[217] To his dying day he thought of everything, especially literature and language, in political and social terms. His purpose was – "to make political writing into an art."[218] Orwell was born into England's most uncomfortable social stratum, the poor but genteel, "lower-upper-middle-class".[219] He was however not a Communist, as is evident from his *Animal Farm* (1945), in which both the capitalists and communists have been satirised equally strongly.

Orwell's novels aim to achieve a frank, detailed and faithful exposure of social experience. He followed Zola, and there are clear signs of the influence of Zola's in the construction of his novels. Everything he deserves, "is grotesque and disgusting, the filth, the stench, the loathsome food, the black-bettles, and worst of all, the sickly, ageing, subhuman people who endure such an existence."[220] The following passage, taken at random, provides a good example of what Orwell observed, and what was his reaction:

"On the day when there was a full champer-pot under the breakfast table I decided to leave. The place was beginning to depress me. It was not only the dirt, the smells and the vile food, but the feeling of stagnant meaningless decay, of having got down into some subterranean place where people go creeping round and round, just like black-bettles, in an endless muddle of slovened jobs and mean grievances."[221]

Here, "The primary subject is Orwell himself, as a representative of his own middle-class generation – repelled by poverty and sentimentally impressed by the workers, ..."[222]

Thus Orwell's novels reflect, "a decade a riot of appalling folly that suddenly becomes a nightmare, a scenic railway ending in a torture chamber."[223] We remember Orwell for his originality and preconceived design. As E.M. Forster comments, "George Orwell's originality has been recognised in this country; his peculiar blend of gaiety and grimness has been appreciated..."[224]

Orwell's novels are documentary for they record recent events with more intimacy and freedom than journalism, but they don't fail as works of art. As a documentary writer, "....his job is not to tell us what he felt, but to be coldly and industriously presenting, arranging, selecting, discarding from the mass of his material to get the significant detail which leaves no more to be said, and implies everything."[225]

The style is flat and descriptive, but it is also an arresting one. He is the 'archetype of romanciers par-necessite'. Cazamian has remarked rightly, "George Orwell's work as a whole is the citizen's manifesto against the powers that be, a sort of despairing cry from the individual crushed by an organizing and technocratic age, the voice in the desert of an outsider who believes in human nature but expects little from men."[226] His blunt, suspicious, no nonsense, anti-romantic attitude, his resolute and ruthless honesty towards himself and the world about him chiefly made him distinguished from other novelists of his time.

ELIZABETH BOWEN

Miss Elizabeth Bowen (1899) is acknowledged as 'one of the most talented of the novelists working in the tradition of sensibility'. She is well known for her gift for rendering states of mind with, quiet precision. The local atmosphere, place, and weather are graphically described in her novels in which mood, region and climate interpenetrate each other. In feelings and techniques she differs completely from her contemporaries. She does not allow 'evil to intrude on her world. It is not the evil, but the experience of others that corrodes the innocent people....'[227] And it is the subject matter of her largest novel, *The Death of The Heart* (1938). One may discern the same thing also in the novel which preceded it, *The House In Paris* (1935). "Her talent for social comedy, her eye for the socially absurd, recall .... Jane Austen. She shares Hardy's love of atmoshphere and design. How soundly, for all their delicacy, her novels are constructed : And what Hardy will make of a woodland, a heath ... she will make of a house or a summer night."[228] Though she is a highly conscious artist yet she condemns 'pre-assumptions'. She says flatly that "Pre-asumptions are bad, because they cause the novel to act immorally on the reader. As the most clearcut example of the pre-assumption at work she cites the detective novel, which works on the single and unchallenged notion that an act of violence is anti-social and that the doer must be traced."[229] But Miss Bowen's reaction against 'pre-assumptions' is a half truth. 'It is pointless to reject a faculty that is common to the whole human race.'[230]

Elizabeth Bowen stands out as a novelist of exceptional individuality among the novelists of the thirties. She had little in common with Graham Greene although both showed their interest in human heart, and both felt the pressure of times upon human character. Like Graham Greene she had also an artistic detachment. Whereas Greene was close to Ernest Hemingway, Elizabeth Bowen was close to Virgina Woolf, "... She does similarly take us into the minds and feelings of her people and thus we again realise that there is no simple black and white about life, but the texture is complex, the constituents everlastingly shifting : There is a continuous ebb and flow, the inrush of the past, the pressure of the "unapprehendable inner wills of the dead', the different influences of a present environment at the mercy of chance."[231] She shows her best skills in developing character and the story by dialogue:

> "While her people talk, they talk on life, they change, and the mechanics of the story move... where Virginia Woolf found it necessary to revolutionise the writing of the novel, Elizabeth Bowen showed how it was possible to employ similar talents in the revivifying of a traditional novel."[232]

Elizabeth Bowen had an active writing life of half a century. Her best known and most widely read novels are *The Death of Heart* (1938) and *The Heat of the Day* (1949); these for different reasons have universal appeal. Her first three novels : *The Hotel* (1927); *The Last September* (1929); and *Friends and Relations* (1931) are small in comparison to their three successors : *To the North* (1932); *The House In Paris* (1935); and *The Death of Heart* (1938). These latter three form the most satisfactorily achieved part of her work. Their themes are related without being repetitive and, in *The Death of the Heart* at least, the theme is handled with great confidence. "They (the themes) are commonly and correctly said to present the confrontation between innocence and experience, but any suggestion of an arid allegorical encounter would be insensitive to the sensuous and intuitive nature of their characters' experience."[233]

Bowen competes with Rosamond Lehmann, her contemporary for first place among the women novelists. Since she has so much of the lyrical poet in her, it is not surprising that she is at her best in short stories. Her fictional writings during the war have been confined mainly to short stories, of which she has published two impressive collections: *Look At All Those Roses* (1941); and *The Demon Lover* (1945). In her novels Bowen is excellent in portraying young, or recently young women of excessive sensibility suffering under the impact of passion. By her skill in describing a scene she can add atmoshphere to the mood of the persons whose behaviour she shows. "She has no lack of humour, and with it she deftly relieves the tension when it might have become oppressive."[234] Her characters work under the social impact because of their sense and sensibility, and their emotional links wih their surroundings. Like many of her contemporaries Bowen is concerned with the middle class, respectable Irish society, or the upper classes in Southern England, whose most glaring defect is 'barrenness of heart'. "The world she creates is our world, solid, real, and undeniable, even though the acuteness of her exploration and the dancing glimmer of her art give it an unusual look. At once clear-cut and many-hued ... but in no way it falsifies the truth of colours."[235]

In summing up Elizabeth Bowen : a self detached artist came into prominence in the early thirties by writing novels which excelled in their craftmanship and vitality. Her poetic gift, sensibility and fine penetrating game made her novels epical in their taste and texture.

C.P. SNOW

C.P. Snow, an eminent physicist both by training and profession, gave up the established career of a scientist in favour of that of a novelist.[236] He himself has remarked, "I knew my own ultimate vocation from the time I was about eighteen," but "I made my way in the most practicable career open to me, as a professional scientist."[237] With fame he has not become a "personality" but something like an institution, a pantocratic sage."[238]

Snow was born in 1905 – that is, within the same ten-year span as Hemingway, Faulkner, Waugh, Graham Greene and Auden, but in terms of literary reputation he belongs to the post-Second World War era. "Although Snow started writing as early as 1932 and published *The Search* in 1934, he seems to us to belong not with Lawrence, Kafka, Steinbeck, but with Bellow, Golding, Styren Amis ... the matters and attitudes which he has been writing for about thirty years have in the nineteen fifties and sixties become central in our thinking..."[239] In 1932 he published a detective story, *Death Under Sail* which was fairly well received. His next venture *New Lives For Old* (1933), was less happy, a work in the Wells' tradition of science fiction about a society that had developed a process of rejuvenation. Though chronologically second, it is, in its lack of sureness, rather more like a first attempt at novel writing.

It is neither autobiographical nor a straight realistic novel. There is none of the fantasy or allegory or concern with technology that is usual in science fiction. Snow is interested in age and youth, in comfortable and discontended temperament, and in the characters second chance of fulfilment. What he has to say about these subjects is said largely within a realistic framework. However, the writer himself was conscious of its many defects, and has condemned it as a "very bad work." *The Search* (1934) is much better written than the previous two, and suggests a number of Snow's later concerns and key ideas. It also gives a good many hints of Snow's further development and the nature of his later achievement. It is a conventional realistic novel, but is not free from certain limitations. Its theme is not clearly defined, and there is total dearth of dramatic actions. Its chief merit lies in the fact that it gives us the fullest and most significant account of the contemporary world. Snow follows the English realistic tradition of Jane Austen, George Eliot and Trollope, and not that of his immediate predecessors like Lawrence, James Joyce and Virgina Woolf. He has emphatically said that the kind of fiction that was called `modern' in his time and more or less ceased,[240] and he sees himself as a spokesman for, "a new tide of realistic and humanistic writing."[241] One of the characteristics of these `modern' novels has been to use D.H. Lawrence's phrase, `putting all the action inside'. The English novel lacks, Snow says, "... not the insight which tells us what it is like to be in certain mood (at which the Americans and English have been pretty good), but the insight which probes beneath the continuum of feeling" and asks, "why should I, of all people, have this mood at all? be driven by these motives? be capable of this action, in both Tolstoy and Dostoevsky, though in different fashions, makes for a complex and enriching interaction between their individual personages and their immense social range. It is probable, I think, that such an insight is inextricably linked with an active insight into society."[242]

Snow reveals character by relating it directly to the plot, by making use of a reflective narrator, by dealing with the psyche as it manifests itself in external action, by relating it public concerns; in short by a more social, objective, and public approach to the character. And in doing this he has bound the public and the private, social fact and character together. He, however, has also his limitations as evidenced by the following extract:

"There was a chance, how good I could not guess, that the

> (atomic) pile would still work quickly; it meant giving Luke even more money, even more men. 'If you are not prepared for that' I said, hearing my voice sound remote, 'I should be against any compromise. You've either got to show some faith now – or give the whole thing up in this country.' 'Double or quits', said Rose, 'if I have n't misunderstood you, my deer chap?'
>
> 'I nodded my head.'

'And again, if I have n't misunderstood you, you'd have a shade of preference, but not a very decided shade, for doubling?'

'I nodded my head once more.'

Rose considered, assembling the threads of the problem, the scientific forecasts, the struggle on his committees, the 'ministerial views'.

'This is rather an awkward one', he said. He stood up and gave his polite youthful bow. "Well", he said, 'I'm most indebted to you and I am sorry to have taken so much of your valuable time. I must think this out, but I'm extremely grateful for your suggestions'."[243]

This example shows "Snow's powers of characterisation, limited chiefly to speech – style, and very often amounting to little more than a few typical phrases per character, are scarcely adequate to the demands of his scheme."[244]

It also shows the convincing nature and accuracy of his observation. The glaring fact remains that C.P. Snow is regarded by many Britons as one of the most important novelists of to-day. Edmund Fuller rightly remarks, "In a period when the senses dominate fiction, when many writers deliberately abdicate reason, he is prominent among the select group who are artists with their minds – not just with their emotions, muscles, or glands. At a time when breakdown, despair, and sickness are pervasive themes, he shows us a large, varied, effectively functioning world peopled by all sorts and conditions of men who are effected by the chaotic elements in their time, but need not inevitably be engulfed by them.[245] In this way C.P. Snow in the thirties interpreted the purpose of the novel in his own way and gave it a new direction as was done by Flaubert and Henry James earlier.

PATRICK HAMILTON

As with the most writers of the thirties, "Patrick Hamilton's work begins to appear in the twenties and continue into the forties and fifties. Nevertheless, the timber of his writing is indelibly of the inter-war years, and his best works are certainly those of the late thirties.'[246] Hamilton, like so many others of his generation, registers in the private, personal crises of individual and small groups, the inner stagnation and decay of his own class in the twentieth century. "Such a metaphorical correlation informs the early poems of Auden, the seedy world of Graham Greene's novels, the observed tone of Orwell's *Coming Up For Air* and *Keep The Aspidistra Flying*, and Christopher Isherwood's early novels of a private hell. And Patrick Hamilton, almost totally disregarded now, also offers ingress to the physical and mental landscape of that ugly and neurotic world."[247]

Hamilton was both a novelist and a playwright. His novels chiefly did for pre-war England what Isherwood's Berlin novels did for Germany. "The world of Hamilton's books is endorsed within a radius of roughly fifty miles of London. It is composed mainly of interiors: of guest houses, boarding-houses, Lyons Cafes, cheap hotel rooms, and ... pubs."[248] The atmoshphere is too much drink laden. The bottle is on the mantle-piece, the bottle in the suitcase, the bottle in the wardrobe. Alcohol is the main motif of Hamilton's novel. It is the chief factor leading to personal crisis, irresponsibility, failure, fear and break down, an inability to face the world, and decline, and inadequacy. Sometimes it also becomes a metaphor for some wide-ranging social malaise. This drunken world is peopled by a homogeneous set of characters. They are frail youngmen of good family, who have a small legacy or an indulgent mother, and viciously attractive and a moral women. It is a shabby, depressed world, often depicted in raw, wet weather. Nothing significant happens here. People do their jobs if they have any and return to black rooms and uncomfortable meals in their boarding houses. They wait at cold city corners for people who usually fail to turn up.

Hamilton's method of presenting the world of his fictions contain strong elements of caricature. This is clearly evident in his successive novels : *Craven House* (1926); *Impromptu In Moribundia* (1939); and *The Slaves of Solitude* (1947). We mark in these novels that the scenes and characters have solid and credible existence, and are not merely hackneyed-type images. 'Indeed, at its best, the depressed world of Hamilton's books bears down on one with a force and actuality that is hard to evade.'[249]

As a literary artist, Hamilton proves himself to be a writer of his time. Like the other young novelists of the thirties, he also evinces a lack of resolution about form, he oscillates between the realistic depiction of the palpable world and the fabulation of contrived worlds; like them he uses fables, allegories and satires. The pressure to expand the novel form seems to represent an attempt, to penetrate and express the shifting inner realms of individual consciousness as a way of comprehending the external world. Most of the English fictions of the thirties offer no positive vision for the future and its chief merit lies in the exposition of the sickness of the world here. There is an interesting passage in Hamilton's *Impromptu In Moribundia*, where the novelist attacks the 'modernistic' literature of Moribundia:

"They are for the most part hopelessly and morbidly turned in upon themselves, and sterile in consequence. But where else are they to turn save upon themselves? In a world which is unchangeable and inexpandable, where is there to gaze save inwards.... For these reasons art, literature, and poetry in Moribundia take on a more and more painfully subjective aspect, more and more the character of meaningless masturbation, there being no future which they can fertilize."[250]

This is interesting if only because it indicates the slant of Hamilton's thinking about literature in the late thirties. One might argue, of course, that the obsession with drink and the depressed mentality of most of his characters is only one more example of much futile introspection.

Craven House (1926) is a very remarkable novel. Like Isherwood's *The Memorial*, it spans the First World war, beginning in the mellow years of Edwardian security and ending in the middle of the twenties; and it too places the responsibility for the war and the post-war society with the middle classes. Although the sense of the parents' liability for the crippled lives of the younger generation is less bitter than in *The Memorial*, the heroine, Elsie is only just rescued from the ferocious cleanliness of her mother's moral piety, and by the end, *Craven House* has been revealed as the hollow sham it is. The house, which takes paying-guests of the decayed genteel variety, is a microcosm of middle class England – a sort of symbolic reverse. One may read the whole in such allegoric terms as : "The movement from Edwardian security to post-war break up ; the house passive, unchanging, apparently secure until the final smash; the various characters acting out aspects of the middle-class way of life-snobbery, insensibility, prudery, hidden sexuality, cowardice, moral flaccidity, prejudice, complacence, under the skin of genteel correctitude ; ... It is a deeply schematic book, and the Dickensian manner of the narration reinforce this."[251]

Hamilton draws his characters with a heavy line and a clear indispensible irony: "Mr. Spicer returned to domesticity with a quantity of little stories (touching or otherwise); a vivid and unutterable sense of the lurid bestiality of his short experience in France, but no sense whatever of it being in any way other than righteous, seemly eternal, and cumulatively expressive of the highest glories achieved by men."[252]

But Hamilton's intrusive manner is by no means ineffective. It is, in fact, the caricature at its best, where the features of the victim are extrapolated:

"Mr. Spicer soon began to peer to the extent of downright nosiness: That his peering was directed towards the numerous young ladies seated, cross legged, upon the chairs lining these avenues; that the difficulties arising from an attempt to combine (1) the intense function of peering sideways, with (2) the perfectly nonchalant function of strolling forward, reduced Mr. Spicer's stride to something uncommonly resembling the crab's."[253]

There are two points about *Craven House* which must be emphasised. Firstly that, Hamilton had already identified the Moribund middle-class world-view as his focus; and secondly that he was developing a particular manner for presenting it. *Craven House* is not a descriptive novel, and in the end it is not really concerned with the mores of the middle-class people in themselves. It is what they mean, rather than what they are, which interests him, and they are already perceived and treated as symptomatic, as metaphors of social dissolution.

The three novels of Hamilton – *The Midnight Bell* (1929); *The Siege of Pleasure* (1932); and *The Plains of Cement* (1934) formed a trilogy and were published in a single volume as *Twenty Thousand Streets Under the Sky* in 1935, with a Preface by J.B. Priestby. This is a large book which is clearly intended to establish a solid and extensive image of the loneliness at the centre of London in the post-war years. It is composed of the interwoven stories of three young people – Bob, the barman, Jenny the prostitute, and Ella the barmaid. The novels are marked by an unfocused realism and authorial commentary, "... Vivid dialogue and speech gestures, fine grotesquerie of characterisation .... and occasionally the suffocating decay of the household lingering on into the new world of the twenties...."[254] But the texture of these novels is weak. The stories seem inconsequential; and the author's voice, with little support from its own fictional world, merely remains one individual's voice, making observations and pointing up significances that cannot be verified. Perhaps because they are the victims of the society that the characters in these novels remain as instances rather than representatives. But there is also no doubt that Hamilton's reliance on reportage and commentary is more culpable for the inconsequentiality of these novels.

Impromptu In Moribundia, a fantasy was published in 1939. This is a significant novel for two reasons : first because it lays on table Hamilton's conviction that in the stagnancy and stupidity of the English middle-class way of life resides the sickness of the society; and second because it employs an uncompromisingly fabular mode to expose this sickness. Hamilton's brilliant strategy in this book is simply to make the people of his fictive Moribundia enact the stereotypes and myths of the English middle-class and lay bare their consciousness.[255]

His Moribundia is –

"The land in which the ideals and ideas of our world, the striving and subconscious wishes of our time, the fictions and figments of our imagination, are calm, cold actualities."[256] The inhabitants are often reified into the images of popular culture : people walk down the road with dripping taps in place of noses or, if suffering from indigestion, with little devils scrabbling round their waists poking them with forked instruments; husbands and wives out shopping become the amazonian viragoes and diminutive hen-pecked males of the comic picture-post card.[257]

Thus these novels of Patrick Hamilton are true to the time-spirit and marvellous in their pattern and execution. Undoubtedly they are journalistic and documentary in their manner and matter yet they are artistic. Their chief merit lies in the exposition of the decaying values of the middle class in the thirties of London.

Thus, the novelists of the nineteen-thirties, who like other literary figures of the decade specially those of new metaphysical poets, worked under the deep impression of social consciousness which coloured and conditioned much of their works. But unlike the poets of the nineteen-thirties (Auden, Spender, C. Day Lewis, MacNeice, etc.) they were not of course anything like school. As it is quite evident that novelists of the thirties discarding atavistic form gave a pragmatic tone and texture to the novels which differed from the novels of twenties which aimed at "recucillement", means recollections, regathering of all the threads of one's life, ignoring a great part of society. We can establish the fact that these careful novelists of the thirties presented in their novels their own method and technique in the devices of narration, in style, in arrangement, in some tricks of contrast and comparison, and all these things made them interesting in their studies.

NOTES AND REFERENCES

1. Widdowson, P.J.– The Saloon Bar Society -- *The 1930s* edited by John Lucas (p. 136), The Harvester Press Limited, 1978.
2. Leavis, O.D. -- *The Fiction And the Reading Public*, 1932, Chatto and Windus (pp. 49-50).
3. Hunter, Jim -- Graham Greene -- *The Modern Novel In English* (studies in extracts), Faber and Faber London, 1966 (p. 84).
4. Allen, Walter -- *Reading A Novel*, Phoenix House (1949), London (p. 19).
5. Maupassant, Guy de -- Le Roman, Introduction To Pierre et Jean, 1888.
6. Benett, Arnold -- Note Book Entry (15 Oct. 1896), *The Journals of Arnold Bennett* (1931).
7. Gillie, Christopher -- *Movements In English Literature* (1900-1940), Cambridge University Press, 1975 (p. 137).
8. Graham Greene In Retrospect -- *Times Literary Supplement* (1971), London University Press (1972) (p. 123).
9. Atkins, John -- *Graham Greene*, Calder & Boyars, 1970 (p. 18).
10. Lodge, David -- *The Novelist At the Crossroads*, Routledge & Kegan Paul (London), 1971 (p. 93).
11. Atkins, John -- *Graham Greene*, Calder & Boyars, 1970 (p. 18).
12. Lodge, David -- *The Novelist At the Crossroads*, Routledge & Kegan Paul (London), 1971 (p. 93).
13. Atkins, John -- *Graham Greene*, Calder & Boyars, 1970 (p. 21).
14. Greene, Graham -- *Stamboul Train* (1974), Heinemann (London), Introductory chapter (p. X).
15. Buchans The Power House -- quoted by David Lodge -- *The Novelist At the Crossroads*, Routledge & Kegan Paul (London), 1971 (p. 94).
16. Greene, Graham -- *Stamboul Train* (1974), Heinemann (London), p. 223.
17. *Ibid*., p. X, Introductory chapter.
18. Lodge, David -- *The Novelist At the Crossroads* (London), 1971 (p. 94).
19. Kingslake, A.W. -- *The Invasion of the Crimes*, 8 vols. (Edinburgh and London): Blackwood, 1863-87, Vol. 5 (pp. 476-7).
20. Hynes, Samuel -- *The Auden Generation*, The Bodley Head (London), 1976 (p. 137).
21. Greene Graham -- *Its A Battlefield*, London : Heinemann, 1934 (p. 174).
22. *Ibid*., p. 237.
23. Greene quotes the note in *A Sort of Life*, Bodby Head, 1971 (p. 210).
24. Greene Graham -- *Its A Battlefield*, quoted by John Atkins : Graham Greene, Calder & Boyars, 1970 (p. 39).

25. *Ibid.*, p. 39.
26. Atkins, John : *Graham Greene*, Calder & Boyars, 1970 (p. 43).
27. Greene, Graham -- *England Made Me* (Penguin Books), London 1964 (p. 207).
28. Hynes, Samuel -- *The Auden Generation*, The Bodley Head, 1976 (p. 230).
29. Greene, Graham -- *Journey Without Maps*, Heinemann, 1936 (p. 262).
30. Hunter, Guy -- The Waste Land in Liberia, *London Mercury*, 34, June, 1936 (p. 178).
31. Greene, Graham -- *Journey Without Maps*, Heinemann, 1936, p. 176.
32. Bergonzi, Bernard -- *Reading the Thirties*, (1971) ; The Macmillan Press Ltd. (London), p. 78.
33. Hynes, Samuel -- *The Auden Generation*, The Bodby Head, 1976 (p. 230).
34. Greene, Graham -- *Journey Without Maps*, Heinemann, 1936 (p. 107).
35. *Ibid.*, p. 107.
36. Greene, Graham -- *A Gun for Sale* (London), Heinemann, 1936 (p. 256-57).
37. Lehmann, Rosamund -- New Novels -- *New Statesman*, 12 (1 Aug. 1936), p. 164.
38. Greene, Graham -- *Brighton Rock*, Quoted by John Atkins : Graham Greene, Calder and Boyars, 1970 (p. 93).
39. *Ibid.*, p. 98.
40. Graham Greene in Retrospect -- *Times Literary Supplement*, London University Press (1972), p. 123.
41. Greene, Graham -- *The Lawless Roads*, authors note, William Heinemann Ltd. (London), 1955 (p. 1).
42. *Ibid.*, (p. 1).
43. *Ibid.*, (pp. 39-40).
44. *Ibid.*, p. 612.
45. *Ibid.*, p. 4.
46. *Ibid.*, p. 289.
47. Lodge, David -- *The Novelist At the Crossroads*, 1971, Routledge and Kegan Paul (London), 1971 (p. 97).
48. *Ibid.*, p. 289.
49. Graham Greene In Retrospect -- *Times Literary Supplement*, 1971, London University Press, 1972 (p. 124).
50. *Ibid.*, p. 124.
51. Bergonzi, Bernard -- *Reading The Thirties* (1971), The Macmillan Press Ltd., London (p. 122).
52. Lehmann, John -- *In My Own Time*, Boston : Little Brown and Company, 1969, p. 233.
53. Woolf, Virginia -- *A Writers Diary*, ed. Leonard Woolf, London : Hogarth Press, 1972, pp. 306-7.
54. Connolly, Cyrill -- Comment, *Horizon*, 1 Feb., 1940, p. 69.

England : Penguin Books, 1940 (pp. 46-47).

56. Symons, Julian -- *Of Crisis And Dismay* -- A Study of writing in the thirties (Rajan, B. & Pearse, A.), Focus one D. Dobson, 1945 (p. 104).

57. Garnett, David -- Books In General, *The New Statesman and Nation*, XXII, March 11, 1939, p. 362.

58. Jones, David Pryce - Isherwood Reassured *Time and Tide*, XLI, Oct. 1, 1960, p. 1162.

59. Isherwood, Christopher -- *Lions and Shadows*, The Hogarth Press, 1938, p. 236.

60. Piazza, Paul -- *Christopher Isherwood : Myth and Antimyth*, Columbia University Press, New York, 1978 (pp. 16-17).

61. Burgess, Anthony -- *The Novel Now*, Faber and Faber (London), 1971 (p. 115).

62. Fryer, Jonathan -- *Isherwood* (A biography of Christopher Isherwood), New English Library, London, 1977 (p. 7).

63. *Ibid.*, p. 16.

64. Isherwood, Christopher -- *Christopher And His Kind*, Methuen & Co. (London), 1976 (p. 10).

65. *Ibid.*

66. *Ibid.*, p. 100.

67. Fryer, Jonathan -- *Isherwood*, New English Library, 1976 (London), p. 100.

68. Isherwood, Christopher, trans., *The Intimate Journals of Charles Bandelaire*, 1930; rpt. Hollywood : Marcel Rodd, 1947, p. 81.

69. *The Times Literary Supplement*, June 14, 1928, p. 452.

70. *Ibid.*, p. 259.

71. Isherwood, Christopher -- *All The Conspirators* (1928), The Hogarth Press (London) (p. 12).

72. *Ibid.*, p. 78.

73. *Ibid.*, p. 235.

74. Connolly, Cyrill -- Introduction to *All the Conspirators.*

75. Isherwood, Christopher -- *Christopher And His Kind*, Methuen & Co. (London), 1976, p. 140.

76. Fryer, Jonathan -- *Isherwood*, New English Library, 1976 (London), p. 219.

77. Piazza, Paul -- *Christopher Isherwood*, New York, 1978 (p. 30).

78. *Ibid.*, p. 30.

79. Isherwood, Christopher -- *The Memorial* (1932), Hogarth Press (London), p. 23.

80. *Ibid.*

81. *Ibid.*, p. 45.

82. Lehmann, John -- *New Writing In Europe*, Harmondsworth: Penguin Books, 1940 (pp. 50-51).

83. Isherwood, Chritospher -- *Christopher And His Kind*, Methuen & Co. (London), 1976, p. 144.

84. Three prominent critics emphasize Norris' Comedic side by placing him in the main stream of renowned comic characters. For instance, W.H. Bantock Calls Norris 'Falstaffian', *The Novels of Christopher Isherwood*, in the novelist as thinker, ed. B. Rajan, London : D. Dobson, 1947, (p. 53).

85. Kermode, Frank : *Puzzles and Epiphanies*, Routledge and K. Paul (London), 1962 (p. 121).

86. Christopher first met Gerald Hamilton in the winter of 1930-31. At that period Gerald's social position was solidly respectable; he was the sales representative of the *London Times* for Germany and had his office in Berlin -- *Christopher And His Kind*, p. 60.

87. Isherwood, Christopher -- *Mr. Norris Changes Trains*, 1956, The Hogarth Press Ltd. (London) pp. 8-10.

88. *Ibid*., p. 239.

89. *Ibid*., p. 130.

90. Times Literary Supplement, 14 March, 1935, 161, William Plomer, Fiction, *Spectator*, 154, 1 March, 1935, p. 346.

91. Isherwood, Christopher -- *Christopher And His Kind*, Methuen & Co. (London), 1976, p. 151.

92. *Ibid*., p. 155.

93. Isherwood, Christopher – Introductory note, *Goodbye To Berlin*, Hogarth (London), 1939, p. 7.

94. Hynes, Samuel -- *The Auden Generation*, The Bodley Head (London), 1976 (p. 354).

95. *Ibid*., p. 354.

96. *Ibid*., p. 355.

97. Isherwood, Chritospher – *Goodbye To Berlin*, The Hogarth Press, 1960, Introductory note.

98. *Ibid*., p. 13.

99. *Ibid*.

100. Piazza, Paul -- *Christopher Isherwood : Myth and Antimyth*, Columbia University, New York, 1978 (p. 93).

101. Isherwood, Christopher - *Goodbye To Berlin*, The Hogarth Press, 1960, p. 130.

102. *Ibid*., p. 180.

103. *Ibid*., p. 2.

104. *Ibid*.

105. *Ibid*.

106. *Ibid*., p. 207.

107. *Ibid*., p. 186.

108. Piazza, Paul -- *Christopher Isherwood : Myth and Antimyth*, Columbia University, New York (1978), p. 119.

109. Mr. Isherwood Changes Trains, *Times Literary Supplement*, Nov. 11, 1949 (p. 727).

110. Isherwood -- 'German Literature in England', *New Republic*, 98, 5 April, 1939, p. 254.
111. Paul Piazza -- *Christopher Isherwood*, New York, 1978, p. 119.
112. Warner, Rex -- *The Cult of Power* (Essays), London, 1946 (p. 129).
113. *The Achievement of Rex Warner* -- Introductory note ed. A.L. McLead, Wentworth Press, Sydney, N.S.W. 1965 (p. 7).
114. Lehmann, John -- *The Achievement of Rex Warner*, Wentworth Press, 1965 (p. 14).
115. Pritchett, V.S. --*Rex Warner*, from *Modern British Writers*, New York, Vanguard Press, 1947 (pp. 304-309).
116. *The Achievement of Rex Warner* -- Introductory note, ed. A.L. McLeod, Wentworth Press, Sydney N.S.W., 1965 (p. 7).
117. *Ibid*., pp. 7-8.
118. *Ibid*., p. 10.
119. Lehmann, John -- *The Achievement of Rex Warner*, 1965 Wentworth Press Sydney (p. 14).
120. Warner, Rex -- *The Wild Goose Chase*, The Bodley Head (London), 1944 (pp. 7-8).
121. Mason, Ronald -- 'The Novels of Rex Warenr', *The Adelphi*, July-Sept., 1945, p. 174.
122. *Ibid*., p. 175.
123. Warner, Rex -- *The Wild Goose Chase*, The Bodley Head (London), 1944 (p. 402).
124. *Ibid*., p. 298.
125. *Ibid*., pp. 115-16.
126. *Ibid*., p. 31.
127. *Ibid*., p. 441.
128. Maini, Darshan Singh -- Rex Warner's Political Novels -- *Indian Journals of English Studies*, II, 1961 (p. 92).
129. *Ibid*., p. 91.
130. Warner, Rex -- *The Wild Goose Chase*, The Bodley Head (London), 1944 (p. 92).
131. *Ibid*., 318.
132. *Ibid*., Chapter XII.
133. *Ibid*., pp. 424-25.
134. Fowler, Roger -- *Linguistics And the Novel*, Methuen and Co. Ltd., 1977 (p. 3).
135. Hynes, Samuel -- *The Auden Generation*, The Bodley Head, London, 1976 (p. 301.)
136. *Ibid*., p. 301.
137. Maini, Darshan Singh -- Rex Warner's Political Novels -- *Indian Journal of English Studies*, II, 1961, p. 96.
138. Warner, Rex -- *The Professor* (1946), Lowe and Brydone Printers Ltd., London, N.W. 10 (pp. 15-16).

139. Hynes, Samuel -- *The Auden Generation*, The Bodley Head, London, 1976 (p. 311).
140. Warner, Rex -- *The Professor* (1946), Lowe and Brydone Printers Ltd. London, N.W. (p. 20).
141. *Ibid.*, pp. 108-19.
142. *Ibid.*, pp. 225-26.
143. *Ibid.*, p. 224.
144. *Ibid.*, p. 13.
145. *Ibid.*
146. *Ibid.*, pp. 280-81.
147. *Ibid.*, p. 290.
148. Mason, Ronald -- *The Novels of Rex Warner*, The Adelphi, July-September, 1945, p. 176.
149. Warner, Rex -- *The Aerodrome* (1956), Lowe and Brydone Printers Limited, p. 70.
150. Maini, Darshan Singh -- Rex Warners Political Novels, *Indian Journal of English Studies*, II, 1961 (pp. 91-107).
151. Waughs Private Diaries, *The Observer Magazine*, 13 May, 1973, p. 50.
152. Waugh, Evelyn -- *Labels*, 1930, Duckworth, (London), p. 40.
153. *Ibid.*, -- *Ninety-two Days*, 1934 (London), p. 13, Duckworth.
154. *Ibid.*, -- *Helena*, 1950 (Penguin), p. 180.
155. *Ibid.*, -- *Brideshead Revisited*, 1945 (London), Eyre Methuen (p. 6).
156. *Ibid.*, -- Fan Fare, *Life*, 6 April, 1946 (p. 60).
157. Myers, William -- Potential Recruits: Evelyn Waugh and the Reader of Black Mischief, an article in the collective work, *The 1930s*, A challenge To Ortodoxy ed. John Lucas, The Harvester Press Limited, Sussex, 1978 (p. 111).
158. *Ibid.*, p. 113.
159. *Ibid.*, p. 114.
160. Waugh, Evelyn -- *Nintey-two Days* (1934), London Duckworth, p. 13.
161. S.J., Father Martin DArcy -- The Religion of Evelyn Waugh, an article in the collective work, *Evelyn Waugh And His World*, ed. David Pryce -- Jones, Weidenfeld and Nicolson (London), 1973 (p. 63).
162. Macaulay, Rose -- Evelyn Waugh, an article in the published work, *Writers of To-day*, ed. Denys Val Baker, Sidgwick and Jackson, Limited, 1948, p. 136.
163. Waugh, Evelyn -- *Decline and Fall*, William Heinemann, Limited (London), 1977 (p. 77).
164. Eagleton, Terry -- *Exiles and Emigres* : Studies In Modern Literature, Chatto & Windus (London) 1970, p. 42.
165. Waugh, Evelyn -- *Decline and Fall*, William Heinemann, Limited (London), 1977 (p. 109).
166. Macaulay, Rose -- Evelyn Waugh, an article in the published work, *Writers of*

To-day, edited by Denys Val Baker (London), 1948, Sidgwick and Jackson, Limited, 1948, p. 137.

167. Hynes, Samuel – *The Auden Generation*, The Bodley Head, 1976 (p. 57).
168. *Ibid.*, p. 58.
169. *Ibid.*, p. 58.
170. Waugh, Evelyn – *Vile Bodies*, Chapman and Hall (London), 1930, p. 223.
171. Hynes, Samuel – *The Auden Generation*, The Bodley Head, 1976 (p. 59).
172. Waugh, Evelyn – *Vile Bodies*, Chapman and Hall (London), 1930, p. 143.
173. Hynes, Samuel – *op. cit.* (p. 63).
174. Jollife, John – 'What's In A Name?' an article, in the collective work, *Evelyn Waugh And His World*, ed. David Pryce Jones, Weidenfeld and Nicolson (London), 1973, p. 232.
175. Waugh, Evelyn – *Black Mischief*, William Heinemann Limited (London), 1977 (p. 138).
176. *Ibid.*, p. 143.
177. William Myers – 'Potential Recruits', an article in the book, *The 1930s'*, ed. John Lucas, The Harvester Press Limited, Sussex, 1978, p. 106.
178. Waugh, Evelyn – *Black Mischief*, William Heinemann Limited (London), 1977 (p. 125).
179. Jollife, John – 'What's In A Name?' an article, in the collective work, *Evelyn Waugh And His World*, ed. David Pryce Jones, Weidenfeld and Nicolson (London), 1973 p. 232.
180. Waugh, Evelyn - *Black Mishief*, William Heinemann Limited (London), 1977, p. 203.
181. Bradbury, Malcolm – *Evelyn Waugh* (Writers and Critics), 1964 (London) p. 55.
182. Macaulay, Rose – 'Evelyn Waugh', an article in the book, *Writers of To-day*, edited by Denys Val Baker (London), 1948, Sidgwick and Jackson, Limited, 1948, p. 142.
183. *Ibid.*, pp. 142-43.
184. Waugh, Evelyn – *Scoop* (1977), William Heinemann, Limited, (London), pp. 74-5.
185. Bradbury, Malcolm – 'The Novel In the 1920s', an article in the book, *The Twentieth Century*, Ed. Bernard Hamilton (London), p. 159.
186. Spender, Stephen – 'The World of Evelyn Waigh', an article in the book, *The Creative Element*, (1953), Hamish Hamilton (London), p. 159.
187. Waugh, Evelyn – *Vile Bodies*, Preface (1954), Chapman and Hall (London).
188. Bradbury, Malcolm – *op. cit.* (p. 216).
189. Wain, John – Essays on *Literature and Ideas* (London), 1963, (p. 43); Amis, Afternoon World p. 619; John Braine, quoted in *Isis*, No. 1507, Feb. 23, 1966 (p. 9).
190. Interview with the author, August, 1965, quoted by John Russe, *Anthony Powell*, Indiana University, 1971 (pp. 6-7).

191. Tucker, James -- *The Novels of Anthony Powell*, 1976, Great Britain, The Bowering Press Limited, Plymouth, p. 4.

192. Lodge, David -- *Language of Fiction* (London), 1966, p. 245.

193. Bergonzi, Bernar -- Anthony Powell, 9/12, Critical Quarterly, XI, Spring, 1969, p. 81.

194. From A Chase To A View, *Times Literary Supplement*, Feb. 16, 1951, p. 100.

195. Powell, Anthony -- *Afternoon Men* (1974), Heinemann, London (p. 2).

196. *Ibid*., p. 2.

197. Tucker, James -- *The Novels of Anthony Powell* (1976), Great Britain, The Bowering Press, Playmouth, p. 10.

198. Powell, Anthony -- *Afternoon Men* (1974), Heinemann, London, p. 183.

199. *Ibid*., p. 18.

200. *Ibid*., p. 88.

201. *Ibid*., p. 117.

202. Tucker, James -- *The Novels of Anthony Powell* (1976), Great Britain, The Bowering Press, p. 18.

203. *Ibid*., p. 21.

204. Powell, Anthony -- *Venusberg*, 1974, Heinemann (London), p. 186.

205. *Ibid*., p. 96.

206. Tucker James -- *op. cit*., p. 24.

207. *Ibid*., p. 28.

208. Messengers of Day -- *To Keep The Bell Rolling* : *The Memories of Anthony Powell*, Vol. II, Heinemann, (London), 1978 (p. 109).

209. *Ibid*., p. 117.

210. George Orwells statement quoted by John Russel in his critical work, *Anthony Powell*, Indiana (1971), p. 77.

211. Blackmur, R.P. -- *The Double Agent*, New York, 1935, p. 83.

212. Alldritt, Keith -- *The Making of George Orwell*, Edward Arnold (London), 1969, p. 2.

213. Leavis, O.D. -- The Literary Life Respectable, Scrutiny, IX, Sept. 1940 (p. 150).

214. Alldritt, Keith -- *The Making of George Orwell*, Edward Arnold (London), 1969, p. 25.

215. Levin, Harry -- *The Gates of Horn*, New York, 1963 p. 339.

216. Wickes, George -- *Masters of Modern British Fiction*, The Macmillan Company, New York, 1963 (p. 359).

217. *Ibid*., p. 359.

218. *Ibid*.

219. *Ibid*., p. 360.

220. Hynes, Samuel -- *op. cit*. p. 17.

221. Orwell, George -- *The Road To Wigan Pier*, London, Gollancz, 1937 (p. 17).

222. Hynes, Samuel -- *op. cit*., p. 17.

223. Powell, George -- *Reviewing the Thirties*, by Malcolm Muggeridge, 25 April, 1940, p. 122.

224. Forster, E.M.,-- *Two Cheers for Democracy*, Edward Arnold (London), 1972, p. 92.

225. Jameson, Storm -- Poignant ironic, penetrating significant, angle -- *Documents*, pp. 15-16.

226. Daiches, David -- *The Present Age*, Indiana University Press, Bloomington, 1958 (p. 116).

227. Reed, Henry -- *The Novel Since 1939*, The British Council, Longmans Green, 1946 (p. 16).

228. *Ibid*., p. 20.

229. Atkins, John -- *Six Novelists Look At A Society*, Calder (London), 1977 (p. 247).

230. *Ibid*., p. 247.

231. Collins, A.S. -- English Literature of the Twentieth Century, University Tutorial Press Ltd., p. 258.

232. *Ibid*., p. 261.

233. Wall, Stephen -- Aspects of the Novel, an article in the book, *The Twentieth Century*, ed. Bernard Bergonzi, Barrie and Jenkins (London), 1970 (p. 255).

234. Scott-James, R.A. -- *Fifty Years of English Literature* (1900-1950), Longmans (1961), London, p. 184.

235. Legouis, Emile and Cazamian, Louis, *op. cit*. (p. 1380).

236. Thale, Jerome -- *C.P. Snow*, Oliver and Boyd Edinburgh and London (1964), p. 2.

237. Sonw, C.P. -- Authors note preceding *The Search*, 1958, Macmillan (London).

238. Thale, Jerome -- *op. cit*., p. 2.

239. *Op. cit*., p. 3.

240. Snow, C.P. -- *The English Realistic Novel*, 1957 (p. 266), Modern Spark, 51.

241. Balliett, W., Biographical note, p. 7, *Saturday Review* 38, II, 8 Jan., 1955.

242. Snow, C.P. -- Science, Politics and the Novelist, *Kenyan Review*, 23 (1961) pp. 5-6.

243. Snow, C.P. -- *The New Men*, 1954 (London), (pp. 123-124), Macmillan.

244. Martin, Graham -- Novelists of Three Decades - *The Modern Age*, ed. Boris Ford, Penguin Books, 1970, p. 412.

245. Fuller, Edmund, 22 April, 1962 p. 25, Quoted by Jerome Thale -- *C.P. Snow*, Oliver & Boyd (London), 1964 (p. 60).

246. Widdowson, J.P. -- Patrick Hamiltons Fiction in the Thirties, *The 1930s*, ed. John Lucas, The Harvester Press, Sussex, 1978 (p. 117).

247. *Ibid*., p. 117.

248. *Ibid*.

249. *Ibid*., p. 119.

250. Hamilton, Patrick -- *Impromptu In Moribundia*, Constable, 1939, p. 250.

251. Widdowson, J.P. -- *op. cit.* (pp. 120-21).

252. Hamilton, Patrick -- *Craven House*, 1926, Constable 1926, p. 103.

253. *Ibid.*, p. 58-59.

254. Widdowson, J.P. -- *op. cit.*, p. 123.

255. *Op. cit.* p. 124.

256. Hamilton, Patrick -- *Impromptu In Moribundia*, Constable, 1939, p. 42.

257. Widdowson, J.P. -- *op. cit.*, p. 42.

FOURTH CHAPTER

TECHNICAL ACHIEVEMENTS

(Plot, Characterisation, Technique and Style)

It is observed that, "... many novels of the thirties show a degree of panic about the form. Where to start and where to end, how much must be believed and how much a joke, a puzzle; how to combine the carefully designed and consequential. The moods of the writers are to admit manipulation and design, to exploit the very act of authorship in the midst of the imagined scene."[1] Evelyn Waugh has expressed this point of view slightly differently in *The Ordeal of Gilbert Pinfold and Other Stories* : "It may happen in the next hundred years that English novelists of the present day will come to be valued as we now value the artists and craftsman of the late eighteenth century. The originators, the exurberant men are extinct, and in their place flourishes a generation notable for elegance and variety of contrivance."[2] Plot to the novelists of the thirties is to denote the invention, and arrangement of events to show their sequence in time and their connections of cause and effect. They took for granted that every novel must have a plot, since language, being extended in time, can't stand still. Therefore they invented a plot which they thought essential for narrative literature to arouse and appease our hopes, fears and curiosity about the fortunes of certain characters.[3]

The novelists of the thirties attempted to create and invent freely as well as to maintain a degree of realistic decorum. They evolved their own fictional mode, "that was serious without being highbrow, using of journalism and the cinema, shot through with sense of social and political crisis, and these devices were best suited to their literary programmes."[4]

Graham Greene's professional skill in designing the plot of a novel is masterly. The stories are avidly interesting, the style relaxed, and almost colloquial, yet capable of conveying great emotions in its understatement. Greene's plots are always set against a convincing background. As a professional journalist, he had been to many trouble-spots; and he has used these places as settings for many of his novels. His skill is such, however, that when we read them we feel that the action could not have taken place anywhere else. The climate, the country, the deeds of the army or the government, all effect the behaviour of the main characters and are inextricably bound up with them, the violence of the action reflecting violent emotions in the characters.[5]

A thriller of Graham Greene is more than action. It is a set of patterns and conventions as firmly established as those of a classical tragedy. "The hunted man who becomes in turn the hunter, the peaceful man who turns at bay, the man who has learned to love justice by suffering injustice."[6] These are the materials of his legends, and as in traditional legends they lend a formality to his violences, and lead us to expect a moral meaning. These legends are expressive narratives, and what happens in the narrative, happens because it carries meaning. In Greene's novels the violence is not there because the world is violent, but because violence satisfies, "that moral craving for the just and reasonable existence of human nature left without belief."[7] His settings are so consistently vivid and actual that they have been given a collective name `Greenland', and a descriptive adjective `seedy'. "... his world is consistently seedy, sordid, violent and cruel. These qualities are part of the legend. They describe not an actual environment, but an image of a spiritual condition – a world abandoned by God."[8] There is therefore a connection between the banality and ugliness of this world and its spiritual emptiness, and this correlation is most powerful and emotionally effective when it appears simply as a legend – that is in the `entertainments'.

The Man Within is about a betrayal, and it is set against a background of sceptical romance. Andrews, the chief character, is often lost in self examination which is an unfamiliar thing in the world of romance. The novel is partly redeemed by having a Conrad for the main character in place of a Swash-buckling hero. The heart searching of Andrews after the trial lifts the book out of the rut prepared for it by easy virtue and hotel beds. Andrews realizes that there is a mystery of self, and this takes us far beyond the normal historical novels of excitement and action. We have the man who deeply delves into his Bible, and goes for long walks by himself because he has sinned of which he is actually aware. When he discovers that the Bible condones his sin, he is satisfied. Then his Bible reading and walks also cease. He even begins to feel the intensity of sexual desire. It is like a dynamo being switched on and off: "There is no doubt, for instance, that he is possessed of a powerful sexual derive, which frequently bursts through the bonds of the narrative to assert itself when the demands would be opposed to it."[9] Technically the novel has many faults. Greene adopts the stream-of-consciousness techniques in the execution of this novel, but he is not happy with it. He is occasionally guilty of verbal abuse, `mingling of concrete and abstract'. the novel comes to its close incomplete, naive, crude and marked here and there by touches of subtlety which does not redeem it.

Stamboul Train is the story of Dr. Czinner, the failed revolutionary. Dr. Czinner feels no longer a doctor, certainly not a believer, not anyone's son; he is simply a socialist and his fighting is for these, "... sad and beautiful faces, thin from bad food, old before their time, resigned to despair ... they were people he had known, whom he had attended and failed to save...."[10] Dr. Czinner is returning to his native country, where a revolution is expected. At the frontier he is checked, and so is coral Musker, an English chorus girl – travelling to take up a job in Istambul. He attempts to pass a message to Coral but both are arrested, and held under guard at the station. He is tried by the Chief of Police, Colonel Hartep. After some thrilling action he is shot while attempting to escape and Coral is rescued by the lesbian journalist, Warren. The story is interesting from beginning to the end. There are depression, failure, sordidness and debauchery. All the incidents are knitted together. The dreams described in the novel at times make its texture surrealistic. Picturesque descriptions outside the train in metaphorical prose gives a naturalistic touch and heightens the poetic sensibility. There is a satisfying symbolism that also makes the plot metaphorical.

Sometimes allegory and factual details fuse together and this slackens the movement, to wit:

> "...that there was the expression of something that loved and suffered for man. Human beings floated like fish in golden water, free from the urge of gravity, flying without wings, transparent in a glass ... ugly faces and misshapen bodies were transmuted, if not into beauty, at least into grotesque forms fashioned by a mocking affection. On that golden tide they rose and fell, murmured and dreamed. They were not imprisoned, for they were not during the hour of dawn aware of their imprisonment."[11] The novelist, here, plays out most of the situations on a narrow stage

> where he directs every movement of his characters. A scene sometimes hampers the progress of the novel, but it becomes necessary for some dramatic purpose. We also mark a taste for psychological subtlety in the novelist, but he has not "the highness of character necessary to restrain him from gloating over man's less attractive features."[12]

It's Battlefield, consists of a number of circlets, in which the soldiers fight in ignorance of what is happening around them. The Assistant Commissioner, the chief character, believes only in his work. He arrests a murderer who affects to be a religious man, playing with belief like a toy shield. Throughout the book runs the question: What can you believe? Conrad, the red journalist, pretends to have a family life. His activities are so much in a mess that he is baffled to distinguish between the real and the false. He has nvever had much to believe in. For him Law, Justice, Police, Jury, Civil servants have all collapsed because they have decided that his brother Jim is a murderer. The Assistant Commissioner, who serves law and justice, is also aware of their hollowness. He has long ago ceased to believe in any great directing purpose. He is always haunted by a sense of waste, of people dying and suffering uselessly. He, therefore, devotes himself fully to, and gets himself lost in his work. His friend, Caroline Bury, also feels the waste and aimlessness of existence equally keenly, but chooses a different way out. She affirms her faith; but it is impossible to say in what. She is in touch with those trifling things which are associated with religion – incense, idols, ikons – and hopes for a solution that would be almost mechanical. She is cleverer than the Assistant Commissioner, but her solution is more nonsensical than his. One can make nothing of life; it is a thing whim and chance. Conrad knows it too well, "They hanged this man and pardoned that; one embezzler was in prison, but other men of the same sort were sent to Parliament."[13] In the general collapse of his world, Conrad feels there is nothing he can do, but still lashes out against his environment. He has been fond of his brother, but now he feels strong hatred for him. Sex is a big fraud and love does not transcand the body. Only time can save men. The novel is in the technique of Joseph Conrad. The lucidity of Conrad's prose is marked here in every line. Greene also adds something of his own, the concrete object producing an appropriate semblance. The plot is so well managed, and the imagery so manipulated that character and atmosphere both are effectively brought into being. The picture of the London streets is nervous and restless, composed of selected Snapshots to make a living pattern. The novelist is equally conscious of the matter as well as the manner, and the two are woven together to provide the texture.

England Made Me is marked for its artistic design. It is a sort of pocket-epic that produces in miniature but in an elevated style some of the serious facets of human life. The episodes move round Anthony and his sister Kate, for whom life is more a tragedy than a comedy. Anthony stands for pain, fear, despair and disgrace. He objectifies these qualities for his sister, who is superior to him, but whose superiority is not moral but technical. She has succeeded and he has failed. Anthony repeats again and again, "I have n't a future, Kate."[14] There is a paradox in Anthony. He has his faults, but he is also responsible, conventional and sympathetic. He is soft and sentimental. Women, in his view, ought to marry for love and bear children. His love for Loo is sincere; and in this he differs from Herr Krogh, Kate's lover and boss, who is a megalomaniac Swedish financier. Herr Krogh wallows and his love for Kate is only superficial. He always thinks in figures; he believes in only one type of value, that is in the business sense. He says to Hall, his henchman, "... value is confidence. As long as we receive money, we're valuable. As long as we're trusted."[15] He is a devil incarnate who takes delight in the misery and poverty of young Anderson, a dismissed worker. The murder of Anthony by Hall makes the story tragic. The narrative includes the elements of seediness, and also does not lack in flippant hot hotel scenes. The style becomes naturalistic in description of such sentimental scenes as the following:

> "A relationship 'so limiting', Loo said. They kissed, and into their kiss crept the desperation, the hunger of departure, the sadness of railway stations; one was going and one was staying; a holiday was over; the fireworks were dead on the grass, other people were watching the pierrots and curling of an evening in their glass shelter on the front, and one had done nothing more complete than this kiss.... She took her mouth away. 'So limiting', she said .... He looked for her mouth and missed it; her cheek tasted salt."[16]

A person's reflection and reverie give an impressionistic touch to the novel. Sometimes it becomes tangible shreds of imaginative experience. The imagery too is significant; sometimes it makes a person look like a cartoon: "His high bald face, like a roll of newspaper, showed at a distance only the bold headlines the smaller types, the little subtleties, obscure fears, were invisible."[17] Thus triviality becomes the subject-matter of the novel which does not lack in symmetry and imaginative colouring. Here life-stuff counts more than its treatment which is intermixed with the former.

Journey without maps was the consequence of the writer's visit to Liberia. Here the journey is a powerful search into the protean power, and an escape from evil. The writing shows the novelist's mood when he set sail for Africa:

''I find myself always torn between two beliefs, he wrote, `the belief that life should be better than it is and the belief that when it appears, it is really worse.''[18] The sex thrill is under no restraint here, although the Liberian women did not excite him. In this book Greene, as the most assertive left winger, has disclosed himself as a harsh critic of imperialism and ''one has to take his criticisms more seriously than many from the professional propagandists.''[19] *A Gun for Sale* is chiefly characterised by the fear of war which is the main device of the story. The impending war evokes strong emotion which everyone experiences in the story. It emerges also from the way the scene of the action is presented from the buildings, the streets, the anonymous crowds that fill them. Its presence in the air of the novel creates war-scare, a compelling reality. Again and again various characters are shown haunted by nightmare of the coming war. There are practices with gas-masks, aeroplanes zooming over London, and hysteric sirens accompanied by drills against air raids. We feel depressed by disgust and other less agreeable emotions. We do not find anything notable and attractive, except the moments of love struggling for expression. The main episode is of detective interest. Raven, a hired murderer is chased by detective sergeant Mather. Irony is piled on irony in the most slapdash manner. The girl Raven gets entangled with is Anna whom Mather loves. Raven is betrayed by Anne and is shot. He muses sadly before he dies:

> ''... he had been marked from his birth for this end, to be betrayed in turn by everyone until every avenue into life was safely closed .... How could he have expected to have escaped the commonest betrayal of all; to go soft on a skirt.''[20]

But Anne is not happy at this betrayal. She treats it as her failure. She says to Mather, ''I did fail''. Before his death Raven murders his Marois and Mr. Davis for they have paid two hundred phoney pounds to him to kill the minister. These deaths make the novel sensational.

The fantasia of unconsciousness forges a dream quality in the novel:

"He (Raven) dreamed that he was building a great bonfire on Guy Fawkers day. He threw in everything he could find: saw-edged knife, a lot of racing cards, the leg of a table. It burnt warmly, deeply, beautifully. A lot of fireworks were going off all round him and again the old war minister appeared on the other side of the fire. He said, `It's a good fire', stepping into it himself. Raven ran to the fire to pull him out, but the old man said, `Let me be. It's warm here, and then he sagged like a Guny Fawkers in the flames."[21]

The dream reveals the unconscious level of Raven's mind, who was forced to murder the war minister because of his desparate financial condition. The novel becomes epical when it introduces some such lines:

"A shadow flits before me,
Not thou, but like to thee;
Ah Christ, that it were possible
For me short hour to see
The souls we loved, that they might tell us
What and where they be."[22]

Sexual and Carnal images suggest libidinous agitation. The essence in this novel as well as in the previous ones is evil. We get the impression that the novelist seeks evil in life and depicts it in his works plainly. Like Fielding, "he considers hypocrisy, malice, cruelty and stupidity as infinitely worse habits than adultery, drunkenness, dope-taking and petty lying he considers it as a part of his duty as a novelist to experience all the pleasures – and certainly many of the pains..."[23] His characters like Raven and Sir Marcus stand for some social malaise. Here actions are less important than the characters who advance the actions further. Deformity and mutation became the dominance symbols.

In *Brighton Rock* the story is symbolic to a degree on the first page we are informed that Hale, who is in the service is a newspaper, had once been a pretty Brighton mobster, and that he bites his nails. The tension in the world of this novel is so oppressive that everyone is reduced to gnawing his nails. We are aware of Anthony Farrant's social pretences and the care he takes with his dress. But the kind of life that he and the others in the novel live, demands release from this tension. As we got into the story, the emotional intensity becomes so strong that we suspended our disbelief and in the end are convinced. Greene tries to raise common events above their familiar level simply to make them stranger than fiction and thus to make novel successful. Pinkie is at times subject to pricks of desire – when he takes Rose into the country, he sees the skin of her thigh for a moment above the silk, and the desire disturbs him like a sickness. But he puts its aside. For him love is a dirty act, leading to, "stuffy room, the wakeful children, the Saturday night movements from the other bed."[24]

The Confidential Agent is carefully planned, but it fails in many respect, we mark symbols of suffering, absurdities, innocent-*cum*-worldly humanity. Such symbols constantly recur in this novel, and they weaken the plot. Some passages like the following, contain parodic allusion to Virginia Woolf:

> "He went into Oxford street; there was no hurry now; nothing to be done until he saw Lord Benditch. He walked, enjoying the sense of unreality – the shop windows full of goods, no ruined houses anywhere, women going into Buzzard's for coffee ... He could not help noticing how well clothed everybody was. A pale winter sun shone and the scarlet lenses stood motionless all down Oxford Street; there was a traffic block... The sky was empty – or nearly empty. One winking, glittering little plane turned and dived on the pale clear sky, drawing in little puffy clouds, a slogan: 'Keep warm with Ovo'. He reached Bloomsbury."[25]

England seems sunk in the bourgeois dream of peace and stability. The character 'D' feels its appeal, but judges it to be ultimately a dangerous illusion. Concealing political tensions and injustices that are being openly fought over in his own country. D breaks into the flat, bringing with him, at gun-point, the agent K who has double-crossed him and who has been partly responsible for the murder of Else. D intends to execute summary justice by shooting K, but has some difficulty in screwing himself up to do the dead. He forces K into the bathroom, shuts his eyes and pulls the trigger, missing his target by a foot. There is a ring at the front door, and he goes to answer the bell. It is his girl, Rose. D tells Rose that he tried to shoot K but failed. When he opens the bath-room door, however, K pitches forward into the room dead from heart failure. They lay him out on the divan and there is another knock on the door. This time it is a youngman called Fortescue, a neighbour. D and Rose pretend that they are friends of the flat's rightful occupier, a Miss Glover, who has loaned them the place for a party and that K is drunk. Given the character of Miss Glover and the absence of any sign of a party such as bottles and glasses, this is a highly implausible story, but Fortescue is too innocent to guess the truth.

All the dynamics of its narrative interest, the suspense, the surprise, the irony – are highly cinematic, generated and expressed through contiguities of space and time ; doors opening on the unexpected, crisis following crisis without respite.

The Lawless Roads is a travel book. It is a Catholic propaganda in place of a novel. But it succeeds to give the sense that for all the hardships and dangers Greene underwent, Mexico remains something of an inner landscape, a metaphor or objective correlative for his obsessions. The novelist in the note to the third edition of this novel refers to the purpose of its writing:

> "... the author dwells too much on a religious situation liable to change at the expense of more permanent sides of Mexican life. My excuse must be that I was committed to write a book on the religious situation, not on folklore or architecture or the painting of Riviera."[26]

Mexico stands for hell to Greene. The first chapter is named as Border which is a recurrent symbol in the thirties literature. The novelist gives an exact idea of the workings of the mind of a man crossing an international border:

> "The border means more than a custom house, a passport officer, a man with a gun. Over there everything is going to be different; life is never going to be quite the same again after your passport has been stamped and you find yourself speechless among the money-changers. The man seeking scenery imagines strange words and unheard of mountains; the romantic believes that the women over the border will be more beautiful and complaisant than those at home, the unhappy man imagines at least a different hell; ..."[27]

The novel in some becomes picaresque, for it includes strange adventures, scenes and people. Some of the things are bizzare indeed:

> ".... a Siamese sheep – eight legs sticking out like octopus tentacles – and calves with so-called human heads (like

> those of morons), and dogs create upside down rolling glass eyeballs towards legs that spronted from somewhere near the backbone and 'a frog baby born to a lady in Oklahoma'. The novelist's self musings save the novel from the monotony of a journalistic work. The novelist also fixes his look on "silent meetings of lovers on square scented with flowers and leaves, a silent fountain, and denumb courtships going on upon every bench in the darkness."[29]

To a novelist, in his narrative, the value of landscapes are different from that of a romantic writer. The novelist introduces the landscape not in terms of picturesequeness but in the perspective of its value to human beings. A romantic would have enjoyed the Mexican scene, describing it as "sublime", but the novelist Greene can give only lip service to its beauty. He never misses to portray the poverty and squalor that is a part of the landscape.

Also the travel account sometime becomes charged with excitement, fun, frolic as well as nausea:

> "... then the Cabaret began – a Mexican dancer with great bold thighs, and the Amercian women lost a little of their remote superiority. They were being beaten at the sexual game ... half a dozen girls in yellow bathing suits did high kicks for a moment and disappeared ... I dreamed that a woman and I had committed a murder and buried the body, but the smell seeped up to us through the ground until the whole world seemed to carry the scent of decay."[30]

Surveying all these novels of the thirties we reach the conclusion that Greene is fully conscious of his craft. He is careful not to overwrite – "in two or three places he has stated that five hundred words a day are quota."[31] Much of Greene's craft is instinctive. His insistence on action makes him different from the writers of Bloomsbury tradition. Greene wrote under the notion that:

> "The act of writing is very like the act of sculpture: One is provided with a rude block of facts, out of which one has to cut the only details that matter."[32]

In fact Greene like a skilled artist gives proper shape and colour to his novels which may be sometimes faulty in form, distorted in the presentation of life, but they never miss the mark. His readability is because,''all his novels involve the use of popular narrative formulas acceptable to a large audience.''[33]

Christopher Isherwood, ''a convenient ventriloquist'[34] shows great dexterity in the construction of his plots through all the stages. As a true photographer he gives photographic reality from different angles. His novels of the thirties incapsulate the socio-political forces which were then operating in Nazi Germany. The narratives are well studded with appropriate scenes and settings which came directly from the reality as we visualise them. The novelist's subjectivity never intrudes on the episodes. Like a senstitive poet he dwells on that which thrills his imagination most:

> ''Erna was a skiny, bobbed-haired woman of about thirty-five ... she had immense, dark, hungry eyes .... The wedding-ring was loose on her boney finger .... the ward was quite dark now. The windows were big pale rectangles in the darkness. Erna, sitting beside me on the bed, felt down for my bed and squeezed it; then she reached behind me and drew my arm around her body. She was trembling violently...''[35]

The novelist gives metaphorical meanings to the trivialities that abound in his novels. Sometimes the episodes of different characters personal lives are presented in one connecting chain. The Berlin stories succeed to sustain our poetic faith, for these are forged out the personal diary of the novelist. The fact and the fiction are fused together. Truth becomes stranger than fiction. In *Mr. Norris Changes Trains* the existing relationships between Norris and William Bradshaw, or between Bradshaw and some of the other characters like Frl. Schroeder, the landlady, Baron Von Pregnitz, Otto and Olga are the main threads that make the texture of the story. The web is woven mainly by the actions of Mr. Norris, the main character. That is, ''simplification of details, a centralisation of incidents into small units of space and time, decorated by a fantastic touch .... The novelist uses the expressionistic technique and exploits the age-old German love for fantasy and the macabre which hundred years before had surged through romantic literature.''[36] Isherwood's technique is identical to that of an actual cameraman in film-making.

Mr. Norris Changes Trains in a serial biography of Arthur Norris who, surrounded by lesser characters, commands the reader's eye. In the first eight chapters William Bradshaw is utterly fascinated, charmed and scandalised by Norris. The novelist narrates the story objectively, camera-wise. The camera could record only outward appearances, actions and spoken words, no thoughts, no feelings, nothing subjective. "The author gives him (the reader) all the necessary objective data, challenging him to interpret it and guess what will happen next. The more often the reader misinterprets and guesses wrongly, the greater is the author's success. This is the technique of classic detective story."[37]

Norris is not a prototype. He is not designed to demonstrate a concept. He is a character in the simplest sense and "meeting him must be its own reward."[38] The novelist wants to make the reader experience Arthur Norris as he himself had experienced Gerald Hamilton. He can do this by writing subjectively, in the first person, describing his own reactions to and feelings about Hamilton, otherwise his portrait may not be life-like. In spite of this strong personal element Christopher not only does make the narrator homosexual, he also scorns to make him heterosexual. Therefore, William Bradshaw, the narrator of the story, can have no explicit sex-experiences. He is a demi-character. It is as if Christopher had told him : "Don't call any unnecessary attention to yourself, don't get more involved with anybody than you absolutely have to."[39] Thus Christopher both acknowledge and disowns his kinship with the narrator, Bradshaw.

Of course, he invents appropriate dialogues, situations and additional characters for the sake of the story. Isherwood wants to keep the reader's attention concentrated on Norris. The reader is encouraged to put himself in the narrator's shoes – to see with the narrator's eyes, to experience his experiences, to identify with him in all his reactions.

Isherwood sets out to write what he calls a 'dynamic portrait'. He uses this term to describe, "a novel whose interest depends on the gradual revealing of a character, rather than on action, crisis and confrontation. What the action of such a novel does, is to remove layer after layer of the skin of outer appearance – thus taking the reader inward from his first superficial impressions, and too hastily formed judgements until he is face to face, at last with the real individual."[40]

In those days *i.e.* during the thirties Isherwood was fond of saying that what most interested him in writing fiction was to present the bizarre as though it were humdrum, and to show events which were generally regarded as extraordinary forming the daily routine of somebody's life. He had chosen Norris for his first subject because of all his Berlin characters, Norris was the most bizarre.

However, in the process of writing the novel, Isherwood makes a deviation from his original intention. Towards the end of the novel, the novelist abandons Norris and his portrait for a whole chapter. He takes the narrator and some minor characters to Switzerland and involves them in an intrigue. Here the bizarre is merely bizarre. This shows that the novelist can invent situations in areas of life, which are quite unknown to him. He does not feel any shame for the betrayal.

Although in his novels about Berlin, Christopher tries to make the bizarre seem humdrum, but actually the humdrum too seem bizarre that is exciting. He intends his readers to feel excitement in Berlin's squalid streets and shabby crowds, in the poverty and dullness of the now overgrown but once Prussian provincial town. The novelist adopts the device of self-musing to disclose a person's character : "Poor Arthur! I have seldom known anybody with much weak nerves. At times, I began to believe he must be suffering from wild form of persecution mania."[41] The novelist makes the story more grim by introducing Schmidt like a villain who enjoys his employer's distress. Bayer, the chief leader of the Communist Party, and Norris with his opposition to British imperialism give a political colouring to the novel. Otto, Anne, Olga and Baron Von Pregnitz are the minor characters who jostle in the episodes to make it variegated in interest.

In Goodbye To Berlin Isherwood composes what he feels he can write best, a sequence of even simpler and more compact individual portraits. These portraits are succinct and direct. It appears as if Isherwood, rather than making a full length feature as he did in Norris, is rest satisfied with, "shooting vivid, loosely joined charts, startling in their severity and power."[42] But what separates Isherwood's from the documentary camera in its sensitivity to nuances – capable because of its selectivity, its angles, its juxtaposition of light and shade, of catching, what Stephen Spender calls "The terrifying mysteries of cities."[43] The narrative is in the first person but the fact is that Isherwood can't by his very nature be a character in a novel. He is simply a kind of scanning device so "the whole I. Christopher experiment is a failure in the last analysis."[44]

Isherwood's main obsession has been homosexuality, and it often breaks out in his sensuous descriptions of male beauty. Also 'Christopher's' selfishness is much less honest, more civilised, more perverse than the writer's. Isherwood went to live with the Mowaks in the autumn of 1931, not 1930 as it is shown in the novel. For this falsification the novelist gives two reasons: "First, from a structural point of view, it seemed better to introduce some of the more important characters – Sally Bowles, Frl Schroeder and her lodgers before the Nowaks. Second, since Isherwood (of the novel) is not overtly homosexual, he has to be given another reason for knowing Otto and another motive for going to live with his family."[45] Isherwood meets Otto through an Englishman named Peter Wilkinson who is Otto's lover. Isherwood becomes the lodger of the Nowaks (belonging to the working class), not because he wants to share a bedroom with Otto but because of his poverty. The novelist takes interest in the delineation of characters from the bourgeois class because he feels that their lives can never be meaningful. And this was a side effect of Christopher's political consciousness.

In December 1930 Isherwood moved again westward, from working class into middle-class Berlin. His new room was in a flat at Nollendorfstrasse 17. The Nollendofstrasse was neither elegant nor in good repair; but it was only middle class shabby, not slum-shabby. The actual landlady of Christopher Isherwood at the Nollendorfstrasse, Frl Meta Thuran, appears as Frl Schroeder in both *Mr. Norris* and *Goodbye To Berlin*. Of all the chief characters in the two books, she is least distorted from the original. Frl. Schroeder's reminiscences of her lodgers are interesting. She is fond of pointing the various marks and stains left by the lodgers who had lived in her room in the past. Her story about Prof. Koch, is very funny. "Sometimes, when he heard me coming, he'd turn out the light and hide behind the door; and then he'd roar like a lion to frighten me. Just like a child."[46]

Through Stephen Spender, Christopher Isherwood got to know another of his chief characters : Gisa Soloweitschik. She was a young Jewish girl who lived with her wealthy parents. In *Goodbye To Berlin*, Gisa is called Natalia Landaner. Natalia is presented as a bossy blue stocking, desperately enthusiastic about culture, sexually frigid and prudish. At first, 'Isherwood' remains mockingly passive towards her attempts to run his life; then he counterattacks by introducing her to Sally Bowles, an actress, a hot stuff. He does this to test Natalia, not Sally: for he knows in advance how Sally will behave. Sally, as usual, boasts about her lovers; and Natalia is prudishly shocked. She has failed Christopher's test. After this he and Natalia become estranged.

In fact Natalia's character is a more caricature of Gisa, as was pointed out by Stephen Spender to 'Isherwood' in a reproachful letter.[47] "Isherwood" in the novel is never emotionally involved with Otto or with anyone else.

It would have been impossible for him to reveal such feelings to Natalia, and thereby give her a chance to show her own warmth and sympathy. Natalia Landauer has a cousin Bernhard Landauer, who helps to run the department store owned by Natalia's father. Again and again Bernhard is presented as being tired and apathetic, suffering from hallucination. He regards his job with weary irony. He even admits to "Isherwood" that the store itself seems unreal to him at times. In the novel it seems to be implied that what Bernhard is hiding is a romantic attachment to 'Isherwood'. The shared trip to China proposed by Bernhard is made to sound like an elopement. The killing of Bernhard is merely a dramatic necessity. In a novel such as this one, which ends with the outbreak of political persecution, one death at least is a must. No other major character in the novel has been killed, and Bernhard is the most appropriate victim being a prominent Jew.[48] However the timing of his death, so early in the persecution, is unconvincing, unless he was murdered by mistake.

'Isherwood's sad self-reflection makes the novel subjective in its treatment:

> "... I begin to feel profoundly unhappy. Where are all those lodgers: Where, in another ten years, shall I be myself? Certainly not here. Now many seas and frontiers shall I have to travel, on foot, on horse-back, by car, push-bike, aeroplane, steamers, train, lift, moving staircase and train? How much money shall I need for that enormous journey? How much food must I gradually wearily consume on my way? How many pairs of shoes shall I wear out? How many thousands of cigarettes shall I smoke? How many cups of tea shall I drink and how many glasses of bear? What an awful tasteful prospect?...."[49]

Sometimes the novel becomes a portrayal of Bohemian life and produces such hot scene as:

> "The couples were dancing with hands on each other's hips, yelling in each other's faces, streaming sweat. On Orchestra in Bavarian costume whorped and drank ...."[50]

Sally's life as a whore is very tragic and touching. She knows that she is of the type which every man imagines he wants until he gets her, and then he finds that he does not after all. Women like her can take men away from their wives but can never keep them for long. Sally thinks that men are always going to leave her.[51] She is tired of her profession.

She undergoes an operation 'to dispel the least whiff of sinister illegality,' but after the operation her conscience pricks her. She tries to imagine how it would feel to be a mother – how, "... her baby would grow up and how she would work for it, and how, after she would put it to bed at nights, she would go out and make love to filthy old men to get money to pay for its food and clothes ..."[52] Her story becomes more tragic when Herr Kommissar, a cheat, betrays her and shatters her dream to be a famous actress in the Hollywood films.

Otto's poverty-stricken life is another touching point in the story. Nobody understands him, nobody sympathises with him, nobody wants him – at least that is how he feels. He, however, strongly feels for his ailing mother, and exclaims with real sorrow:

> "Poor mother! .... It's terrible. I can't bear to think of her working like that, everyday. You know, Christopher, she is very ill. Often, at night, she coughs for hours and hours. And sometimes she spits out blood. I lie awake wondering if she is going to die."[53] Frau Nowak, his mother, in turn is equally worried about her family. She is to be sent to the sanatorium, but reflects very sadly, "I'm sure I shall enjoy being there, if only I can stop myself worrying about the family. What they'll do when I'm gone, goodness only knows. They are as helpless as a lot of sheep."[54]

Mythopoeic description of persons and things at times becomes surrealistic:

> "They all thronged round us for a moment in the little circle of light from the panting bus, there lit faces ghostly like ghosts against the black stems of the pines. I had an absurd pang of fear that they were going to attack us – a gang of terrifyingly soft muffled shapes – clawing us from our seats, dragging us hungrily down, in dead silence. But the moment passed. They drew back – harmless, after all, as mere ghosts – into the darkness..."[55]

Thus the novel in six chapters, "Berlin Diary" (Autumn 1930), "Sally Bowles", "On Ruegan Island" (Summer 1931), "The Nowaks", "The Landaners" and again "A Berlin Diary", is roughly a continuous narrative, and also a loosely connected sequence of diaries and sketches. It is neither purely autobiographical, nor are the characters exact portraits of living persons. Its chief merit lies in the fact that it stands in recognisable relation to real life, but the relations are various: the life can be heightened or burlesqued or antithesized; it is in any case a selection of specially purposive sort from life.[56]

Rex Warner's *Wild Goose Chase*, *Professor* and *The Aerodrome* are classified as novels of symbolism expressing the modern problems in terms of fantasy. In these novels we find inter-dependence of characters and action. The narratives grow out of the personalities involved. There is less of superimposition than of a scheme of controlled analysis. "The author is completely successful in his representation of the forces whose conflict is even tearing humanity to pieces."[57] Fantasy is sufficient for his purpose. He distorts a known theme or situation to give point to a new force or one aspect over another; but he always keeps the nature of his material in his memory.

Warner's symbols, which are the constituting essence of his narrative, are simple, direct and applicable within narrow limits. He aims at the creation of a clear-cut allegory to show certain facets of men's struggles in life. There is no transcendentalism and no authentic mysticism. "All his values take their validity from their application to human relationship. The drama is played entirely on an earthly plane and there is no chance that any of the characters are gods in disguise."[58]

The Professor is a tragedy. Prof. A becomes a tragic figure when he is finally driven back to seek refuge with low humanity, out of bullet range of Colonel Grimm and his raiders. He now not only understands, but feels the horrible truth that crude force all too frequently wins out over idealism and scholarly wisdom. His devotion to abstract justice becomes the cause of tragic death. So far we can see nothing but strictly classical form mixed with a Kaftesque technique: "For half a second he again had the sensation that he was an actor in a nightmare, that the whole circumference of his world might at any moment crack and that all which he saw would be dispelled as phantoms in the air."[59] This Kafkesque technique makes the Professor's tragic stature also ridiculous: "There was no room for him on the floor, unless he were to stand face to face, as close as though dancing with one or other of the present occupants of the small area, and as he remained with one foot on the arm of old Jinkerman's chair and the other on the window-still, raised above the others as if he were an orator or some important figure in a tabbau on the stage."[60] In this Kafkesque realm the death of a man is like the death of a rat, meaningless and insignificant. The old Jinkerman dies in his room and his death reminds Professor A of his own death.

Mr. Cough, one of the survivors, a pacifist, lying on the floor, on his hands and knees in the room of Jinkerman, gives us the sense of "some wounded rat, surrounded by a circle of sticks, and searching for an outlet in the ring of his enemies."[61] This caricature of Dr. Cough shows man's magnificence in the nightmarish land, a subject of bathos and laughter.

Here the tragedy is a compound of plot and character. It has the unities of time, place and action. An infected context, an evil milieu which is indispensable to tragedy, exists. Professor A opposes the facist forces and meets his final tragic end. A tragic man is pre-occupied with his own suffering. At the beginning of the action Professor A does not have this preoccupation. He is not aware of the real issues. The tight form of the plot requires, however, that every action be an additional recognition of the evils; one dare not ignore any clue to one's destiny, for he does so only on the pain of his own destruction. Tragic irony arises not only from undercutting and multiplicity of interpretations but also from the protagonist's awakening to these evils: "One is not destroyed until he has thoroughly faced the difficulties that he has minimised or thought non-existent."[62] The book emerges in all dimensions as a composite product of ancient and contemporary forms and material. *The Professor* reveals the context of our problem that we are not secure. Our old ideals have proven to be false. Warner shows us that once again we live in a time when self-courage, a leap into faith in the human condition, is the only thing which may save human consciousness from decay.

Again and again Warner introduces absurdity in *The Professor*, yet this element does not detract from the essential tragedy of the protagonist. Professor A jumps out of the bushes and sings an Elizabathan love-ditty to his son and a girl friend, an action silly and inappropriate on the eve of his country's loss of freedom. Professor A shamefacedly dons a scarlet dressing gown to receive his cabinet members, who in turn squabble over trivialities and descend to insults just when the country is falling under enemy dictatorship.

The narrative becomes surrealistic when the novelist transports Professor A to the dream-land. "... a dream to see a huge monument on a hill and beyond the hill, the sea in the distance, slopes covered with heather, and flight of fleecy clouds passing over a wind washed sky. For a moment he sought in his memory to remember the name of the person in whose honour the monument had been erected, and then he observed that a file of men and women, as numerous and, in the distance, as tiny as auto, was approaching the monument over hills and valleys for as far as he could see....''[63]

Dreams reflect not only the unconscious but also the conscious mind of Professor A, which is aware of periodical crises:

> ''....The Professor observed that a fight was on the point of breaking out between the demonstrators and the police, one of whom was attempting to wrest the banner from the hands of the man who held it.''[64]

Warner has not flinched from describing even gruesome details when needed for verisimilitude, to wit:

> ''His great body was convulsed for some moments with a fit of coughing. Blood came from his mouth. His eyes were contracted and his lips over which he seemed to have lost control, were trying to enunciate words. A spasm passed up with the length of one leg and died away, as though the limb had been flicked into immobility by lightning. His mouth, with pretruding tongue, felt open and lay on the carpet like a huge sponge.''[65]

The book lacks in dramatic dialogue. Sometimes there are boring arid arguments of one person covering several pages. There is little action. Ideas instead of form and characterisation predominate. Hence the plot is very thin and characters are merely sketches.

In *Wild Goose Chase* the matter is more important than form. Here passion does not spin the plot. Episodes within episodes are linked together. The form of the novel is picaresque in conception. George, the hero, goes on an expedition across the border where he meets strange peoples and adventures. The Kafkesque technique makes the novel in a 'waking dream'. The novel opens with a bleak view of a landscape which gives us a horrid sense of no man's land. There are occasions for laughter, *e.g.* at the clownish antics of Bob.[66] Bob like the Shakespearean 'Fool' pleases us by his witty song.[67] He is there because he has been exiled on a charge of bigamy. Gruesome details and ghastly scenes are not lacking in this novel too. Cleobyle and Pyrrha, the two devoted attendants of Antonio appear anything but pleasing to the eyes of George.[68] Similarly, the description of the dead body of Antonio, after his brutal suicide, flanked by his two female devotees in all their nakedness, is terrifyingly nauseating.[69]

The novelist transports George and Bob with the waving of a magic wand to a new country, "Where they found a mile stone denoting the distance 30,000 miles away from the town of George."[70] George wants to ask something from the countrymen, but Bob says, "... you could never trust a countryman and for all one knew these countrymen might be cannibals, ..."[71] George's meeting with Joe and his daughter Joan at the farm building is a crucial point in the story. Joan is in the habit of sleeping with every stranger who comes to stay there in the night. When George asks if her father ever objects, she replies, "Oh no. Why should he? He knows that there is no risk of that kind. All who comes this way, are sterile."[72] Joan is glad to see George; therefore, she proposes to marry and settle down. But George could not sleep with Joan. He starts up in bed hearing a noise that grew louder and louder. The scene becomes hallucinatory as the wild geese approach and then pass by the window:

> "... Now they were passing the windows and the room trembled, quivered as though about to be swept away by that deluge of air and sound ... George sprang out of bed, though Joan clang to him, and swang back, the window letting into the room a high wind which blew the clothes off the bed, ... wild geese! wild geese!" he shouted ... his heart bursting with joy."[73]

But George does not run after them because his goal is the city that would open the gate through which he could reach near these wild geese. The scene becomes dramatic when George disengages himself from Joan and sits out for the city. He is misunderstood and reproached by Joan who accuses him of being after town women.[74]

George's journey to the city in the company of Bob is like a journey through a dreamland. George finds himself in a Kafkian city where intellectuals are like Tiresias enjoying both sexes. George wishes to go to the convent; therefore, he is led to an operation for changing his sex:

> "You have no idea how valuable it is to feel the reactions of a woman. And then, of course, you can be a man at the same time. You can synthesize or analyse."[75]

George observes in the city that men and women are like shadowless spectres moving to and fro swiftly. George succeeds to see the 'Stuffed Goose', an object of reverence for the citymen. David had taken it as a real goose. George meets Pothimere a Professor of love, Harold the games master, Humberto the chief statistician, and Humberto's wife Marqueta. George feels boredom and disgust in their company. The football match between pros and cons with George as the referee is a horrible one. All the players of the former team are shot dead.

The novelist does not miss to portray the horrid facts of appalling poverty and privations of the proletarian class.[76] He also adopts the Kafkesque device to describe George's encounter with the king's soldiers.[77] Sometimes storming nature becomes the appropriate scenario to the coming catastrophe[78], and at others, as in describing a dream, specially when a number of persons are introduced therein, the narrative becomes highly imaginative.[79] George fails to reach the wild geese through the city as he had expected. Hence, after five years he returns to the village of Joan who is already married to Bill. Joan is not at rest with her married life. She still longs for George. This time Joe increases our surprise by revealing the fact to George that Don Antonio was his brother and Freda Harrison, his wife whom Antonio wanted to marry. Pushkov's death in the country jail produces pity and terror. George "looked at the dead agitator's features, stone-rigid in death, remembering that, for whatever motives, he had constantly opposed the government, that he had refused bribes, been subjected to insults, and now had lost his life in captivity."[80]

George with a peasants' army attacks the city, and captures it. There is no fight. The city has bombers and fighters, but the pilots have been dead for many years. George's proclamation to the students of the convent is significant:

> "... 'each student should within twentyfour hours – decide upon his or her sex' ... these still dressed bisexually, locked with contempt at the soldiers..."[81]

The story ends on a note of harmony, "Now looking upwards, they saw the whole blue sky ... very slowly and in complete silence the birds passed, going like galleons, huge ships with sails set and filled majestically by some wind that blows beautifully on the sea, though the watcher on the shore stands in admiration with not the smallest breeze to fan his cheek."[82]

Thus, the fabulous tale is in consonance with the novelist's purpose which lies in the exposition of some of the contemporary warring elements like Fascism and Communism. Ideas take wings and soar above, rushing the reader along in a frenzy or ecstacy of language. All other fictional ingredients such as plot, character and humour fade away for the moment, or are sometimes subordinated to long overwhelming dialogues which are swollen with thought, and go hurtling along at a breathless speed.[83]

Of all the novelists of the thirties, Evelyn Waugh is the most entertaining and perhaps the most gifted. The world he invented and adorned with extravagant *jeux d'esprit* is a comic world. In it he moves, "with the blandest security and ease; from within its circumference he can utter any commentary on life, create and manipulate any beings who inhabit there."[84] In *Decline and Fall* the story is gay, grim and amoral. Its vicissitudes are catastrophically logical, its ingenious hero, Paul Pennyfeather, is the victim of the most shocking turpitudes and betrayal. He is landed in prison, helped out of it by intriguing friends, and ends officially dead and lastly resuming life in disguise. We do not see here either vulgarity, refinement or morality; the atmosphere is that of irreverent and essentially anarchic fantasy to produce the irony of anticlimax the novelist focuses attention on the thoughts of Paul.

In the novel the prison is really a joke, the processes of law are preposterous, and Paul finds his weeks of confinement to be among the happiest in his life: "There was no need to shave, no hesitation about what tie he should wear, none of the fidgeting with studs and collars and links that so distracts the waking moments of civilised man."[85] Paul's vision makes jail a dreamland: "No words can describe the splendour of it. It was all crimson as if it were carved of ruby, hard and glittering, and the warders and the prisoners creeping in and out like red ladybirds."[86] There is ambivalence about the crime and fraud within the upper-class world itself. Its point is to suggest the real depradation and brutalities which underlie the glittering surface. Paul finds attractive, but the sharp edge of that criticism is blunted by the grotesque enormity of the crimes themselves; white slave traffic, poison and conspiracy. These forms of corruption are so extreme as to be unreal. They reflect less a considered satiric criticism than an uncontrolled sense of nightmare and absurdity. Paul Pennyfeather is protected by a comic good fortune that takes away his identity, but allows him his survival. It is true to say that *Decline and Fall* is in fact a kind of modern history of Tom Jones in which the realm of comic fortune sustains the characters in an otherwise anarchic world. Paul Pennyfeather, the intelligent, well educated youngman is allowed to exist in the novel only as a shadow; he can revert only to his state of simple innocence away from the big wheel which turns the world. At the beginning of the book Paul is taken out of the state when he is unjustly sent down from the college; he then suffers a succession of other injustices, largely at the hands of 'Metropolitan Smart set', which he enters first by spending a `very modern night of love', with Margot Baste-Chetwynde. The lesson he learns is that he does not have the powers necessary for survival in the constant frays that constitute life in the modern world, those comic powers that Margot and the unkillable Grim possess, "powers which Waugh explicitly links with Dionsian and anarchic dimension of comedy."[87] Thus the action of the novel takes place in a devised comic universe in which the laws of probability are slightly suspended where special codes of comic fortune and misfortune work, where comedy's wild laws have precedence over hopes, values and ideals.

"The action of the book", says the author's note in *Vile Bodies*, "is laid in the near future, when existing social tendencies have become more marked ... I have assumed a certain speeding up of legal procedure and daily journalism."[88]

Parties, rackets, vices, chatter and jokes are the main ingredients of the novel. The novelist's imagination is more constructive than descriptive. The giddy whirl of *Vile Bodies* snatches up in its dances at least a dozen separate groups of people, each within their own story. "The mass effect of unsteady, extravagant fantasy and sick and squalid reaction is breath-taking. The moralist has looked in, the smell of dust and ashes hangs on the circus air; irony has become less bland, the death's head grims among the roses"[89]. Every now and then Waugh disengages himself from his tale and becomes a commentator, pointing at a social moral, with `Oh bright young people!' But the comments are too infrequent to damage the relevancy of the plot which follows its course, Kaleidoscopic, various and irresistibly funny. Wit, here, seldom flags; situations and persons are flung on the scene with lavish extravagance. "He (author) saunters tranquilly among sudden fortune and catastrophes, love, loss, customs officers ... drunken majors who take these young women as debonair and luckless as himself. He has no more moral sense than anyone else in the book but rather an appealing innocence."[90] The world is urban in which all hopes, values, traditions as well as permanence belong to the past and exist only to be violated. Waugh takes delight in a world where changes occur at an accelerating speed – `faster-faster' – world of motor races, flimsy marriages, brief affairs and parties.

In *Black Mischief* the novelist makes savagery the chief motif. Waugh is not interested so much in analysing a character as in the use of language. Actions, speech and events are his main interests. The story of the novel is set in Abyssinia. It is really a funny fantasia, but several of the characters are quite convincing – the ingenious and aspiring black emperor, the helpful Armenian rascal, the enterprising English Cad, the British and French envoys. There are descriptions of a few London scenes, of rather dreary rivalry and social life, faintly and less gaily recalling *Vile Bodies*, and dealing with many of the same people. All the author's gifts are in evidence unceasing wit, economy in language, quick fire dialogues and a background of absurdity.

The story becomes thrilling when in Matodi everybody is apprehensive of an assault by the enemy. The novelist's imagination creates a real grim picture.

"The darkness pulsed with the drumming of unknown conquerers. In the narrow streets of the city the people were awake-active and apprehensive. Dark figures sped to and fro on further errands, hiding from each other in doorways till the way was empty. In the houses they were packing away bundles in secret places, little hoards of coins and jewellery, pictures and books, ancestral sword hills of fine workmanship ... silk shawls, scent bottles, anything that might attract attention next morning when the city was given to loot..."[91] The victory of Seth is an exhilarating event. Prince Achon's death, immediately after being made the king, is quite ironical. Sometimes the novelist looks into the mind of a person simply to make the work real and convincing, as is illustrated in the case of Seth after his victory.[92]

In *Fanfare* Waugh tells us that *A Handful of Dust* was begun at the end : "I had written a short story about a man trapped in the jungle, ending his days reading Dickens aloud ... then after the short story was written and published, the idea kept working in my mind. I wanted to discover how the prisoner got there, and eventually the thing grew into a study of other sorts of savages at home and the civilised man's helpless plight among them."[93]

In this work Waugh succeeds to create a situation close to tragedy. He does so without sentimentalising his main characters, who are both detestable and real. In their different ways, Beaver, Tony Last and Brenda are all selfish and self-absorbed. Waugh succeeds in making us realize that despite their heartlessness, two of these characters, Tony and Brenda, really suffer. But the tragedy is borne by their son's unfortunate death in a hunting accident.

Thus, though the novel deals with the dealings of civilized barbarians, yet the author is not without compassion for their heartlessness. The innocent talks and simple ideas of child John Andrews make the reader chuckle.[94] The novel also contains appropriate scenes and situations synchronising with the assuring end. The essential method of this work does not greatly differ from the early farces, *Decline and Fall* and *Vile Bodies*. The farce is evident and cruel, and it coexists with an intense pathos. The characters, however, do not have a sufficient degree of humanity to support tragedy. In presenting their inability to do so, Waugh is making a sharp though implicit comment on the empty world of the Lasts and Beavers. The title of the novel comes from *The Waste Land*, and both the denizens of Eliot's unreal city and the characters in Waugh's novels do not have any deep feeling. At the end of the novel farce turns into horror, as we leave Tony Last imprisoned for ever in South American jungle reading aloud Dickens to the recluse, Mr. Todd.

Both Anthony Powell and Evelyn Waugh are satirically interested in the London circles, partly fashionable, partly artistic that had been more cheerfully described and exposed in the early novels of Aldous Huxley. Yet of the two Waugh is more cruel, hysterical and gay. The world Powell is describing is "dull, incurious and barbarous, judged from the outside, but very funny to read about."[95] Much of the matter and method of Anthony Powell's first novel, *Afternoon Man* is caught in the following comically becalmed exchange between Fortheringham, a struggling, drink-hazed journalist, here blindly seeking deeper truths, and William Atwater, the novel's hero who so blankly refuses guidance:

"I am not a religious sort of chap. I don't know about that sort of thing. But there must be something beyond all this sex business."

"Yes."
"You think so."
"Oh yes, quite likely, why not?"
"But what?"
"I can't help."
"You can't."[96]

The *Afternoon Men* is a book of continuously mannered style whose entertaining surface is broken now and then by a brief but clear form of a method which Powell will follow in all his works of the thirties. Fortheringham's insight that there must be something beyond this sex business is central to the novel. The book presents some young people of London society, obsessed with their social and sexual lives. The picture is not without genuine feelings – but Powell's purpose is mainly satiric. Atwater's love for Susan Nunnery is a subject of ridicule. Susan shows that if emotion is outlawed in favour of pleasure and excitement, emotion finally becomes impossible. "No, don't be a bore. I'm tired", she says, fending off Atwater in the taxi whilst returning after dinner. 'A love': it is the rebuke for off-colour social behaviour not for the over-eagerness of a would-be lover. Atwater's search for something substantial and deeper has come to naught in the final scene. The warmth, vitality and feelings prized in Powell's novels are rarley suggested in *Afternoon Man*. And in its offhand way, the book mourns their absence from the characters' lives. The message is reinforced by Atwater's inability to find love with another woman. He pursues a model named Lola in an uncommitted manner. Sex is dull and boring. His affair with Lola ceases without any outburst of strong feelings. His affairs with Harriet Twining, the mistress of his friend Raymond Pringle, an artist, is also a farcical one. Between Atwater's set and that of the working class, a brutally emphatic demarcation exists. This great gulf is typical of Powell's early novels. Most of the working-class characters in the book are flunkeys, and they come in for very rough handling. They may be repulsively ill, like the doormen in V, who has a birth mark on his face; or ugly and ill Ethal chalk who looks anaemic, or the boy in Atwater's museum, who is conditioned and overgrown, with a cauliflower ear; or ugly and stupid like the 'ape-faced dotard' who is at the door at Pringle's art exhibition; or the waiter at Atwater's dinner with Susan whose face was 'furrowed with the minor dishonesties of uncounted years', or the commissionaries outside the club where we first meet Atwater, who look like 'two Shakespearean murderers' minor things from one of the doubtfully ascribed plays whether these cheap, savage views of people are the hero's or the author's is not clear.

Afternoon Men's construction and style catch admirably the mood of drifting inconsequence seen in its characters' lives, Minor characters, such as, the comically nuisance Dr. J. Crutch, and background action (such as boxing) are given sizeable space, without having too much bearing on the main theme. Characters like the American publisher Scheigan, always searching for some impressive party, come and go, providing comic entertainment. Powell is, of course, writing here and in most of his other works about a group which conceals, plays down and even avoids feelings. But feelings cannot be entirely excluded from life, nor have they been from the novel. We are given a credible portrait of a few members of a social group whose failings are special to them, yet which, because these are to do with trivialisation of life, hint at the feelings of men everywhere.

Venusberg too is a love story. Its plot is more conventional than Afternoon Men's. It contains no elaborate pieces of a comic set, and skilfully uses several minor characters in linked roles. Because of symmetry and form, *Venusberg* is an advance on *Afternoon Men*. Lushington, the hero, does get his girl at last, as well as another with whom he occupies the waiting time. But the novel's happy ending emerged out of a sad, farcical accident, and amounts to no rhapsody of fulfilment. The avowals pulsate with compromise.[97] The book's irony is remarkably complicated, beginning with the basic agonies of those who yearn only for love. The narrative method is unemphatic, oblique, dead pan. Rarely does the author seem interested in describing incident with force and immediacy; it is the result that concerns him. Lushington kisses Ortrud for the first time in their outing. On a boat. This is a significant moment. Ye, we are given no details of what actually happened, nor of Lushington's feelings at the time; there is only mention of it by Ortrud.[98] Even when she goes to his cabin, and they make love, a deliberate abstractness in the few sentences of description indicates a lack of urgency and passion. We are told that Lushington felt as if he had been carried unexpectedly off his feet. And we need to be told of it; we have seen no evidence of such turmoil for ourselves. The book's climax – the shooting of Ortrud and Da Costa – is recounted to Lushington, sometimes after the event by Pope and two other minor characters. It would not have been difficult – might even have been dramatic – for Powell to have left Lushington actually see the shooting and so provide an eye-witness account. But Powell does not seek such an impact. Some might argue that "his technique is self-protection only, enabling him to include the material of melodrama while disguising it with the soft pedal."[99] We feel as inability of the style to cope with the action. But the flash-back treatment of the killings does come off. It has its own drama and suspense. Lushington is awakened out of a nightmare by a telephone call from Pope and told that there has been a serious, unspecified accident.

As a character, Lushington has possibly even less definition than Atwater. About his appearance we learn no more than he has 'a pink and white face'. We are not told much directly about his personality. Of course, in a book whose theme is that men are creatures of circumstance there would be little place for a hero bursting with decisiveness. Lushington, on the whole, is someone to whom things happen, not who makes them happen. He is also, of course, an ironic observer and listener. Passive qualities are implied. The unemphatic portrait of Lushington is well compensated by the vividness and complexity of other characters.

This novel provides a surprising advance in Powell's creation of people. Even caricatures like Pope and Bobel have some stature and poignancy. It is however, in Ortrud that we may see the chief development. Sexually, arrogance, coquettishness, vulnerability and a touch of doom combine marvellously in her, creating a far more credible, beguiling and complex woman than Susan Nunnery in *Afternoon Men*. She has no equal in Powell's other novels. Powell shows, too, the attractive gift of producing now and then some piece of remarks sparkling with insight: "Lushington noticed Count Bobel dancing with an elderly woman, who showed by her demeanour that she was paying for the evening's entertainment."[100] Lastly it is his skill that works throughout his work.

Zouch, the hero of *From A View To A Death* is not like Atwater and Lushington. He represents only a partial turn towards the dynamic hero. Powell shifts the narrative between several groups of characters and Zouch, and his viewpoint disappears for sizeable stretches. And this loss of allegiance to one character makes Zouch a more complicated hero than his predecessors. He is certainly no superman. "He has about him the glint of low-level creative talent – he is a painter of `bright, hopeless portraits' – and brings an occasional feel of intelligence to a milieu where craftiness and aggression are more customarily the chief product of male thought."[101] He occasionally seems genuinely inspired during a love affair, but these decent feelings are swiftly drowned by self-interest.

Vernon Passenger is a superman, a little irresolute behind the apparantly egomaniac exterior. He is possibly more sensitive than Zouch, the artist. Passenger may be an unwilling country gentleman; but when threatened, he will defend himself and his position furiously. Passenger provides a link to the general thesis of Powell's novels that pretension, ambition and role-playing suppress the human essence of people; reduce them, and take away their natural decency and warmth.

Lacking in a consistent method of presentation, the opening chapter of this book is a little feverish for comic effect. Confronted within a few pages with the deranged Major Fosdick, his two clownish sons: Joseph and Torquill, the highted, unstable oprhans, and grandiosely self-obsessed Mrs. Banden, we may wonder if the author knows where he is going. And this doubt continues till quite late, when Zouch's situation takes on a more urgent and compelling tone:

> "The early sections seem designed more like clever, very sharp, witty sketches than the organised stages of a novel,

> and may remind us of Powell's affection for the portraits, often of eccentrics...."[102]

The surface stories of *Agents and Patients* and *What's Becoming of Waring* are almost inconsequential. Blore Smith is the hero of *Agents and Patients*. Maltravers and Chipchase are the two other interesting figures in the story. Significantly we hear, though very briefly, references to the contemporary economic depression. Motives centre not on class but economics for a change, whom, finally, Maltravers picks two knaves out of a pack of cards and throws them across the table. Powell is offering a metonymic comment on his and Chipchase's roles. They represent shallowness and self-obsession. They do it too well and bring degree of aridity to the book. The description of events as they occur tends to be less important than the placing of them in the overall scheme. It is one of the novelist's objectives to convey the flavour and freshness of a moment and possibly not the chief objective. "As a result, he needs a specially devised style ... it is a style which rarley strives for narrative pace, and which may down-play and blur the impact, edge and immediacy of events as they happen."[103] The scenes can be called compositional scenes that set the pattern of life and its texture, that present or help define the values examined in the novel. The novel, like any other extended work of art, acquires a rhythm which is created by repetition and variation of activities or situations throughout.

Although *What's Becoming of Waring* reveals an interest and craft in pure story-telling, here it would be wrong to say that Powell follows the conventional requirements of a plotted novel. On the face of it, he has written a mystery story about an author who conceals his private life, and who, as it turns out has good reasons for his behaviour. The novel is capable of light weight exercise and represents a pause in Powell's progress.

George Orwell's fictions like Greene's combine strong, even obsessive, personal preoccupations with direct social observations. In the novel *Coming Up For Air*, Orwell's middle-aged, middle class hero, George Bowling, takes a few days' holiday from his nagging wife and the dull suburb where he lives. He goes to the village of Lower Binfield, where he had enjoyed the pleasures of rural life as a boy, and where he had enjoyed the pleasures of rural life as a boy, and where he hopes to recapture the spirit of his youth. But Lower Binfield, he finds, has been quite spoilt; built ones, modernised, and turned into yet one more expense of uniform semi-suburbia.[104]

George Bowling is very much a vehicle for Orwell's vision of English life, as Bowling looks at the town, the factory and the bombers.[105] *Coming Up For Air* (1939) published just before the outbreak of war in 1939, is both a farewell to the thirties and an anticipation of the war of the forties. It is Orwell's masterpiece. There is clumsiness in its construction and lack of cohesion in its central character. The author is too intrusive; he lifts the mark too openly for us to be able to delude ourselves for long.[106] George Bowling's evocation of the part is a catalogue of bare personal experiences, with little or no figurative elaboration.[107]

The metonymic technique is used throughout the book. Boyhood, for instance, is evoked thus:

"It's a kind of strong, rank feeling, a feeling of knowing everything and feeling nothing, and it's all bound up with breaking rules and killing things. The white dusty roads, the hot sweaty feeling of one's clothes, the smell of fennel and wild peppermint, the dirty words, the sour stink of the rubbish dump, the taste of the fizzy lemonade and the gas that made our belch, the stamping on the young birds, the feel of the fish straining on the line – it was all part of it."[108]

It is evident that Orwell's avoidance of metaphors is because he is using as his narrator an ordinary sort of man to whom any fine writing of the Proustian kind would be quite unsuitable. There is in fact a mythopoeic, metaphorical level in his works, but it is concealed under the prosaic surface. As a child, George tells us, he had a passion for fishing, a pursuit which for him symbolises the healthier state of culture and society in the pre-World War I days; 'fishing is somehow typical of that civilisation.'[109]

The way things happen sum up George Bowling's rueful, stoical pessimistic attitude towards life, an attitude that the realistic novel is well adopted to express:

> "Life as a sequence of accidents, a plot without a Providence directing it, a chain of local cause and effect, the general pattern of which can only be seen in retrospect, when it is too late to do anything about it."[110]

George takes his girl friend, Elsie into the grounds of Binfield House. He leaves her for a while and goes to have a look at a Carp pool. He returns to Elsie and they have sex for the first time. When he goes back to lower Binfield some twenty-five years later, hopefully carrying a newly purchased fishing rod, he finds that the grounds of the old house have been turned into a middle-class housing estate and that the Cap pond has become a rubbish dump. "I'd learned the lesson all right. Fat men of forty-five cannot go fishing. That kind of fishing does not happen any longer, it's just a dream, there'll be no more fishing this side of the grave."[111] Behind this story there is a visible but faint outline of a myth. The carp-filled pool in the heart of the wilderness is a kind of paradise, sacred and innocent, from which the hero is expelled by a double fall into social conformity and sexuality, a paradise which he is unable to regain. George attributes historical connotations to fishing – the very idea of sitting all day under a willow tree beside a quiet pool belongs to a time before the war.

The lower middle class hero is not allowed to introspect and analyse his own condition, for it is precisely the lack of ability to 'totalise', and so actively transcend his situation that lies at the heart of his problem. "He is intelligent enough to react correctly, but not to perceive the whole condition of which, for his author, he is merely an interesing symptom."[112]

Orwell's failure as a novelist is the emergence of his efforts to write, "... in accord with the symbolist manner, misguided because the assumptions of symbolism were intellectually and temperamentally uncongenial to him. The symbolist technique that he endeavoured to use were thoroughly incomapatible with his real concerns as a novelist, that is to say with the stories that he wanted to tell and the effect upon the reader that he wanted to achieve."[113]

Miss Elizabeth Bowen is at home in a world with tradition of space and privilege. She has a story of the 'upper class' to tell, and tells it on the whole in what strikes the ordinary reader as a "sound, old fashioned way". Her interest in experimentation shows itself more in the shaping of paragraphs and sentences, the freshening up of the language, than in the structure of the novel as a whole. Her most popular novel *The Heat Of The Day*, is a study of London life during the war, in the days of great German air raids; and it evokes the tense, exalted atmosphere of that period better than any other book. Its story seems almost to be a dramatic one. It is of a woman (a lady in the old sense) who discovers that her lover is a traitor and who is blackmailed by a Government secret agent, who offers to spare the lover, if, as a reward, the lady will yield herself to him. Miss Bowen has erected a living structure of words which allows us to grasp not only a particular scene at a particular time, but a general pattern running through the English life. No character in the novel is made wholly hateful. We are shown enough of the unhappy family background of Robert, the traitor, to realise that what has led him into a terrible and fatal course of action is not any real evil in his nature, but rather a disgust at what he conceives to be the purely commercial, purely materialistic, purely sordid and empty atmosphere of English life. Even for the Government secret agent, who appears both to be neglecting his duty and to be making a most caddish use of his power, we feel sorry. He is the kind of men who has efficiency without personality, usefulness without joy. Nobody will ever love him, he will never be happy in any personal relationship, even as a menace to the heroine's happiness, he is strangely without colour or impact. Robert, the unfortunate hero saves the situation by committing suicide. But of a kind of pity, the heroine is still willing to let the secret agent spend the night with her; but love was what he wanted, and love, he now realises, he will never get; so he retreats into the drab everyday danger and routine of his life. The heroine herself is one of the most attractive characters in recent English fictions, a person whose traditional kindness and decency is bewildered by the queer inner twistedness of the two men she has to deal with. The portrait of the heroine's son is a wonderfully vivid and attractive portrait. He embodies in the rather sad and troubled world of the story, the spirit of hope.

Elizabeth Bowen is a highly conscious artist who has evolved over the year, "... a prose style that has the elaboration, the richness of texture, the allusiveness of poetry, a prose as carefully wrought, as subtle in its implications, as that of Henry James in his last phase. She has, too, an intense awareness of, and sensitivity to, place and weather to the living character of the houses, for example, and the indefinable yet readily palpable relation set up between them and the people who dwell in them."[114] Her characters are always people living in particular places during particular seasons and in particular climatic conditions; and she uses her settings in place and time symbolically, to further our responses to the characters that move in them. We remember the brilliant opening scene of *The Death of The Heart*, of Ana Quayne and her friend the novelist at Quentin walking in Regent's Park. However, it is more than a vivid description of a winter scene in London. The frozen lake in Regent's Park connotes the frozen heart of Anna Quayne. The tragedy here is the unfortunate destiny that awaits, fastidious people, weighing most heavily on the weak, upon helpless children and adolescents. The young girl Portia, immersed in solitude, looks around in vain for the affection of which she is desperately in need. But she meets only indifference, hypocrisy, conformism, stupidity, and egoism. Her primary function in the novel is revelatory, enabling us to detect poverty of emotion.

Elizabeth Bowen is careful to avoid taking sides. She does not intervene. Perfectly clear-sighted, detached, and impartial, she shuns advocacy no less than lamentation and recrimination.

C.P. Snow gives us 'some insight into society', by relating the stories of several individuals over a period of time, roughly 1920 to 1950. Snow follows the moral growth of Lewis Eliot, the narrator of these stories, as he experiences the struggle for power, both private and public. Each novel can be separately read, but they are all closely linked, not only by their common themes, but by the persons, incidents, and places used in the narration. Eliot's presence is of course the main connecting link. He is more than a narrator. As an observer, Snow is accurate and painstaking rather than sensitive. He has little success in conveying any mood or atmoshphere which does not fall within the reflective sensibility of Lewis Eliot; so that between us and the portrayal there is a certain remoteness. But the accuracy is convincing:

> "He was propounding the normal foreign office view that, since the amount of material was large, it was the sensible thing to distribute it in small portions, so that no one should be quite left out, we should thus lay up credit in days to come. The extreme alternative view was to see nothing but the immediate benefit to the war, get a purely military judgment, and throw all this material there without any side-glances. There was a whole spectrum of shades between the two, but on the whole Edgar tended to be isolated in that company and had to work very hard for small returns. It was so that day. But he was surprisingly effective in committee; he was not particularly clever, but he spoke with clarity, enthusiasm, pertinacity and above all weight. Even among sophisticated men, weight counted immeasurably more than subtlety or finesse."[115]

This social documentation is only one aspect of Snow's novels. Into each account of public events in his novels Snow interweaves a personal story. But the private histories are the least successful parts of the these novels. Snow's powers of characterisation is limited chiefly to speech-style, and very often amounts to little more than a few typcial phrases. The novels are very thin in their physical and emotional content. The various events, considered apart from the local use that Eliot makes of them, resolve into mere aggregate of social-documentary details. Eliot's morality dominates the novels, becomes in fact the felt morality of the novelist. The novelist of social conscience is not near here, and is so static that Snow defeats his own purpose.

NOTES AND REFERENCES

1. Harwick, Elizabeth -- Reflection on Fiction, *New York* Review of Books, 13 Feb. 1969, p. 50.
2. Quoted by Lodge, David – *The Novelist At the Crossroads*, Routledge and Kegan Paul (London), 1971, p. 25.
3. *Ibid*., p. 61.
4. *Ibid*., p. 97.
5. Manners, Penelope, J. -- *Novels of To-day*, University of London Press Ltd., 1967 (pp. 22-27).
6. *Times Literary Supplement* -- Graham Greene In Retrospect, London University Press, 1972, p. 121.
7. *Ibid*., p. 124.
8. *Ibid*., p. 124.
9. Atkins, John -- *Graham Greene*, Calder & Boyars (London), p. 19.
10. Greene, Graham -- *Stamboul Train*, 1974, William Heinemann Bodley Head (London), p. 198.
11. *Ibid*., p. 48.
12. Atkins, John, *op. cit*., p. 36.
13. *Op. cit*., 40.
14. Greene, Graham -- *England Made Me*, Harmondsworth, Penguin. Books (London), 1977, p. 29.
15. *Ibid*., p. 133.
16. *Ibid*., p. 122.
17. *Ibid*., p. 17.
18. Atkins, John – *op. cit*., pp. 65-66.
19. *Op. cit*., p. 68.
20. Greene, Graham -- *A Gun For Sale*, Harmondsworth, Penguin Books (London), 1977, p. 145.
21. *Ibid*., p. 131.
22. *Ibid*., p. 67.
23. Atkins, John -- *Graham Greene* (1970), Calder & Boyars (London), pp. 214-15.
24. Greene, Graham – *Brighton Rock* (1977), Penguin Books, Harmondsworth, (London), p. 90.
25. Greene, Graham – *The Confidential Agent*, Harmondsworth, 1962, pp. 42-48.
26. Greene, Graham – *The Lawless Roads* (1955), William Heinemann Ltd. (London), Authors note.
27. *Ibid*., p. 15.
28. *Ibid*., p. 24.

29. *Ibid.*, p. 41.
30. *Ibid.*, p. 90.
31. Atkins, John, *op. cit.*, p. 183.
32. *Op. cit.* p. 71.
33. Wall, Stephen – Aspects of the Novel *The Twentieth Century*, edited by Bernard Bergonzi, Barria and Jenkins (London), 1970, p. 228.
34. Isherwood, Christopher – *Goodbye To Berlin*, The Hogarth Press, 1960, Introductory chapter.
35. Isherwood, Christopher – *op. cit.*, pp. 208-213.
36. Rotha, Paul – *The Fiction Till Now*, with an additional section by Richard Griffith, 1949, rpt New York : Twyne Publishers, Inc. 1963, pp. 254-56, 257-709.
37. Isherwood, Christopher – *Christopher And His Kind*, Eyre Methuen Ltd. (London), 1976, p. 141.
38. *Ibid.*, p. 141.
39. *Ibid.*, p. 142.
40. *Ibid.*, p. 143.
41. Isherwod, Christopher – *Mr. Norras Changes Trains*, 1956, The Hogarth Press Ltd. (London), p. 59.
42. Piazza, Paul – *Christopher Isherwood*, Columbia University Press, New York, 1978, p. 119.
43. Spender, Stephen – *World Within World*, p. 109.
44. Personal Communication received by Leon Surmelian from Christopher Isherwood, printed in *Techniques of Fiction Writing : Measure and Madness*, New York, Actor Books, 1968, p. 81.
45. Isherwood, Christopher – *Christopher And His Kind*, 1976, Eyre Methuen & Co. Ltd., pp. 44-45.
46. Isherwood, Christopher – *Goodbye to Berlin*, Hogarth Press, 1960, p. 19.
47. Isherwood, Christopher – *Christopher And His Kind*, 1976, Eyre Methuen & Co. Ltd., p. 54.
48. *Op. cit.*, p. 59.
49. Isherwood, Christopher – *Goodbye to Berlin*, Hogarth Press, 1960, pp. 19-20.
50. *Ibid.*, p. 67.
51. *Ibid.*, p. 68.
52. *Ibid.*, p. 91.
53. *Ibid.*, p. 180.
54. *Ibid.*, p. 198.
55. *Ibid.*, p. 215.
56. Warren, Austin – The Nature and Modes of Narrative Fiction, – *Perspectives On Fiction*, ed. Jane L. Calderwood and Harold E. Toliver, New York, Oxford University Press, London, 1968, p. 73.
57. Focus One, ed. by Rajan and A. Pearse (London), Dennis Dobson, 1945, pp. 7-65.

58. Woodcock, George -- Kafka and Rex Warner, Focus One, pp. 59-65.
59. Warner, Rex -- *The Professor* (London), Lowe and Brydone Printers Ltd., N.W., 1946, p. 241.
60. *Ibid*., pp. 242-43.
61. Curry, Elizabeth, A.R. -- Rex Warner and Modern Tragedy, Theme and Method in the allegorical novels of Rex Warner, Dissertation Graduate School, University of Wisconsin Ann. Arbov, Michingan Universtiy Micro Films, 1963 -- *Ibid*. Dissertation abstracts XXIII, 1964, pp. 3370-71.
62. *Ibid*., pp. 65-66.
63. Warner, Rex -- *The Professor* (London), Lowe and Brydone Printers Ltd., N.W. 10, 1946, p. 131.
64. *Ibid*., p. 166.
65. *Ibid*., p. 124.
66. Warner, Rex -- *The Wild Goose Chase*, The Bodley Head 1944 (London), p. 39.
67. *Ibid*., p. 52.
68. *Ibid*., p. 53.
69. *Ibid*., p. 67.
70. *Ibid*., p. 79.
71. *Ibid*.
72. *Ibid*., p. 96.
73. *Ibid*., p. 100.
74. *Ibid*., p. 135.
75. *Ibid*., p. 162.
76. *Ibid*., p. 215-16.
77. *Ibid*., p. 230.
78. *Ibid*., p. 216.
79. *Ibid*., p. 316.
80. *Ibid*.; p. 284.
81. *Ibid*., p. 378.
82. *Ibid*., p. 441.
83. Political Novels -- *Indian Journal of English Studies II*, 1961, pp. 91-107.
84. Macaulay, Rose -- Evelyn Waugh -- *Writers of To-day*, ed. Denys Val Baker (London), Sidgwick and Jackson Limited, 1948, p. 135.
85. Waugh, Evelyn -- *Decline and Fall*, William Heinemann Ltd. (London), 1977, p. 101.
86. *Ibid*., p. 108.
87. Bradbury, Malcolm -- The Novel In the 1920s -- *The Twentieth Century*, edited by Bernard Bergonzi, 1970, p. 216.
88. Waugh, Evelyn -- *Vile Bodies*, Authors note (London), Chapman and Hall, 1930.

89. Macaulay, Rose -- *op. cit.*, p. 138.
90. *Ibid.*, p. 138.
91. Waugh, Evelyn -- *Black Mischief*, 1977, William Heinemann Ltd. (London), p. 143.
92. *Ibid.*, p. 206.
93. Waugh, Evelyn -- *Fan Fare,* Quoted by Frederick J. Stopp -- *Portrait of an Artist* -- Evelyn Waugh Chapman and Hall Ltd., 1958, p. 90.
94. Waugh, Evelyn -- *A Handful of Dust*, Harmondsworth, Penguin Books (London), 1977, p. 83.
95. Pritchett, V.S. -- *The Working Novelist*, Chatto and Windus (London), 1965, p. 173.
96. Powell, Anthony -- *Afternoon Men*, Heinemann (London), 1974, p. 63.
97. *Ibid.,* -- *Venusberg*, Heinemann (London), 1974, p. 192.
98. *Ibid.*, pp. 34-35.
99. Tucker, James -- *The Novels of Anthony Powell*, 1976, The Bowering Press Limited, Plymouth, p. 23.
100. *Ibid.*, p. 25.
101. *Ibid.*, p. 28.
102. *Ibid.*, p. 30.
103. *Ibid.*, p. 103.
104. Orwell, George -- *Coming Up For Air*, Harmondsworth, 1967, p. 80.
105. *Ibid.*, p. 90.
106. Legouis, Emile and Cazamian, Louis -- *History of English Literature* (London), 1964, J.M. Deut and Sons Ltd., p. 1401.
107. Orwell, George -- *op. cit.*, p. 33.
108. *Op. cit.*, p. 65.
109. *Op. cit.*, p. 74.
110. Lodge, David -- *The Modes of Modern Writing*, Edward Arnold (London), 1979, p. 192.
111. Orwell, George -- *op. cit.*, p. 105.
112. Eagleton, Terry -- *Exiles And Emigres*, 1970, Chatto and Windus (London), p. 75.
113. Alldritt, Keith -- *The Making of George Orwell*, Edward Arnold (London), 1969, p. 4.
114. Allen, Walter -- *Tradition and Dream*, Phoenix House (London), 1964, p. 188.
115. Snow, C.P. -- *The Light And The Dark*, Harmondsworth, 1964, pp. 333-4.

FIFTH CHAPTER

TRADITION AND NEW TRENDS

The immediate predecessors of the novelists of the thirties can be conveniently grouped under two heads – the modernists like James Joyce, Virgina Woolf and Dorothy Richardson, and the Edwardian realists like H.G. Wells, Arnold Bennett and John Galsworthy. The two are clearly distinct from each other, but there is also a defineable continuity in technique between them that leads back eventually to the classical nineteenth century realism. The novelists of the thirties adopted the realistic technique but in them there is informational saturation of the Edwardians. They were to mere copyists of the art of the Edwardian realists. The 'materialist' battle cry of Arnold Bennett had become subdued by the criticism of Virginia Woolf. "His (Bennett's) acquiescence ... in the values and assumptions of a capitalist class-society, is clearly not embraced by the nineteen-thirties novelists."[1] The novelists like Orwell, Isherwood and Graham Greene had learnt much from the modernists who were their immediate predecessors. They had learnt to replace a plethora of factual details by a much more artfully selective use of documentary ones.

The fictions of Orwell, Isherwood and Greene like the fictions of George Eliot, Thackeray and Jane Austen, is based on the assumption that there is a common phenomenal world that may be described by the methods of empirical history; although to the latter writers what this world means is much more problematical. From this assumption is derived their kind of novel form : "...The blending of public and private experience, inner and outer history conveyed through a third-person past tense authorial mode of narration, or the autobiographical-confessional mode."[2]

The post-World War II period has, indeed, been dubbed as an age of reaction against experiment in English novels,[3] as though it had not occurred much earlier. The reaction had actually set in before the war. Experimentation in English novels was a phenomenon of the twenties, and reaction against it had set in towards the end of that decade itself. In *Lions and Shadows*, published in 1938 but written much earlier Christopher Isherwood described and disowned the artistic assumptions with which he had composed his first novel, *All the Conspirators* (1928) when experienment was still fashionable:

"I thought of the novel (as I hoped to learn to write it) essentially in terms of technique, of conjuring, of chess. The novelist, I said to myself, is playing a game with his reader; he must continually amaze and deceive him, with tricks, with traps, with extraordinary gambits, with sham climaxes, with false directions.... I saw it (novel) as something compact, and by the laws of its own nature, fairly short. In fact my models were not novels at all, but detective stories, and the plays of Ibsen and Tchekov. *War and Peace*, which I read for the first time a few months later, disarranged and altered my ideas."[4] Tolstoy's realism still seemed valid and viable to a young writer in the thirties.[5]

George Orwell deplores the indifference to contemporary reality displayed by the writers of the ninteen-twenties and their obsession with form to the neglect of content: "Our eyes are directed to Rome, to Byzantium, to Montparnasse, to Mexico, to the Etruscans, to the subconscious, to the solar plexus – to ever where except to places where things are actually happening. When one looks back at the twenties, nothing is queerer than the way in which every important event in Europe escaped the notice of the English intelligentsia.... In 'cultured' circles art-for-art's sake extended practically to a worship of the meaningless. Literature was supposed to consist solely in the manipulation of words. To judge a book by its subject matter was the unforgivable sin, and even to be aware of its subject matter was looked on as a lapse of taste."[6]

Graham Greene, though of different ideology, joins the chorus of Isherwood and Orwell, as Lehmann, the literary historian of this period opines, "... as emphatically as Pritchett or Isherwood, he has pursued speed in dialogue, simplicity in prose and colloquialism in his diction.... And he is as interested as any of the 'Birmingham School' in the ordinary urban and suburban scene of working lives. He has, in fact, exactly the same claim to be called a realist as they – and can make squalor small as efficiently as Orwell."[7]

Graham Greene's essay on Francois Mauriac is particularly interesting, for it sheds light on the changing trends of English novel after the death of Henry James :

"After the death of Henry James a disaster overtook the

> English novel .... For with the death of James the religious sense was lost to the English novel, and with the religious sense, went the sense of the importance of the human act."[8]

Greene reacted against the modernist or symbolist mode of writing for two reasons : One was literary and was shared by most of the literary men of his time. They deplored the emphasis on individual consciousness and sensibility in modernist writing because it seemed to dissolve and deny, the empirical reality of the 'visible world'; and the other reason was moral and religious, and was largely peculiar to Greene and Waugh. C.P. Snow, like Greene also felt repulsion towards experimental novels. His opposition was due to the fact that the essence of the method of Joyce, Virginia Woolf and Dorothy Richardson, "was to represent brute experience through the moments of sensation' and it "effectively cut out precisely those aspects of the novel where a living tradition can be handed on. Reflection had to be sacrificed; so did moral awareness; so did the investigatory intelligence."[9]

The central tradition of the English novel, came down through the Victorians and Edwardians. It was temporarily diverted by the modernist experimentalism, but was subsequently restored by Orwell, Isherwood, Greene, Waugh, Powell and C.P. Snow.

The thirties was not conducive to vigorous imaginative activity, and besides many of the writers who had distinguished themselves during the previous decade, were in one sense or another removed : Lawrence died in 1930, and Forster had written his last important novel – *A Passage to India* – in 1924; Virginia Woolf was in decline and James Joyce had become arcane. Eliot and Yeats were still achieving great works, but they now dominated the skyline rather than the immediate scene. The younger generation of new talent who came to replace them did not match either the originally or the distinction of their ideas. However, it is a fallacy to assume that the interest of a period depends on its production of masterpieces or at least works of imaginative originality. It may also depend on how far a writer belongs to an age, and how far he is a part of the age, and how authentically he presents his age. The work of George Orwell, Graham Greene and Evelyn Waugh is in its total effect pessimistic. The picture of the human situation that emerges from the novels of these writers is in the last degree one of despair. They write about a society which manifests all the classic aspects of decadence; what is significant is that the writers themselves partake overwhelmingly of the values of the society they depict. "They are not simply writers describing decadence, they are decadent writers."[10]

Broadly speaking what happens in the nineteen-twenties is the redistribution of the forces of modernism in the face of a different kind of world, a post-war and modernised world, and a consequent challenge to its capabilities and resources. We usually take modernism to mean the internal stylization of the arts, the distortion of the familiar surface of observed reality, and the disposition of artistic content according to the logic of metaphor, form or symbol, rather than according to a linear logic taken from history or story. The 'modern' writer is concerned not so much with revolution in the world as with revolution in the word. But in the thirties fiction becomes, "a record of recent events with more intimacy and freedom than journalism .... It tells you a great deal, and vividly about the lives of all kinds of people, most of them wage-earners, in different parts of the world, plasterers, sailors, Vienna socialists, men smuggling arms into Spain, front door convassers in Paris, and so on. In brief, all these stories are documented."[11] Some of the writers have used the documentary facts as spring board to leap from reality into imagination and they form the majority. In selecting, shaping and arranging incidents to make a story instead of asking, 'Is this necessary to the design I am making in my imagination?' have asked "Is this true to life, does this stick to the facts?..."[12] They all, however, have adjusted their art to the changing order, faced in new directions, suggested new patterns of experience, or generally, became in any important sense, prophets or pioneers.[13]

We actually find in the fiction of this decade : "an insistence upon the merely painful, an utter joylessness – devoid of passion, even its negations. Some writers come to no sort of decent terms with life, make no sort of peace."[14] The novelists are less confident of the glorious possibilities of man and feel more at home when making studies of the ordinary, the weak, the morbid, or even the ignoble. They appear to be more often impressed by the pettiness than by the magnificence of man, by the futility of his efforts than by the splendour of his aspirations. They distrust the grand passions. Pessimism which seethes in the lives of the characters makes impossible the novel as a great work. "Pessimism makes of all idealism at best a gloomy consolation, a mere whistling in the dark."[15]

With the rapid growth of a large middle-class reading public, however, and the accompanying rise of prose fiction, literature came to dwell more and more on the plains of every day life. Victorian novelists treated more or less realistically the lives of average middle-class folks. But the range of their realism was limited. They seldom followed their hero into his work-a-day, and the lower classes they introduced as comic figures or occasionally as objects for the exercise of fine sentiments. But the hero in the fiction of the thirties is commonly a proletarian who is treated honestly, sympathetically and without condescension, in the conviction that the ruin of the ordinary man is a poignant and a noble theme like the spectacular downfall of the great. The social setting was somewhat chaotic, and the novelists were immortalizing the chaos. "They did not turn their backs on their society nor seek surcease from its ills in a dream world. They did not destroy the realistic spirit or even aim to destroy it."[16] The hero is likely to be less an agent or spokesman than a patient who always wishes to die, his story less a drama than a case history, his world a kind of psychopathic world:

> "There is in general a tendency in poetry as in fiction, to mistake seeing life minutely for seeing it whole, to blur the main outlines of experience while exploring its shadows or exhibiting its many bright or curious bits, to make these subtle studies an end in themselves and not bring them to bear on the major choices, actions and conflicts that organise human lives."[17]

In the thirties the novelists were aware of a world breaking up around them, and in their own several ways they searched for some myth with which to express the unprecedented crisis of their time. Some also sought a way in which they could effect a solution. The novelists of the twenties had concentrated on technique because they had no urgency of conviction, but those of the thirties felt that the theme was more important than the technique, and at the same time they had an urgent desire to be understood. No longer did the author delight in the bewilderment of the audience, for he had behind him a cause, and urgently he wished the readers to join on his side.[18] So the novelists in the thirties were a voice interpreting its need, voicing, if never explaining its perplexity, and using a new Colloquial, and supremely unacademic style to figure out the phantoms of uncertainty and horror that lay ahead. "It was a generation of novelists that felt entrapped. In a desire for sympathy it stretched out its hands more frankly than its elders, anxious to feel a communal unity in society..... It had, unfortunately, little knowledge of its own national tradition, and it turned upon the past of England and its present institutions in cheap and inept satire."[19]

From Hardy these novelists inherited a legacy of poetry and architecture; from Henry James a legacy of subtlety and psychological curiosity; from Joyce a rejuvenation of language. But there were two other writers working on a much smaller scale, who also formed part of the background : E.M. Forster and Virginia Woolf. E.M. Forster's influence is clearly perceptible on younger novelists like Chirstopher Isherwood and Elizabeth Bowen.[20]

The novelists of the pre-war generation, Galsworthy Bennet and Wells, shirked the problems arising out of sordid and loathsome anarchism of the capitalist state by laying enormous emphasis on the fabric of things. The novelists of the thirties did not overlook this fact. They peered into the seething souls behind the fabric before presenting it. They were concerned not only with the creation of a new society but with the condition of their own survival. The proletarian novels of this time deal perforce largely with the misery and wretchedness of the poor and their struggle for better life. By their nature they are novels of conflict and bitterness.

Galsworthy wanted to attack his contemporary society but he did not know what to put in place of what he loathed, being himself devoid of all vital values. The trouble with H.G. Wells is that most of his social criticism is as slapdash as his treatment of personal relations in his novels. He has never penetrated to the reality of human relationships. Aldous Huxley also 'as a novelist walks round his characters, pointing out their weaknesses and most obvious absurdities with an almost impish relish but he never really succeeds in getting inside them."[21] Conrad and D.H. Lawrence wrote about men and women as in the last resort isolated from society, alone against fate, chance or the sea. The novel of the thirties aim at, "not the abolition of individuality, but the creation of a society in which the individual will for the first time stand out in his true proportions as the master of his environment. It will be anti-capitalist...."[22] and an advance upon the bourgeois novel, with all its shallow cynicism and sterile metaphysical conflicts, in so far as it contributes to an understanding of human relationships. It is indeed only on the basis of a new humanism that the novelists of this period tried to restore to the novel that richness and vigour which characterize the finest productions of human mind.

The novel of the thirties records the illusion that snobbery generates, and tries to penetrate to the truth which, as the novel assumes, lies hidden beneath all the false appearances. Money, war, unemployment, snobbery, the ideal of status – all these become in themselves the objects of fantasy, the support of love, freedom, charm and power. The novelist's eyes are "not only on the external world but also on the audience, which he hopes to delight or instruct, giving it either what it wants or what he thinks it needs."[23] Thus the novel becomes a union of the fictional and empirical, representational and illustrative. The novelist is not a mere recorder of births, deaths and marriages. "He is concerned with the mystery of words and their music, and with events as representing something larger than our social comprehension can envisage."[24] The novelists "applied novel to critical purpose, holding it up as a mirror, if only a distorting mirror of their own times."[25] Joyce Cary, Elizabeth Bowen, Graham Greene, Isherwood and others made their novels "a special kind of mirror that reflects not merely the external features of the age but also its inner face, its nervous system, the coursing of its blood and the unconscious promptings and conflicts which sway it."[26] They have their command of life, thier grasp of character, their knowledge of human affections and manners ; they have a certain range and strength and depth; we can penetrate their minds and detect the ideas that ruled there. Men and women of Rex Warner represent often spiritual and social forces which are more powerful and significant than a simple individual in his ordinary relationships. And so they are exaggerated often almost out of recognition and set in an environment where fantastic lights and darkness throw certain objects into unnatural relief, or totally submerge others. As we observe in Dickens and Dostoevsky a passion for dreams, visions, grotesqueness and madness; so also in the novelists of the thirties these became prominent features. There is however no "psychic distance between the author and his readers as such, making sure that a work is neither "overdistanced" nor "under-distanced". The novel does not seem improbable, artificial, empty or absurd, and the reader finds no difficulty in responding to it. The work is not underdistanced in the sense that it is not too personal and hence it can be enjoyed as art. But there is no energy, variety and abundance which characterise the very greatest novels. Language in symbolical novels of the thirties in its nature metaphorical, being largely composed of vital metaphors.

The realistic novel appear to be perfectly obvious; they seem to require no interpretation. We do not read them as documents although they have documentary elements in them. Certain feelings are aroused in us by the novels, and we find that these feelings are relevant to the life that we know. But the work does not impress as being a work of art, a whole without complexity, sufficient achieved form. Characters, objects, places are recognizable, as similar to those which we actually know.

The novels of the thirties are called "pseudo novels",[27] because most of them are disguised history, rhetorical or autobiographical. But they are good novels in the sense that they are expressions of the author's excitement about life, about experience. They form a recognizable period, and they all reflect, in their varying ways, a recognizable way of life. They attack on the obscurity, allusiveness and elitism of the modernist-symbolist tradition. Stephen Spender published a pamphlet called, *The New Realism* in 1939, in which he said that: "... there is a tendency for artists today to turn outwards to reality, because the phase of experimenting in form has proved sterile. If you like, the artist is simply in search of inspiration, having discovered that inspiration depends on there being some ground of understanding between him and his audience about the nature of reality, and on a demand from that audience for what he creates."[28] The result was the formation of a very distinctive and homogeneous period – style, underlying the surface idiosyncracies of personal styles. There was a pronounced swing back from the metaphoric to the metonymic pole of literary discourse.

As has been said in chapter second the decade of the thirties was inevitably heading to the catastrophic war of the Forties and many of the novelists of the thirties had not only a premonition of this catastrophe, they also had their ideas of the ways in which it might be averted. They wanted to convey their premonition and the remedy to as many people as possible through their novels, and found that the documentary or realistic technique to be inadequate for their purpose. They, therefore, adopted the form of allegory, sometimes referred to in the criticism, of the period as 'fable' or 'myth' or 'parable'. They were not romanticists, they were actually realists, but they had to adopt this essentially romantic form because of the exigencies of the time. Violence and distortion in style are a heritage from which there is no escape, although these also cause a marked decline in the quality of the writing. Therefore, many novels of these writers contain stylistic and structural flaws that twenty years earlier would have been regarded as evidence of lack of craftmanship and sheer laziness.

NOTES AND REFERENCES

1. Lodge, David -- *The Modes of Modern Writing*, Edward Arnold, 1979 (London), p. 46.
2. *Ibid.*, p. 47.
3. Rabinowits, Rubin – The reaction against experiment in the English novel; quoted by David Lodge -- *The Modes of Modern Writing*, Edward Arnold, 1979, p. 47.

4. Isherwood, Christopher -- *Lions and Shadows*, Signet edn., 1969 (pp. 159-60).
5. Lodge, David, *op. cit.*, p. 48.
6. Orwell, George -- Inside The Whale, Collected Essays, Journalism and Letters (Harmondsworth, 1970, vol. 1, p. 557).
7. Lehmann, John -- *New Writing In Europe*, Harmondsworth, 1940, p. 134.
8. Greene, Graham -- Collected Essays, 1969, pp. 115-16. Quoted by David Lodge -- *The Modes of Modern Writing*, Edward Arnold, 1979, p. 50.
9. Snow, C.P. -- *Sunday Times*, 27 December, 1953, quoted by Rubin Rabinowitz, *The Reaction Against Experiment In The English Novel*, 1968 (p. 98).
10. Kettle, Arnold -- *An Introduction To The English Novel*, Vol. II, Hutchinson University Library (London), 1967, p. 150.
11. Brophy -- New Fiction -- The Need For More Imagination, *Daily Telegraph*, 20 Oct. 1936, p. 10.
12. *Ibid.*, p.10.
13. Muller, Herbert J. -- *Modern Fiction*, Funk and Wagnads, New York, 1937 (p. xiii).
14. *Ibid.*, p. 29.
15. *Ibid.*, p. 31.
16. *Ibid.*, p. 49.
17. *Ibid.*, pp. 60-61.
18. Evans, B. Ifor -- *English Literature Between The Wars*, Methuen and Co. Ltd., London, 1951, p. 83.
19. *Ibid.*, p. 127.
20. Reed, Henry -- *The Novel Since 1939*, Longman Green, The British Council, 1946, p. 12.
21. Henderson, Philip -- *The Novel Today*, John Lane, The Bodley Head, London, 1936, pp. 118-19.
22. *Ibid.*, p. 185.
23. Scholes, Robert -- *The Nature of Narrative*, Robert Kellong, Oxford University Press, 1968, p. 15.
24. Church, Richard -- *The Growth of the English Novel*, Methuen University Paperbacks (London), 1957 (p. 2).
25. *Ibid.*, p. 173.
26. Allen, Walter -- *Reading a Novel*, Phoenix House, London, 1949, p. 14.
27. Atkins, John -- *Six Novelists Look At Society*, Calder (London), 1977 (p. 11).
28. Spender, Stephen -- *The New Realism*, 1939 (p. 8), quoted by David Lodge, *op. cit.* (p. 190).

CONCLUSION

The nineteen-thirties was not stagnant in the growth of English novels. Although many of the novels of this period were thrillers dealing with crime, adventure and romance, there were quite a few of literary importance also. The latter contributed vitality and force justifying the continuance of the novel as the dominant literary form of the time. Some novelists like Graham Greene poured out their hearts with full throated ease like Keat's nightingale, whereas others like Isherwood, Waugh and Powell proceeded with scientific deliberateness worrying their way between matter and manner. They never trusted their own inspiration.

These English novelists of the thirties did offer a serious criticism of life. They adjusted their art to a changing order, faced in a new direction, suggested a new patterns of experience. They followed their own formulae; and selected and organised their matter according to that formula. They leave us brooding over such burning topics as war, unemployment and slums. They searched out new myths and symbols to express the crude truths of the time.

The novel once again resumed its previous role which was neglected in the twenties, once again experimenting both in narration and the creation of characters. The novelists felt that the theme was more important than the technique. They had a keen desire to be explicit; so, to the bewilderment of the audience they shunned all that was merely delightful. They had a cause, and wished the readers to join in their chorus. They interpreted the need of the people, and voiced their anxiety. They used a new colloquials which was well suited to give an exact expression to the phantoms of uncertainty and horror that lay ahead in the forties. In their novels we notice sordid places where people have to spend their dismal lives, where they are born, where they return tired after a day's work, where they rot without work, where they love and marry, breed children and at last die. Thus these novelists expressed of that section life which was known to them through experiences.

The English novels of the thirties were in fact "an advance upon the contemporary bourgeois novel, with all its shallow cynicism and sterile metaphorical conflicts, in so far as they contributed to a greater understanding of human relationship."[1] Of course only on the basis of a new humanism towards the craving shapes of slum-dwellers and their ilk that these novelists of the thirties could restore to the novel a fresh richness and vigour so necessary for the continuance of an art form. They also imposed a beginning, a middle and an end on the flux of experience to give the novel a more aesthetically satisfying form. In the nineteenth-century novels, we may say, the pull was most strongly towards life; in the early years of the twentieth century, more attention was paid towards craft and convention; in the fictions of the thirties an effort was made to arrive at a balance between the two.

In the thirties the novelists' eyes were not only on the external world but also on the audience, which they hoped to delight as well as instruct. They were the spoksmen of the age; or at least of the most important section of the society, the midddle class. The audience of course was not homogeneous. Intellectually it was divided into the highbrow, middlebrow and lowbrow; and the novelists had to keep this important factor in their minds in order to achieve any degree of success in their efforts. They could not produce double-decker novels; nevertheless they succeeded to draw attention and sympathy from a large segment of their readers. Their reputation is still based on their works done in the thirties.

We can call the fiction of the thirties apocalyptic for it portrays English society on the verge of destroying itself. The novelists chose incidents and situations from common life, and related or described them, as far as possible in a language really used by men. Virginia Woolf has called the writers of this decade, "not Ivory Tower writers", but "Leaning Tower writers", meaning that, "they were still shut up in their own artists' worlds, but had at least realised that worlds were threatened."[3] It was an important gain that the novelists became socially conscious and planted their feet on the earth once more. With the forging of closer bonds between writers and the people, the hope of a deep understanding and support of art on the part of millions who had been indifferent before came to be realised.

Eighteenth century fiction gave a fairly accurate picture of the eighteenth century society. Nineteenth century fiction was less successful in this, for it undervalued industrialism and ignored sex. The early twentieth century fiction was somewhat different in that whereas the picture of the society therein is more or less fictitious accurate, the people of the time could scarcely recognise it as such. The fiction of the thirties reverts to the eighteenth century type and is fairly representative of its generation. The novels of the thirties do not merely instruct, delight, and move, but also embody the myths of the society. They serve as the sophisticated scriptures of an underground religion. The novelists tried to find the appropriate formula to transform their fancies, amusing freaks and bogies into valid symbols of the evils of the society.

It goes without saying that in the thirties there were good poems, good sociological works, brilliant pamphlets but practically no fiction of equal stature. From 1933 onwards the social climate and intellectual preoccupation were not favourable for the creation of great works in fiction. In fact, "it was a time of labels, slogans, and evasions but not a time of good novels which are not written by orthodoxy-sniffers, nor by people who are conscience-stricken about their own unorthodoxy."[5] But the main distinguishing feature of the fiction of the thirties is the realistic depiction of the actual conditions in which the down-trodden lived and laboured. Furthermore the novelists have successfully communicated to the readers the plight of this down-trodden section of humanity in a fast changing socio-political situation. The seedy world of Graham Greene's novels, the obsessed tone of Orwell's novels, and Isherwood's Berlin stories of private hell intermittently dispaly horrid snapshots of the life of these unfortunates.

Some novelists of this decade oscillated between the realistic depiction of the palpable world and fabulation of their contrived worlds through the use of fables, allegories, satire and dystopia. We can mark this oscillation in the fantasies and allegories of Rex Warner's *Wild Goose Chase* and *Aerodrome*, in *Upwards Railway Accident*, in Evelyn Waugh's *Black Mischief* and *Vile Bodies*, and in the fables of Orwell's *Animal Farm* and *Nineteen Eighty-Four*. These novelists in their painstaking attempts aimed through allegories and fables to accurately report the prevalent and political forces and the tensions between them. Graham Greene and Isherwood reconciled these two in their works.

Though the novels of the thirties offered no positive vision of the future yet they effectively revealed the sickness of the present. The novelists adopted potent symbols for the revelation of social mores and malaise. The fog in Dickens's novels is again seen sprawling in the London-legends of Graham Greene. The chaos of an individual's life is the chaos of the age and the novelists of the thirties tried to immortalise this chaos. They could avoid sketching full and lively portraits of their characters, but they could not avoid depicting what was rotten in the society. Some of their characters are nameless and faceless but none of them are phantoms of imagination. They are real common Londoners. Some of them are unidentified hooded hords of the waste land, but we recognise them and feel with them. The action in the novels of the thirties is very thin and sometimes dull and flat. There is no momentous happenings in them. Heroes are mostly neurotic. They are presented indulging in nail biting. They are the present-day Hamlets. They don't inspire but depress us.

Thus the English novels in the thirties presented a fragmented life. The novelists could not give any integrated view of life because the society itself was not stable and homogeneous. The form of the novel was no more conventional than in the immediate past. Some of the novelists followed the surrealistic method to show the fantastic and illogical layers of human mind. Some followed the Kafkesque technique to tell the truth of the time symbolically. They introduced new metaphors and metonymes to make their novels deeper in their meanings. And this saved their novels from the monotony of a documentary work. Most of the novels of the thirties were topical, hence they lost much of their appeal after the thirties; but because some of the novelists were true artists, quite a few of their works are still capable of sustaining our interest. The thrillers of Graham Greene, the Berlin stories of Isherwood, the social comedies of Powell and Waugh, and the political allegories of Rex Warner and George Orwell are still read for their fidelity to life. They are serious criticism of life; and therefore, we do not mind their flatness, dullness and feebleness. They (the novelists) dealt with such unpleasant facts as masturbation, paederasty, intimate family relationship, psychological complex and neurosis. They were not dilettante; they had a serious social purpose to serve. But this does not mean that art was a means of propaganda to them. Though these novelists did not form any school yet many of them were alike in their tastes and temperaments. We still remember them as the social chroniclers like Defoe and Swift. Furthermore, the novelists have successfully communicated to the readers the plight of down-trodden section of humanity in a fast changing socio-political situation.

NOTES AND REFERENCES

1. Henderson, Philip -- *The Novel To-day*, John Lane, The Bodley Head, 1936, p. 188.

2. Allen, Walter -- *The Novel To-day*, 1960, Longmans Green and Co., p. 12.
3. Lehmann, John -- *New Writing in Europe*, Harmondsworth, 1949, p. 142
4. Atkins, John -- *Six Novelists Look At Society*, Calder (London) 1977, p. 251.
5. Wicks, George - *Masters of Modern British Fiction* (p. 378), The Macmillan Company, New York, 1963.

BIBLIOGRAPHY

Allen, Walter. *The English Novel*, Harmondsworth, 1963.

—. *Reading A Novel*, Phoenix House, London, 1949.

—. *The Novel To-day*, rev. ed. London, Green & Co., 1980.

—. *Writers on Writing*, Phoenix House, 1948.

—. *Tradition And Dream*, Phoenix House, London, 1964.

—. Atkins, John. *Graham Greene*, Calder and Boyars (London), 1957.

—. *Six Novelists Look At A Society*, Calder, 1977.

Alldritt, Keith. *The Making of George Orwell*, Edward Arnold, London (1969).

Auden, W. H. *The Dance of Death*, London : The Hogarth Press, 1933.

—. *Forewords and Afterwords*, Faber and Faber, 1973.

Auden & Plumb. 'Preface', *Oxford Poetry*, 1926, Oxford : Basil Blackwed.

Adams, Robert Martin. *After Joyce*, New York Oxford University Press, 1977.

Allot, Miriam. *Novelists On the Novel*, London, 1959.

Beach, Joseph Warner. *The Twentieth Century Novel*, 1965, India.

Bergonzi, Bernard. *Reading The Thirties*, London : The Macmillan Press Ltd., 1971.

—. *The Twentieth Century*, London : Barrie and Jenkins, 1970.

—. *The Turn of a Century*, Macmillan, London (1970).

—. *The Situation of the Novel*, London: Macmillan (1970).

Burgess, Anthony. *The Novel Now*, London : Faber and Faber, 1971.

Baker, Denys Val, ed. *Writers of To-day*, Sidgwick and Jackson, Limited, 1948.

Bradbury, Malcolm. *Evelyn Waugh* (London), 1964.

Blackmur, R.G. *The Double Agent*, New York, 1935.

Bell, Anne Oliver. *The Diary of Virgina Woolf*, Vol. II, 1978, London: The Hogarth Press.

Boulton, Marjorie. *The Anatomy of the Novel*, Routledge & Kegan Paul (London), 1975.

Bradbury, Malcolm, ed. *The Novel To-day*, Manchester University Press, 1977.

Bowen, Elizabeth. *The House In Paris*, London : Cox and Wyman, 1976.

Booth, W. *The Rhetoric of Fiction*, University of Chicago Press, 1961.

Collins, A.S. *English Literature of the Twentieth Century*, University Tutorial Press, 1967.

Calderwood, Jane L. and Toliver, Harold E., ed. *Perspectives on Fiction*, Oxford University Press, London, 1968.

Curry, Elizabeth A.R. 'Rex Warner and Modern Tragedy', 'Theme and method in the allegorical novels of Rex Warner', Dissertation Graduate School, University of Wisconsin Ann Arbov, Michigan University Micro Films, 1963.

Church, Richard. *The Growth of the English Novel*, London : Methuen & Co. 1957.

—. *Speaking Aloud*, London: Heinemann, 1968.

Collins, Malcolm Muggeridge. *The Thirties* (1930-1940), London : Collins, 1967.

Cavalcade, Noel Coward. *Century Blues*, London : Bloomington, Heinemann, 1932.

Daiches, David. *The Present Age After 1920*, London : Bloomington, Indiana University Press, 1958.

—. *The Novel and the Modern World*, Chicago University of Chicago Press, 1960.

Dobree, Bonamy. *The Lamp and the Lute*, London : Frank Cass and Co. Ltd., 1960.

Davie, Michael, ed. *The Diaries of Evelyn Waugh*, London : Weidenfeld and Nicolson, 1964.

Dyson, A.E. *Between Two Worlds*, London : Macmillan Press, 1972.

Eastman, Max. *The Literary Mind*, New York : Charles Scribner's Sons, 1935.

Eagleton, Terry. *Exiles and Emigres*, London : Chatto and Windus, 1970.

Evans, B. Ifor. *English Literature Between the Wars,* London : Methuen & Co., 1951.

Eisinger, Chester E. *Fiction of the Forties*, The University of Chicago Press, 1965.

Fisher, William J., ed. *American Literature of Nineteenth Century*, Eurasia Publishing House Pvt. Ltd., Ram Nagar, Delhi, 1970.

Fielding, Henry. *Tom Jones*, London : Collins, 1955.

Forster, E.M. *Aspects of The Novel*, Harmondsworth, Penguin, 1970.

—. *Two Cheers For Democracy*, London : Edward Arnold, 1972.

Fraser, G.S. *The Modern Writer And His World*, Rupa & Co. Calcutta, 1964.

Fryer, Jonathan. *Isherwood*, New English Library, London, 1977.

Fox, Ralph. *The Novel and the People*, London : Lawrence & Wishart, 1937.

Ford, Madox Ford. *The March of Literature*, London : George Allen and Unwin, 1937.

Finney, Brian. *Christopher Isherwood*, Faber and Faber, 1979.

Farmer, Una Ellis. *Masters of Reality*, London : Methuen & Co., 1942.

Freud, Sigmund. *Collected Papers*, Vol. IV, London : Hogarth Press, 1925.

Friedman, Alan. *The Turn of the Novel*, Oxford University Press, New York, 1967.

Freud, Sigmund. *Civilization*, War and Death, London : Hogarth Press, 1953.

Greene, Graham. *A Gun For Sale*, Harmondsworth : Penguin, 1977.

—. *Stamboul Train*, Heinemann, 1934.

—. *It's A Battlefield*, Heinemann, 1934.

—. *A Sort of Life*, Bodley Head, 1937.

—. *England Made Me*, Harmondsworth, 1964.

—. J*ourney Without Maps*, Heinemann, 1936.

—. *Brighton Rock*, Heinemann, 1964.

—. *The Lawless Roads*, Heinemann, 1955.

—. *The Lost Child and Other Essays*, London : Eyre & Spottiswoode, 1954.

Groddeck. *The Unknown Self*, second ed., C.W. Daniel Company, 1932.

Gilli, Christopher. *Movements In English Literature* (1900-1940), Cambridge University Press, 1975.

Glendinning, Victoria. *Elizabeth Bowen*, London : Weidenfeld and Nicolson, 1971.

Grigson, Geoffrey. *Psychology and Art To-day*, London: John Lane, The Bodley Head, 1935.

Gascoyne. *A Short Survey of Surrealism*, London : Sauderson,1935.

Gasset, Ortega Y. *The Dehumanization of Art*, Princeton University Press, 1948.

Holloway, John. 'The Literary Scene' . *The Modern Age*, ed. Boris Ford, Harmondsworth, 1964.

Hynes, Samuel. *The Auden Generation*, The Bodley Head, 1976.

Hight, Gilbert. *The Classical Tradition*, London : Clarendon Press, 1949.

Hunter, Jim. *The Modern Novel in Europe*, Faber and Faber (London), 1966.

Hamilton, Patrick. *Impromptu In Moribundia*, Constable, 1939.

—. *Craven House*, Constable, 1926.

Henderson, Philip. *The Novel Today*, John Lane, The Bodley Head, London, 1936.

Hewison, Robert. *Under Siege* (1939-45), London : Weidenfeld and Nicolson, 1977.

Harvey, W.J. *Character and the Novel*, London : Chatto and Windus, 1965.

Huxley, Aldous. *Ends and Means*, London : Chatto and Windus, 1937.

—. *Literature and Science*, London : Chatto and Windus, 1963.

Heinmann, Margot and Noreen, Brenson. *Britain In The Nineteen Thirties*, London : Weidenfeld and Nicolson, 1971.

Henkle, Roger B. *Reading The Novel*, London : Harper and Row Publishers, 1977.

Hewitt, Douglas. *The Approach to Fiction*, London 1972.

Hamalian, Leo & Karl, Frederick. *The Shape of Fiction*, McGraw-Hill, Printed in U.S.A. 1978.

Isherwood, Christopher. *Christopher And His Kind*, London: Methuen & Co., 1976.

—. *All The Conspirators*, London : The Hogarth Press, 1928.

—. *The Memorial*, London : The Hogarth Press, 1932.

—. *Mr. Norris Changes Trains*, London : The Hogarth Press Ltd. 1956.

—. *Goodbye to Berlin*, London : Hogarth Press, 1939.

—. *Lions and Shadows*, London : The Hogarth Press, 1938.

—. *Down There On A Visit*, London : Methuen & Co., 1962.

Issacs, J. *Assessment of Contemporary Literature*, London : Sacker and Warburg, 1952.

Hicks, Granville, ed. *The Living Novel*, New York, 1957.

James, R.A. Scott. *The Making of Literature*, London : Sacker and Warburg, 1970.

Joyce, James. *A Portrait of the Artist*, Harmondsworth, 1969.

Jones, David Pryce. *Evelyn Waugh And His World*, London : Weidenfeld and Nicolson, 1973.

Hermode, Frank. *Puzzles and Epiphanies*, London : Routledge and K. Paul, 1962.

Kettle, Arnold. *An Introduction To The English Novel*, Vol. II, Hutchinson University Library, London, 1967.

Kermode, Frank and Hollandef, John. *Modern British Literature*, Oxford University Press, 1973.

Kiely, Robert. *The Romantic Novel In England*, Harvard University Press, Massachusetts, 1972.

Law, Rachael. *The History of the British Film*, Vol. 3, London : Allen & Unwin 1950.

Legouis, Emile and Cazamian, Louis. *History of English Literature*, 1964, J.M. Deut and Sons Ltd.

Leavis, F.R. *The Great Tradition*, London : Chatto, 1962.

Leavis, F.R. and Thompson, D. *Culture and Environment*, London : Chatto and Windus, 1948.

Lawrence, D.H. *Fantasia of the Conscious and Psychoanalysis and the Unconscious Life*, London : Heinemann, 1961.

Lucas, John, ed. *The 1930's*, The Harvester Press, 1978.

Leavis, O.D. *The Fiction and the Reading Public*, London : Chatto and Windus, 1932.

Lodge, David. *Language of Fiction*, London, 1966.

—. *The Novelist At the Crossroads*, London : Routledge & Kegan Paul, 1971.

—. *The Modes of Modern Writing*, Edward Arnold, London, 1979.

Lehmann, John. *In My Own Time*, Boston Little Brown & Company, 1969.

—. *The Open Night*, Longmans, Green & Co., 1952.

—. *New Writing In Europe*, Harmondsworth, 1940.

Levin, Henry. *The Gates of Horn*, New York, 1963.

Lewis, C.D. *The Buried Day*, London : Chatto and Windus.

Lubboek, Perey. *The Craft of Fiction*, London, 1966.

Marshall, Perey. *Masters of the English Novel*, London : Dennis Dobson, 1962.

Morineth. *Selected Writing*, London, 1972.

Messengers of Day. To Keep The Bell Rolling, *The Memories of Anthony Powell*, Vol. II, Heinemann, London, 1978.

Manners, Penelope J.. *Novels of To-day*, University of London Press Ltd., 1967.

Muller, Herbert J. Modern Fiction, New York : Funk and Wagnads, 1937.

Maugham, W. Somerset. *The Summing Up*, The New American Library, 1961.

Mizeneh, Arthur. *The Sense of Life In the Modern Novel*, Boston University Press, 1964.

Nin, Anais. *The Novel of the Future*, Peter Owen, London, 1969.

Orwell, George. *The Road to Wigan Pier*, Gollanez, London, 1937.

—. *Coming up For Air*, Harmondsworth, 1967.

—. *Inside The Whale*, Collected Essays, Journalism and Letters, Harmondsworth, 1970, Vol. 1.

—. *Keep The Aspidistra Flying*, London : Gollaneze, 1936.

—. Burmese Days, Heinemann, 1934.

—. *Nineteen Eighty-Four,* Harmondsworth, 1978.

Powell, Anthony. *Afternoon Men*, London : Heinemann 1931.

—. *Venusberg*, London : Heinemann, 1964.

—. *From A View To Death*, London : Heinemann, 1974.

Piazza, Paul. *Christopher Isherwood*, Columbia University Press, New York, 1978.

Pritchett, V.S. *The Working Novelist*, London : Chatto and Windus, 1965.

Plimpton, George, ed. *Writers At Work*, Fourth Series, The Paris Review Interviews; Seeker & Wardbury, London, 1976.

Russel, John. *Anthony Powell*, Indiana University, 1971

Reed, Henry. *The Novel Since 1939*, The British Council, Longmans Green, 1946.

Rotha, Paul. *The Fiction Till Now*, Twyne Publishers, Inc. 1963.

Roadway, Allan. *The Truths of Fiction*, London : Chatto and Windus, 1970.

Sartre, Jean Paul. *What is Literature*?, translated by Barnard Fratchman, London : Mathuen & Co., 1948.

Stopp, Frederick J. *Evelyn Waugh*, London : Chapman & Hall Ltd., 1948.

Swinden, Patrick. *Unofficial Selves*, Macmillan, 1973.

Spender, Stephen. *Poems*, London : Faber and Faber, 1933.

—. *The Destructive Element*, London : Cape, 1935.

—. *The Thirties And After*, London : William Collins Sons & Co. Ltd., 1978.

—. *The Creative Element*, London. Hamish Hamilton, 1953.

—. *World Within World*, London : Hamish Hamilton, 1951.

Scholes, Robert & Kellogg, Robert. *The Nature of Narrative*, London : Oxford University Press, 1968.

—. *Structuralism In Literature*, New Heaven and London, Yale University Press, 1974.

Sussex, Elizabeth. *The Rise and Fall of British Documentary*, University of California, 1975.

Sampson, George. *The Concise Cambridge History of English Literature*, Cambridge University Press, 1972.

Symons, Julian. *The Angry 30's*. Picture File, Eyre Methuen, 1976.

—. *Of Crisis And Dismay*, ed. Rajan, B. & Pearse, London, A.D. Dobson Focus One, 1945.

—. *The Thirties – A Dream Revolved*, London : Faber and Faber, 1975.

Snow, C.P. *The Search*, London : Macmillan 1958.

—. *The English Realistic Novel*, Modern Spark, 1957.

—. *The New Men*, London : Macmillan, 1954.

—. *The Light and the Dark*, London : Harmondsworth, 1964.

—. *Death Under Sail*, London : Heinemann, 1932.

Sandison, Alan. *The Wheel of Empire*, A study of imperial idea in some late nineteenth and early twentieth century fiction, London : Macmillan, 1967.

Tindall, W.Y. *Forces In Modern British Literature*, Vintage Books Inc., 1947.

Tucker, James. *The Novels of Anthony Powell*, The Bowering Press Limited, Plymouth, 1976.

Thale, Jerome. *C.P. Show*, Oliver and Boyd, London, 1964.

Tindall, W.Y. *The Literary Symbol*, Newyork, Columbia University Press, 1955.

Thomson, David. *England In the Twentieth Century*, London : Jonathan Cape, 1964.

Taylor, A.J.P. *England* (1914-1939), Oxford University Press, 1965.

Trilling, Lienel. *The Liberal Imagination*, New York : The Viking Press, 1951.

Thiher, Allen. *The Novel As Delirium*, Rutgers University Press, New Jersey, 1947.

Tobin, Patricia Orechsel. *Time And the Novel*, Princeton University Press, 1978.

Thomson, J.A.K. *The Classical Background of English Literature*, London: George Allen and Unwin Ltd., 1948.

—. *Classical Influence on English Prose* (London), 1956.

Upward, Edward. *Sketch For a Marxist*, interpretation of literature, in C. Day Lewis, ed., *The Mind In Chains*, London : Frederick Muller Ltd., 1937.

—. *The Railway Accident*, Harmondsworth Penguin, 1972.

Vinson, James. *Contemporary Novelists*, London : St. James Press, 1976.

Wickes, George. *Masters of Modern British Fiction*, New York : The Macmillan Company, 1963.

Williamson, T.A. *The Evolution of England*, Oxford University Press, 1931.

Walpole, Hugh and Others. *Tendencies of the Modern Novel*, George Allen & Unwin Ltd., 1934.

Woolf, Virginia. *Contemporary Writers*, London : The Hogarth Press, 1965.

—. *Granite And Rainbow* (Essays), The Hogarth Press, 1960.

—. *The Moment And Other Essays*, The Hogarth Press, 1960.

—. *A Writer's Diary*, ed. Leonard Woolf, London : Hogarth Press, 1972.

Ward, A.C.. *Twentieth Century Literature*, London : Methuen & Co., 1959.

Wimsatt, J.R., William K. and Brooks, Cleauth. *Literary Criticism* . A Short History, 1964, Oxford I.B.H. Pub. Co., Calcutta.

Warner, Rex. *The Cult of Power* (essays), 1947, New York.

—. *The Professor*, Love and Brydone, London, 1946.

—. *The Wild Goose Chase*, London : The Bodley Head, 1944.

—. *The Aerodrome*, London : Lowe and Brydon, 1966.

West, Paul. *The Modern Novel*, Vol. II, London : Hutchinson & Co. Ltd., 1967.

Waugh, Evelyn. *Labels*, London : Duckworth, 1930.

—. *Ninety-Two Days*, London : Duckworth, 1934.

—. *Helena*, Harmondsworth, 1950.

—. *Brideshead Revisited*, Eyre Methuen, 1945.

—. *Decline and Fall*, William Heinemann, 1977.

—. *Vile Bodies*, Chapman and Hall, 1930.

—. *Black Mischief*, William Heinemann, 1977.

—. *A Handful of Dust*, Harmondsworth, 1977.

—. *Scoop*, William Heinemann, 1977.

Ziolkeuski, Theodore. *Disenchanted Images*, Princeton University Press, New Jersey, U.K., 1977.

PERIODICALS AND JOURNALS

Adelphi (*The*), London. Mason, Ronald . 'The Novels of Rex Warner'. July-Sept., 1945.

Bookman Review (*The*), London, Vol. LXXXIV, 1933, p. 160.

Cousins, E.G. 'Cinema and Propaganda'. Vol. LXXXIV, Oct. 1933.

Lewis, Wyndham. 'Classical Revival, In England'. No. 517, Vol. LXXXVII, Oct. 1934.

Joanna Cannan. 'The New Trend In Fiction' Vol. LXXXIV, Oct. 1933.

C.P. Snow. 'Science of the Year'. Vol. LXXXIV, Oct. 1933.

Norah Hoult. 'The Novel and the Contemporary Civilization'. Vol. LXXXIV, Oct. 1933.

Geoffray Dearmer : 'The Decline of Inspiration In Modern Literature'. No. 499, Vol. LXXXIV, Oct. 1933.

Wyndham Lewis : 'Classical Revival In England'. No. 517, Vol. LXXXVII, Oct. 1934.

Collins Brooks . 'Europe In Transition'. May, 1931, Vol. LXXX.

Blackwood, London. Kinglake, A.W. 'The Invasion of the Crimea'. 8 vols. (Edinburgh and London) vol. 5, 1863-87.

Critical Quarterly, London. Bernard Bargonzi . 'Anthony Powell', XI, Spring, 1969, p. 81.

Critic (*The*), London. Bruce Cook . 'The Trouble with George'. XXIII, Oct-Nov., 1964, p. 65.

Cambridge Journal, London. Richard Mayne. 'The Novel and Mr. Morris', VI, June, 1953.

Contemporary Review (*The*), London. George Glasgo . 'Politics as an international disease'. July-December, 1930.

Daily Worker, London J.K. . 'Explodes on Illusion'. 30 December, 1936, p. 7.

Daily Telegraphy, London. Brophy : 'New Fiction' . The need for more imagination, 20 Oct. 1936.

Foreign Affairs, London. Croce, Benedette : 'Of Liberty', New York, Oct. 1932, p. 17.

Fortnightly Review (*The*), London and New York. G.K. Chesterton. 'The Spirit of the age in Literature.' Sept. 1, 1938.

Earnest Baker. 'The Movement In National Life', May, 1935.

Horizon, London. Connolly, Cyrill . 'Comment, 1 Feb., 1940.

International Surrealist Bulletin, London. Davies, Hugh Sykes: Extracts from the lecture. 'Biology and Surrealism'. 4 Sept. 1936.

Herbert Read's Speech at the Conway Hall, 4 Sept. 1936.

Kenyan Review. C.P. Snow . 'Science, Politics and The Novelist', 23 June, 1961 (pp. 5-6).

Indian Journal of English Studies. Maini, Darshan Singh . 'Rex Warner's Political Moves,' Vol. II, 1961.

London Mercury, London. 'Ivoy Tower', December, 1938.

James, R.A. Scott. Editorial Note. April, 1935, pp. 522-23.

Hunter, Guy. 'The Waste Land' in Liberia' . 24 June, 1936.

Forster . 'Credo', 38 Sept., 1938.

Life. Waugh, Evelyn : 'Fan Fare', 6 April, 1946.

Listener, London. Fryer, T.R. 'Problems of the Modern Novelist', 21 April, 1955, p. 708.

Left Review, London. C.D. Lewis . 'The Road These Times Must Take', 1 Nov., 1934.

New Republic (*The*), London. Auden, W.H. . 'The Means of Grace'. IV June 2, 1941.

Isherwood Christopher. 'German Literature In England', 5 April, 1938.

New Statesman And Nation (*The*), Garnett, David. 'Books In General', XXII, March 11, 1939.

New Stateman, London. Lehmann, Rosamund. 'New Novels', 1 August, 1936.

Bell, 'Politics In Cambridge', 6 December, 1933, p. 731.

Stonier – 'An Exceptional Story', 12 December, 1936, p. 998.

Observer Magazine (*The*), London. Waugh's Private Diaries, 13 May, 1973.

Oxford Outlook, London. Blunden. 'An Institution and a Moral', 11 Nov. 1931, pp. 191-2.

Review of Books, London. Elizabeth Hardwick : 'Reflection on Fiction', 13 Feb., 1969.

Spring, London. Anden . T.E. Lawrence, 'Now and Then', No. 47, 1934, p. 30.

Surrealists Left (*The*), London. Lord Hastings, 2 Jan., 1936, p. 186.

Scrutiny, Cambridge. O.D. Leavis, 'The Literary Life Respectable'. IX, Sept., 1940, p. 150.

Saturday Review, London. Balliet, W., Biographical Note, 38, II, 8 Jan., 1955.

Spectator (*The*), London. William Plomer, 'Fiction', 1 March, 1935.

Tamarack Review (*The*), Clifford Solway . 'An Interview with Christopher Isherwood'. X, Spring, 1966, p. 29.

Times Literary Supplement (*The*), London. 'The Air of Bloomsbury'. Friday August 20, 1954, p. 523.

'Science and Literature'. Editorial Note, July, 1954.

J.B. Priestley . 'Jung and the Writer'. 6 August, 1954.

Prof. Niebuhr, 'The Two Cities'. Sept. 17, 1954.

'From A Chase To A View', Feb. 16, 1951.

Anthony Powell . 'Temporary Kings', 22 June, 1973.

D.A. Willis, 'New Life For The Novel'. 8 Feb., 1934.

Johnson, Pamela Hansford : 'Modern Fiction and the English Understatement.' 7 August, 1959.

Time and Tide, London. Jones, David Pryce, 'Isherwood Reassured', XLI, Oct. 1, 1960.

Index

To Important Authors and Titles

J

K

L

M

N

O

P

S

T

V

W

Z